Short Stories
in a Long Journey

What It Takes to End
and Prevent Homelessness

Richard R. Troxell

www.HouseTheHomeless.org
www.UniversalLivingWage.org

Praise for *Short Stories in a Long Journey*

"For 40 years, Richard has been a leader in the charge to defeat the national disgrace we call homelessness. He brings to the table specific and viable **solutions** in the name of justice and has done it while calling for dignity and fairness for all. Awesome!"
—**Alan Graham**, President/Founder Mobile Loaves and Fishes
  and Community First! Village, Austin, TX

"This book is just a few chapters of Richard's life with the homeless and both of their struggles. He tells you of his own background, which is a wonderful portrayal of him. I was there in Austin with him during some of these times. This book lays out the issues of homelessness and many solutions. It is just amazing and wonderful...a must read."
—**Judge Philip Sanders**, Assistant and First Assistant DA, Travis County
  US magistrate for the Western District of Texas

"*Short Stories in a Long Journey* is Richard R. Troxell's chronicle of the shaping of a tenacious advocate for the men, women and children experiencing homelessness. Never afraid of fighting City Hall, Troxell narrates his efforts to convince the power brokers of Austin, Texas to recognize the unique issues impacting the homeless and address them with common sense, dignity and fairness. Using meticulous research, wry humor, and dogged stubbornness, this is an account of a visionary effort to convince, cajole or drag his weird city to a higher ground."
—**Tracey Whitley**, Attorney, Texas Rio Grande Legal Aid

Also by Richard R. Troxell

* *Looking Up at the Bottom Line: The Struggle for the Living Wage*
* *Austin Affordable Housing Guide*
* *Homeless to Housed Continuum: Dual Housing Track*
* *Jobs + Plus*
* *Permanent Housing of Homeless People in Philadelphia*
* *Prevent Homelessness...at its core The Universal Living Wage*
* *Project Fresh Start: A Continuum of Care for Homeless People*
    (still in use by the City of Austin)
* *Striking a Balance! Revitalization/Displacement from Gentrification*

Short Stories in a Long Journey

What It Takes to End and Prevent Homelessness

Richard R. Troxell

www.HouseTheHomeless.org
www.UniversalLivingWage.org

Plain View Press, LLC
1101 W 34th Street, STE 404

www.plainviewpress.net
Austin, TX 78705

ISBN: 978-1-63210-088-7
ebook ISBN: 978-1-63210-095-5
Library of Congress Control Number: 2021947742

Cover art: *Man with Dog*, with permission from Pets of the Homeless
Cover design by Pam Knight

We Find Healing In Existing Reality
Plain View Press is a 40-year-old issue-based literary publishing house. Our books result from artistic collaboration between writers, artists, and editors. Over the years we have become a far-flung community of humane and highly creative activists whose energies bring humanitarian enlightenment and hope to individuals and communities grappling with the major issues of our time—peace, justice, the environment, education and gender.

To all the children, women, and men who have had the misfortune of experiencing homelessness.

- *To any child who has been made fun of for having outdated shoes, jacket, dress, etc., or having simply been identified as being homeless.*
- *To anyone who has had their camp and tent, bulldozed along with all their personal belongings: medications, important papers, including letters from their loved ones thrown into the trash.*
- *To every homeless person kicked awake by anyone.*
- *To every woman who has ever woken in violent darkness with their best friend and "protector" on top of them.*
- *To everyone who has ever gotten a ticket for "criminal sleeping," loitering, panhandling (asking for help), sitting, or lying down.*
- *To anyone who has found themselves in a jail cell for being unable to pay a $200-$500 fine for violating a "quality of life" law.*
- *To all the other folks who escaped having their skulls crushed in the middle of the night as happened to seven human beings in Austin, TX, in the 1980s.*
- *And to all the guys and gals from the streets of Austin, who stood with me and took the hill over and over again.*

100% of all proceeds from the sale of this book will benefit these folks...our friends and family, to fight homelessness. Buy two copies and give one to a friend!

Acknowledgments

Undoubtedly, this book would not exist without the support of my wife, Sylvia, and my publisher, Pam Knight, and the following:

Book Editors: Pat Hartman, writing coach, sweetest gal, sharpest tongue; Tracey Whitely, confidant; Sue Watlov Phillips, inexhaustible advocate; Greg Gibson, highly valued unique perspective; Patti Prieb, best next-door neighbor and cheerleader; Gene Stickley, brother-in-law and by choice.

Professor Edgar S. Cahn valued visionary, "We're on the same page".

Alan Graham, a friend, pulling on the same rope and in the same direction.

Cecilia Blanford, Co-founder, and current House the Homeless President, like my adopted sister.

Jim Harrington, slayer of dragons/Civil Rights brother in the field.

Mike Urena, Texas Rio Grande Legal Aid Attorney, Americans with Disabilities Act visionary.

Will Hyatt, House the Homeless Field Manager, most prayerful, also on the same page.

Jon Sullivan, best moral support and Senior Massage Therapist.

Steve and Heather Dubov, sculptors, mentors, and friends.

Timothy P. Schmalz, best international telephone sculpting buddy.

Tony Frey, best sculpting project-head.

Linda Bugarsky, very best "Girl Friday".

Colleen Troxell, my daughter and inspiration.

JoAnn Koepke, Heart and Soul of House the Homeless. Helped me launch the ULW Campaign, tracked down 42,000 potential supporters before the internet ever existed and caused HtH to adopt two Uganda girls.

Kathie Kimbrel, author, who helped me build the Universal Living Wage website.

Karen Gilbert, my Legal Aid secretary who privately typed many House the Homeless documents.

Terrance Flowers, Role Model, a good Christian, who stood tall as a plaintiff in the No Camping case in Austin, Texas.

Contents

Crystal Clear

...and the note read,
"Give my brothers a home, bread to eat, water to drink, and
let the Homeless learn to be citizens in a foreign land."
—And the note had been wrapped tightly about a stone.
—And he flung it, full force, through the priceless glass,
crystal window.
—And the act had shattered its beauty forever.
—And he had said that he would do it again and again
until they treated his brothers and sisters with love.
—And he said he would do it again. And he would do
it again, and again, and again, and it shattered their
priceless lives like crystal again, and again, and again,
and again, and again, and again and again...

Richard R. Troxell Director
Legal Aid for the Homeless
Founder of House the Homeless

Note: This poem was inspired by a true incident that occurred in
Austin, Texas, in March 1991.

Introduction

Is this a book about a formerly homeless man who spends his life helping the homeless? Is this a book about universal minimum wage and the fight to make it happen? Is this a book about short stories that speaks for people along the way who have lived on our streets? Or, is this a book about a sculpture that has provided a monument for those who are homeless? It is all of the above and more. As someone who works for the poor as my ministry, I highly recommend this book. I learned a lot.

Father John
Rev. Msgr. John J. Enzler, President and CEO
Catholic Charities of the Archdiocese of Washington

Richard R. Troxell, a longtime fearless and fearsome advocate for homeless people, has put together a series of short vignettes that weave together, in panoramic view, his life in an ever-pressing community reality that Americans don't want to face. Richard also offers practical solutions, which, though, may be outside current political will. He is not one of those society architects who think they know what to do and impose their views. Richard stands with homeless people inside the circle of exclusion that communities draw around them. *Short Stories in a Long Journey* shows the passionate journey of Richard's life with those who live on our streets. The breadth of homelessness in the country is staggering and relatively new in American history from the time of World War II vets living on the streets. Richard, in my view, correctly looks at homelessness as an economy-driven phenomenon, the result of severe systemic structural imbalances ("injustice" and "oppression") in our capitalist system.

A few chapters particularly stand out. One is Richard's battle against the Austin city ordinance that criminalized homeless people for sitting and sleeping on sidewalks and similar areas and how deft use of the Americans with Disabilities Act essentially gutted the ordinance.

Another chapter details the four-year struggle to memorialize homeless individuals in sculpture, culminating in erecting a pair of statues of homeless people at Austin's Community First! Village, a 51-acre property in Austin where once chronically homeless people live in tiny houses and trailers. The town has received widespread praise and is a fitting home for beautiful works of art.

The group of sculptures named *The Home Coming* tells the story of a chance encounter between a veteran, John, and his daughter, Colleen, and an African American woman, Ms. Anateen," Troxell said. The story, which Richard called emblematic of his advocacy, is "about people who don't have anything, but are willing to share whatever they have, the warmth of their fire and their humanity with others."

At the sculptures' dedication, U.S. Congress Member Lloyd Doggett called them "a reminder that our homeless are not nameless and faceless. They're real people." Richard Troxell has lived his life, reminding us sometimes fiercely, and always passionately, who these real people are that live among us.

James C. Harrington
Texas Civil Rights Lawyer and
    Founder of the Texas Civil Rights Project

Preface

Livable incomes is presented in two pieces. First, it analyzes how inadequate and flawed our present efforts are—and second, it provides a set of carefully reasoned, well-buttressed proposals that could make a real dent in both reducing and preventing economic homelessness.

The recommendations focus on our outdated American poverty standards, a minimum wage far below a living wage, and the extent to which payments to those unable to work due to age or disability are grossly inadequate. For Troxell, preventing homelessness begins by enabling people who can work, earn enough to have a roof over their heads. He reminds us how Henry Ford created the consumer market for his product. If everyone earns more, everyone spends more. Higher take-home pay lifts all boats. Troxell would guarantee a sufficient income for those who can't work to enable them to pay their rent.

Troxell is not naive about the odds. Given his decades in the trenches on behalf of the homeless, he documents how we have criminalized homelessness, tried to banish the homeless from sight and conscience, and then fall back on blaming the victim. He knows that market theology pervades much of our political discourse. Looking at compelling cost-benefit analysis was all that mattered; Troxell has provided the data and the argument.

Troxell divides the world into two categories: those who can work and those who can't. And we both believe that everyone has the capacity to contribute to our well-being, that we all need each other. A monetary definition of economics tends to omit what it takes to raise children, care for the elderly, make democracy work, hold officials accountable, advance social justice or keep the planet sustainable. I regard such contributions as work, even if the market does not value vast amounts of essential contribution.

Livable incomes focus on what should be done within the monetary system. Both of us agree that the present distributive system does not enable all who work to earn a sustainable livelihood. We agree that people who work, who contribute, who produce value should be able to enjoy a decent standard of living and a roof over their heads. We call for change. If all we have is the present monetary system, there are few options. We can rely on charity, transfer payments, entitlements—we can move toward some version of Troxell's recommendations regarding minimum wage, cost of living, and social security. But we think once we begin to think of the homeless and other groups—children, teenagers, the elderly, the disabled, veterans—as a vast underutilized asset—other possibilities emerge, such as Community First! Village for those who cannot work. There are substantial numbers of homeless veterans who have been unable to access the very rights conferred upon them by a nation that owes them so much. But new efforts are underway to remedy that. There are ways in which student debt can now be forgiven in return for extended public service. In the past, teachers and doctors who worked critically in underserved communities have received loan forgiveness.

Time Banking—a complementary currency earned by helping others and addressing critical needs—radically expands the available options. One hour spent helping another human being earns one (1) time credit, regardless of the market value of the work being done. All hours are equal in value. In effect, this turns a community or a membership group into a vast extended family through an exchange system that is not commercial, that advances charitable objectives, and that the IRS has ruled is different from barter. We are trapped right now by our definition of value as that which is measured by money and must be compensated with money.

The chapter on Livable Incomes is more than a set of recommendations. It is an indictment of a system that relegates millions to needless suffering, deprivation, and demoralization—and that defines the homeless as a burden rather than an invaluable asset.

This piece clarifies the distance we must travel to realign our wage and benefit systems to our core values. The gravity, the scale, and the seeming intransigence of the problem should inspire us to reach across present divides and find additional ways to enlist all to address intolerable disparities. It is time we undertook community by community to honor all contributions made day in day out by the homeless, by those working at unlivable wages, by those who have returned from national service, by those who are unable to find employment but still committed to helping each other. Even now, there are ways to reward ongoing contributions that could reclaim habitat for all our brothers and sisters. I hope that this document will increase our readiness to map alternative paths and our willingness to declare "No More Throw-Away People." We can do it.

Thank you, Richard R. Troxell.

Edgar S. Cahn
Distinguished Professor of Law, University of the District of Columbia
    David A. Clarke School of Law
Ashoka Fellow, Founder of TimeBanks USA

1 The Condition of Homelessness

An Overview by Sue Watlov Phillips, M.A.
President, National Coalition for the Homeless
Executive Director, Metropolitan Interfaith Council
on Affordable Housing

Discharged to Homelessness became a phrase utilized to describe people being discharged from various mainstream programs, including but not limited to hospitals, MI/MD/CD treatment settings, and prisons/ jails, U.S. military with no place to go called home. This phrase became popular in the late 1990s and early 2000s as we completed the second decade and entered the third decade of this episode of homelessness in our country.

Unfortunately, the responses to homelessness have continued to be cobbled together. Oftentimes, motivated by special interest groups to promote specific data collection that blamed homelessness on individual problems, creating short-sighted plans to address ongoing societal structural issues through the homeless system, and creating a very expensive, limited, and often segregated housing system called permanent supportive housing that has maintained many people, now in supportive housing for over 5-20 years.

To get into supportive housing, you have to meet HUD's restrictive definition of homelessness and have an additional disability diagnosis. Suppose you have been homeless continuously for one year or 4 times in the last 3 years. In that case, you're classified as "chronic," a medical term that has inappropriately been used and continues to blame homelessness on the individual instead of addressing the structural causes of homelessness.

These inappropriate responses have helped maintain stereotypes, which are often perpetuated by the media; a person is homeless because of their personal problems. It has drained valuable resources and has significantly impacted the availability of resources to prevent homelessness and rapidly exit/rapidly re-house people out of homelessness into appropriate housing. It created a new form of segregated housing. This inappropriate and inadequate response has allowed our society to ignore its responsibility to address the structural changes required to ensure each person in our country has a home.

To Bring America Home, we need to create and maintain these structural changes:

- create, maintain, and rehab safe, decent, affordable, and accessible housing for all.
- create livable income employment and livable incomes for those unemployed and/or unable to work.
- create a single-payer universal healthcare for all.
- create access to education and job training for all.
- honor, protect, and enforce the civil rights of everyone.

As long as we continue to blame homelessness on individuals' problems and on mainstream systems that are doing their jobs—providing treatment, rehab services, and then discharging people...it allows us as a society to not address the fundamental structural issues in our society that are causing and maintaining homelessness for millions of our people in this country and allows the general society to identify people experiencing homelessness as "those people" instead of our people.

Societal Changes

The major societal changes that have occurred over the last 5 decades in our country have significantly impacted access to housing, livable incomes, healthcare, education, and civil rights enforcement and racism. These changes have been instrumental in causing the growth and maintenance of homelessness as we are now in our fifth decade of growing homelessness, a phenomenon that, while historical in the world, has never occurred in our country's short history.

Major Structural Issues: Housing

Until the early 1970s, most people could rent an apartment just about anywhere in the country working a part-time or full-time job (systemic racism of redlining and other discrimination was and continues to create barriers to diverse people/people of color). Housing availability and access were impacted by:

- The demolition of housing without one-to-one replacement of housing.
- The changes in the tax codes in 1986 made it difficult for Ma and Pa landlords to stay in business.
- The white flight to the suburbs and new lot sizes, zoning codes which increased housing costs, and the push by the real estate industry to build larger homes and expansion of gated communities to keep certain types of people out.
- Increased costs of all building products.

- The implementation of electronic criminal and credit checks to keep people with more difficult histories from accessing housing.
- The growth of urban areas as rural areas lost jobs.
- Income.
- The rapid increase in pace of moving from an agrarian society to an urban society.
- Intentional think-tank plans that have destroyed the family farm and create corporate farms.

In1970s-1980s, the loss/reduction of mining, timber, fishing industries. The decision to sign international trade agreements without U.S. worker protections such as tariffs—thus significant number of manufacturing jobs were outsourced to third world countries, which resulted in a reduction of good union paying jobs.

The real estate and banking deregulations that led to one of the largest scams and stripping of equity of homeowners in the mid -2000s to now have resulted in millions of people who have lost their homes due to the risk or actual foreclosure and threatened millions more as the credit requirements have tightened up and many people owe more on the house than it is currently worth. This has driven millions of previous homeowners into the rental market, thus creating greater demand than supply of affordable units in most communities.

The expansion of our outsourcing jobs to temporary services within the country has decreased the employer-employee loyalty relationship.

Wages and assistance to those unemployed or unable to work because of a disability (SSI) or being elderly did not maintain pace with the cost of housing, food, healthcare, and transportation. In other words, all people need Livable Incomes.

Healthcare

In the 1980s, we changed from having the family hometown doctor to a system called Managed Care. It was promoted in the 1980s to be the new idea to make health available to all at an affordable price by setting up a major nonprofit healthcare system. In reality, it drove out of business the family doctors and community mental health providers and replaced it with a system that did what its name said—Managed Care. In other words, the individual had limited choices of who they could see and for how long the system was based on averages vs. individual needs. Thus, many people didn't or couldn't access services because they were inaccessible, not culturally appropriate, or just denied care because they didn't meet HMO standards. We made many CEOs millionaires at the cost of many people not receiving proper, medical care, physical, mental and physical health. There is a high correlation with those experiencing homelessness due to the inability to address their healthcare needs and/or because they couldn't pay the medical bills, their HMO wouldn't pay, or were unable to get into an HMO plan due to pre-existing conditions.

Treatment of the Mentally Ill

In the 1950 and 1960s, people in the United States began to demand that people with mental health disabilities have a community-based option instead of being "warehoused" in mental health institutions. Often, caretakers with no schooling and no formal training act as surrogate parents 24 hours a day for people with serious mental illness. The conditions of overcrowding, abuse, and neglect were rampant. Civil liberty groups filed a number of lawsuits that led to a civil rights' movement for people with disabilities. The Civil Rights of Institutional Persons Act empowered the United States Justice Department to file civil suits on behalf of residents of institutions whose rights had been violated.

The advent of psychotropic drugs such as Thorazine and Haldol caused mental health service providers to believe that they could successfully treat people on an outpatient basis. *However, people's internal systems would make chemical adjustments over time, and the invisible cords of connection would sever.* As a result, and in combination, many institutions, having lost their clientele (their economic base of support), were closed down, and tens of thousands of mentally ill persons became homeless. The Community based residential settings were not funded at a level to address the numbers of people that were released with nowhere to go. The lack of community-based residential settings not only impacted people being released but also those who need help now and have limited options in the community. With limited inpatient beds comes difficult access to long-term care. Many individuals have had to wait for months for an inpatient bed to become available.

Today, as many as 40% of the unsheltered people experiencing homelessness have serious mental health concerns. Even if they are lucky enough to receive a stipend (Supplemental Security Insurance), SSI for their disability, the amount is merely $794.00 per month across the nation. This is about half ($7.25 per hour) of the Federal Minimum Wage, which is wholly insufficient for a person to get into and keep basic rental housing.

Unfortunately, our nation's prisons have become the de facto housing facilities for many of our nation's mentally ill. This is especially true for the "not guilty by reason of insanity" group.

Education/ Job Training

Until the end of the 1970s, State Universities were typically affordable for many in our society. Those unable to pay were often able to access student loans or grants. Over the last 5 decades, the cost of education has increased by over 31X while income and loans/grants have not kept pace. *The value placed on sports in our college systems often overshadows the need for strengthening resources for training for our medical, scientific, research, educational and humanitarian professions.* The lack of access to affordable housing for students impacts their personal stability and ability to do well in school. Subsidized Job Training for unemployed and/or people with disabilities to assist them in obtaining livable income jobs has been replaced, oftentimes, with Job Search.

Civil Rights

While our Society made great gains in protecting and honoring Civil Rights in the 1960s and 1970s, we have been on a steady decline of enforcement of civil rights through a variety of tactics in our society since then.

Voting—needing ID or an address to vote—limits people with limited income or who have moved or who have no home to exercise this fundamental right.

Criminal and Credit checks are used as *discriminatory tools* to limit people's access to housing rental and homeownership and jobs, including jobs requiring being licensed: (Doctors, Social Workers, Psychologists, therapists, etc.).

Homeless Management Information Systems (HMIS) is Congress's way of tracking the effectiveness of their funding to address homelessness. HMIS is required by the Federal Department of Housing and Urban Development (HUD). It has created significant barriers for people choosing to use the homeless systems that may be available, and in this writer's, opinion violates many state and federal Data Privacy Laws, including Health Insurance Portability and Accountability Act, (HIPAA) in the sharing of private information about people at risk of experiencing homelessness.

Coordinated Entry is often another form of how people experiencing homelessness are discriminated against by information requested and process in attempting to get basic needs met.

Prison Reform

Shift in governmentally owned and operated prison institutions to privatization and a for-profit setting. This has led to an explosion of the creation of new prison facilities throughout the nation. Additionally, this transfer led to further cost-saving measures, including the reduction in prison healthcare and the reduction and elimination of educational opportunities for reforming inmates. Change in laws included enhanced penalties for cocaine derivative use (crack) affecting Black and poverty-encased communities.

Note, parolees not eligible for federal housing, food stamps, TANIF, etc., further exacerbates the challenge of escaping poverty. Failure to address causes of recidivism.

Moral Outcry

Walt Leginski (Retired HHS), in his writing about the historical perspective of homelessness in our country, described the episodes of homelessness, points out two key differences in our response to this episode of homelessness in our country.

The lack of moral outcry to address this ongoing issue in our society. This is the first time we have talked about ending homelessness while many faith communities were actively involved in a movement in the late 1970s and early 1980s, as the growth of this new episode of homelessness dramatically increased, advocating for a society to address the structural issues while providing some direct services to people at risk or experiencing homelessness.

Over the last 3 decades, this movement has been co-opted and became a major industry of providers oftentimes, and more focused on increasing homeless resources through the McKinney Vento Act (federal legislation) "researching people experiencing homelessness and their personal issues" versus addressing the structural issues causing and allowing people to become homeless. (See GAO 2010 Report). The homeless industry is now, in my opinion, the second greatest obstacle to our goal to end homelessness.

The primary obstacle to ending homelessness is you and me. We have failed those in our community who lack the resources to access housing, healthcare, livable income education, and job training, and we continue to discriminate and scapegoat them as being different from "us." Much of this is rooted deeply in the seeds of racism as a result of slavery reaching back to 1619 as evidenced by the fact that people of color are clearly over represented in the ranks of homelessness.

We the privileged masses have enough resources—legally and illegally to get into housing and purchase the services we need. We have little regard for those who can't and blame them for not being like "us." As a Country founded on and our pledges each day to be: ONE nation under God, INDIVISIBLE with Liberty and Justice for All. We are now a nation of haves and have nots. If you *have*, then you are good. If you *have not*, then you are to blame for being in that situation.

As long as our response to people at risk or experiencing homelessness is based on that philosophy, I believe we are doomed to continuing to see the ongoing growth of homelessness.

If we dare to stand up again and be the Nation that our Pledge of Allegiance says we are, we will be able to look at our faiths' moral principles as a guide: to love and treat others the way we want to be treated.

I challenge anyone reading this to try to apply for public benefits, get into the homeless system, and live in a shelter or outside in your community for 1 week. Then ask yourself: Is that how I would want to be treated if I lost my financial, family, and health resources?

If the answer is NO; which I believe most of you will say...then join us in a national outcry/demand to use our tax resources, including tax expenditures, appropriations, bonding, and require businesses to pay living wages to make the structural changes to *prevent and end homelessness* in our country while providing a loving and caring response (the way we would want to be treated) to meet the immediate needs of people at risk or experiencing homelessness and *Bring America Home Now!*

The National Coalition for the Homeless invites you in our 2021 campaign—*Bring America Home Now!*

We are collaborating across the nation to Prevent and End homelessness. We are crafting legislative bills in five areas:
1) Housing
2) Health Care
3) Livable Incomes
4) Education and Training and
5) Civil Rights and Anti-racism.

Join us today by going to https://nationalhomeless.org/.
Thank you Richard for helping to open the door for change.

2 A Glimpse at a Truly Long Journey

My timeline here reveals my long journey, full of many personal short stories. Somehow, all the little pieces fit together and got me to where I am; an ex-homeless veteran dedicated to ending and preventing homelessness. Some highlights are as follows: At the age of five or six, I put on my superman cape and flew from my parents' roof in Twin Brook, MD. As a birthday "gift," I was sent to Porter Military Academy. My father received a military transfer to Wappoo Creek, SC. With my sister Lynn on board a boat we found on said creek, and nothing but a poled crab net for a paddle, I drifted us into the inter-coastal waters (and all but out to sea). An old fisherman saved us and allowed the story that you are reading to keep on going. In 5th and 6th grade, I lived in Canada for two years, where we played street hockey, ice hockey, football, went tobogganing, sledding, curling, ice skating, and built an endless number of snow tunnels.

Young Richard Troxell as Superman

These were the last best years of my youth. In the years that followed, I...
- survived high school in the 1960s.
- became a United States Marine that started at Paris Island, SC.
- later became a Vietnam Veteran.
- lived in Japan off base for nearly a year.

- railed against the U.S. Government.
- created and operated M&M Enterprises (Catch-22) in Iwakuni, Japan.
- led a mini-revolt about the intolerable conditions regarding the Nixon pullout from Vietnam, of which I became part.
- returned to the "World," a life that no longer fit.
- got a job with the Montgomery County government picking up trash on the sides of rural roads that led to a lifetime hobby of collecting bottles that finally focused on Colonial Black Glass.
- attended community college in Montgomery County, MD, for little over one year.
- found and lost my dog Russell, "Rusty," who came and went.
- mixed mortar, carried hods, and apprenticed as a brick mason at Larry Keeler Brick Mason Inc. in Montgomery County, Maryland.

Then, suddenly and violently, my father died. In the aftermath, I hitch-hiked across America and back with my Springer Spaniel and amazing friend, Buddy (or Buddy Trucker, because he so loved riding in the big rigs), who came into my life. I then...

- experienced homelessness first hand for 3 years, lived in the woods, a car, a truck, and lots of abandoned buildings.
- apprenticed as an auto mechanic with Garland and Cliff Dempsey in the City of Brotherly Love, PA.
- lived in an all-Black North Philadelphia community for over a year and felt gloriously free.
- became a consumer activist.
- studied under the late, great Max Weiner at the Consumer Education and Protective Association, CEPA, and helped launch the Consumer Party in Philadelphia, PA.
- crammed a political speech into one and a half minutes, over and over again while standing in front of the Philadelphia city hall speaking to citizens through a bull horn while they waited for a stoplight to free them.
- found that my homelessness had come to an end when Garland Dempsey gave me permission to remain in the house where I had been "squatting" with Buddy.

Then things went into high gear. I moved to the historic Germantown section of Philadelphia, sharing a co-op house with the La Salle University Rowing Crew. I became the District Director for CEPA International, for the Philadelphia District of CEPA. During a political dispute with the Department of Housing and Urban Development, HUD, I was handcuffed by police and thrown into the back of a paddy wagon, along with 5 other brethren. We had taken over Independence Hall to secure deeds to 22 abandoned, boarded-up HUD houses. The deeds were presented to the squatters.

Richard with his Reagan poster

I was hired right out of street activism by Legal Services Corporation, Law Center North Central as a paralegal with no schooled experience. I created a mortgage foreclosure intervention program with me as a self-made "Mortgage Foreclosure Preventionist." Along the way, I...

- became a sport parachutist, first with my friend Penny Scott, then with many others for a total of ten jumps to earn my jump wings.
- traveled with my new best friend Eric into the spectacular 40,000-acre wilderness of Canada's Algonquin Park for a portage trek where I honed my wilderness survival skills.
- Sept. 1983, received my NAUI Scuba certification.
- traveled with Eric into the Arctic Tidal Basin.
- rough traveled with Eric into the Amazon, Egypt, Turkey, Peru, and Bolivia
- led a successful mule team expedition with Eric into the Semien Mountains in Ethiopia in search of the Falashas (Black Jews).

Back in the States, I squatted and partially rehabilitated another house. I then bought and shared a house co-operatively. I went on to rehabilitate a 6-bedroom, 1896 Flemish Revival, twin house, in Germantown, PA., with Sylvia Stickley. In 1986, while riding my bicycle to see Sylvia, I was run down by a truck, breaking my neck and leading to a lifetime of spinal procedures, fused vertebrae, and titanium plates. Sylvia and I were married in 1988 in the house that we so loved and worked on together.

Having honed my home rehabilitation skills, I became the Housing Director for a 55-square-block neighborhood known as the Penn Area Neighborhood Association (PANA). Then, the United Nations decreed it the International Year of Shelter for the Homeless. I wrote the proposal: "Philadelphia Stabilization Program," which was acknowledged from HUD's search for the U.N. for examples of best practices for housing people experiencing homelessness. Then I...

- received my Pennsylvania real estate license and practiced with Wissahickon Realty for a brief period.
- created the concept and secured funding for the Mobile Mini-Police Station funded by the late, great Senator John Heinz—with the concept being adopted in at least 6 cities since then.
- became heavily involved in Community Urban Gardening in Germantown, PA., as a way to bring folks together as a community.
- was invited in the mid-1980s to join a small group of friends who reached out to people who had been released from Byberry, the Pennsylvania State Hospital. Severely mentally ill and homeless, these former patients were living wrapped around the steam grates that heated the sidewalks of downtown Philadelphia in winter.
- was recognized for my homeless/poor/community activism work by (Sylvia's alma mater) La Salle University.
- was recognized by the Philadelphia Bar Association as Man of the Year.
- was recognized by the Pennsylvania Senate.

When Buddy, my dog and best friend ever, died, I buried him on the sacred grounds of the Leni Lenape Native Americans in Germantown, MD. In 1989, my mother contracted congestive heart failure ending my Pennsylvania real estate career. Miraculously, Sylvia and I sold our beloved home at a profit in about a month and a half and moved to Austin, TX. Having rushed to give emotional support to my mother, we arrived with no jobs. I camped out on the doorstep of Legal Aid Attorney Regina Rogoff and Attorney Rod Nelson until they finally hired me to stop my everyday sit-in. Sylvia and I bought a house on Hard Rock Road outside of Austin, TX. I then went on to...

- found/create Legal Aid for the Homeless within a month of arriving in Austin in 1989. I assisted homeless/disabled people and helped secure their disability benefits for 40 years.
- co-founded House the Homeless Inc., HtH, with my life-long friend and cohort, Cecilia Blanford. HtH is a 501(c)(3) nonprofit based on the principles of advocacy and education around the issue of homelessness. We set up the Board of Directors with no less than 60% of its Board of Directors being either homeless or formerly homeless.

- lead the fight against the no-camping ordinance in both the court and the court of public opinion for five long years along with hundreds of my very best friends, including our champion, attorney Cecilia Wood.
- supported Sylvia when in 1990, she gave birth to our daughter, our beloved Colleen Regnier.
- become a self-taught stonemason. I "rocked-in" our house on Timberline Dr. in Austin and built a stone carport with the help of Sylvia and the "supervision" of our daughter Colleen, then age 5.
- delighted in my sister Gail moving to Austin.
- enjoyed five very fine years with my mother before she left to go help sort things out in heaven.

In 1992, I...
- paddled my kayak on Town Lake in search of Diane Breisch Malloy and discovered her body and uncovered the fact that 23 other brothers and sisters had lived and *died* on the streets of Austin.
- led a march of 100 guys who were suffering in agony and pain from the loss of their brothers and sisters, onto the grounds of the state capitol, without a permit. See the full story in *Looking Up at the Bottom Line–The Struggle for the Living Wage*. You will never be the same again.

Next, I created the Homeless Memorial on Auditorium Shores by planting a live oak tree, The Tree of Remembrance, in concert with the City of Austin Parks Department. My good friend Skip Baird and I cracked the cap on a pint of whiskey, raised a toast to Diane Breisch Malloy and all our sisters and brothers lost, and we buried the rest of the bottle under its plaque. The next day, the surface of the plaque was unveiled, and its damning words were vicariously sanctioned in the presence of Mayor Bruce Todd, who, at that time, was leading the initiative to pass the no-camping ordinance against the homeless citizens of Austin. Fifty of our brothers and sisters were present at the unveiling. See: *Looking Up at the Bottom Line*. It will get you up and out of your chair.

I went forward with my life and...
- anticipated the closing of 100 military bases and wrote a proposal to convert part of the Bergstrom Military Base (hospital, two dorms, and the NCO club) to become a drug and alcohol rehabilitation, grounds—maintenance jobs program for people experiencing homelessness. I received approval for the Bergstrom project from the Austin City Council, who had passed and authorized the ordinance to proceed, so long as it didn't interfere with new plans to convert the majority of the 2,000 acres into an International Airport.
- entered college as a sociology major at St. Edwards University in Austin.

Richard with baby Colleen and Sylvia

- was invited to Washington, DC to receive the Beverly "Ma" Curtis Award for homeless activism at the recommendation of Michael Stoops, national organizer for the National Coalition for the Homeless. Michael would later become my close friend.
- struggled for two years to keep the Bergstrom Detox/Jobs project alive in the middle of ever-changing plans of the city for the Austin Bergstrom Air Base that was being developed into Bergstrom International Airport more and more every day.
- received a Certification of Recognition of Programs for Dealing with Homelessness from Governor Ann Richards.
- published two homeless newsletters in Austin—North Star Legal Update and Notes from the Blues Box, which continues today as The Challenger, under the editorship of Valerie Romness.
- received the Distinguished Service Award from Mayor Lee Cook for my work in the area of homelessness.
- provided Bill Clinton, who was running for President the first time, my proposal, which he touted as continuing solutions to deal with homelessness by converting U.S. military bases into job training centers and living quarters across America.
- felt monetarily faint of heart when the Austin City Council retracted the use of the Bergstrom Air Base for our housing and jobs program.
- graduated from St. Edwards University in 1997 with honors and received a B.A. in Sociology.

Between 1995–2010, I received many awards, including...

- KVUE Five Who Care Award–National Jefferson Community Service Award, Austin Area Homeless Coalition Certificate of Appreciation for Outstanding Community Service, J.C. Penny Golden Rule Award, Beverly "Ma" Curtis Award, United Way Community Collaboration Award, Austin Chamber of Commerce Community Legacy Award, American Civil Liberties Union of Texas Outstanding Civic Contributions Certificate, City of Austin Human Rights Commission Recognition and Award,
- 2005 Texas Homeless Network Outstanding Homeless Advocate,
- 2006-2007 The Heritage Registry of Who's Who,
- 2009 Texas Homeless Network Homeless Community Service Award,
- 2009 Community Action Network Fred Butler Leadership Award,
- 2010 Runner-Up, Citizen of the Year, City of West Lake Hills

With the help of Attorney Cecilia Wood, I then arranged for House the Homeless to sue President Clinton, the U.S. Government, and the City of Austin. This was accomplished under the 1988 McKinney Act/Law that says that "...unused or underutilized military property, should be made available to the homeless community..." I discovered that they had failed to fulfill a requirement to advertise the availability of the Bergstrom land parcels in the Federal Register.

Richard receiving Beverly "Ma" Curtis Award

This was when I devised the Universal Living Wage Formula to fix the Federal Minimum Wage. This formula is designed to ensure that if a person puts in 40 hours of work (be it from one job or more), that person will be able to afford basic food, clothing, shelter, phone and public transportation, in whatever location that work is done throughout the United States. I then...

- actively participated in Leadership Austin.
- wrote and published *Striking a Balance*, a book about the pending gentrification of East Austin, which, at that time, was inhabited almost entirely by Black and Hispanic people.
- created **Project Fresh Start**, a seamless Continuum of Care, Social Service Network linking existing homeless services in the city and identifying missing links, including a living wage jobs program. The document continues to be the blueprint for ending homelessness in Austin.
- crafted the Homeless Protected Class Resolution at the urging of Michael Stoops National Coalition for the Homeless, NCH, field organizer.
- orchestrated the three-time ratification of the resolution by the National Coalition for the Homeless.
- was awarded the City of Austin Community Collaboration Award and Community Legacy Award with Katie Grau, my Vista Volunteer and dear friend who died in her 20s.
- created in 1998 the Plastic Pocket Guide, a city-wide resource for people experiencing homelessness, as well as social service providers. This multi-paneled, laminated, folding, pocket-size information resource guide is now in its 17th printing.
- became a certified massage therapist in the State of Texas.
- launched the Thermal Underwear Drive, now in its 20th year of winterizing homeless Austinites.

In 2001, I built and launched the Universal Living Wage website with the help of my good friend Kathie Kimbrel. I launched the Universal Living Wage (ULW) Campaign with the help of my friend JoAnn Koepke, who gathered contacts while I hand-signed, addressed, and mailed 42,000 letters to potential supporting organizations that included unions, faith-based entities, nonprofits, and businesses. This created our letters of support and ULW database throughout the entire United States. This was before most people had really come to utilize the internet, let alone have email accounts. Despite being physically challenged, JoAnn has "risen to the occasion" her entire life. House the Homeless helped get her off the streets in the early 1990s. She led House the Homeless to virtually "adopt" two young orphan girls from Uganda and financially assist and emotionally support them as they entered adulthood. I then...

- went to Houston, TX, and urged the Texas Greens to vote to help form and become part of the National Green Party and then vote to support the Universal Living Wage. They did both.

- traveled with Eric in 2007 to Inner Mongolia in China on an Earth Watch Expedition. With Dr. Gu, we searched water in the Gobi Desert.
- published in 2010, my second book, *Looking Up at the Bottom Line: The Struggle for the Living Wage*. It is about the economics of homelessness and includes my formula to fix the federal minimum wage. After a five-year search for a publisher, I was told by the founder of Plainview Press that the book was, "too important not to be published."
- crafted the Criminalization of Homelessness Cycle—Austin. The cycle clearly shows that businesses paying people so little that they fall into homelessness and are then fined for their condition of being homeless, such as sleeping outside because they can't afford housing, and are then arrested for being unable to pay the fine, only keeps people impoverished and living on the streets.
- crafted a formula to fix the Supplemental Security Income, SSI stipend, commonly known as Disability Benefits, to ensure access to housing.

In 2012 after one full year of negotiation with the City of Austin, we reached the nation's first settlement over the No Sit/No Lie Ordinance. This brought the city ordinance into compliance with the Federal Americans with Disabilities Act...and then some. I then...
- wrote the white paper, "Prevention of Homelessness...at its Core."
- needing to find another medium to reach out to our citizenry about homelessness, I secured permission of the HTH Board of Directors to learn to **sculpt** in bronze, and I studied under Steve Dubois for one year.
- published the e-book, *Livable Incomes that Stimulate the Economy*.
- launched the city-wide/city endorsed House the Homeless, Let's Get to Work initiative based on Livable Incomes.

Then I sculpted and fired a clay version of *The Home Coming*. My vision of a chance encounter of a homeless veteran with his daughter and her dog with an African American woman on the edge of a woods. They share what little they have, the warmth of their fire and their humanity.

In 2014, I was approached by Timothy P. Schmalz, who has been called the "Michelangelo of our time." Together, over 4 1/2 years, we sculpted *The Home Coming* by phone and through the internet.

In 2015, I raised funds for him to create a 2 ½ foot high plaster cast of *The Home Coming*. In 2016, I raised funds to order and secure 200 maquettes, or miniature statues, which would be used to raise funds to create the life-size statue in bronze.

I successfully raised funds to cover all the costs of bronze casting *The Home Coming*. In 2019, at Austin's Community First! Village, my new friend Larry Crawford-Director of Maintenance, and I installed the sculpture so that the characters appear to be walking on the earth, not a pedestal. Community First! Village, vision borne from the Bergstrom jobs program effort, was revived by the visionary founder Alan Graham. In its second stage of development, the 51-acre community became a place where the disabled homeless can live with dignity and fairness. On May 18th, 2019, my friend Will Hyatt pulled off the tarp and unveiled The Home Coming. I immediately started to raise funds for a second statue to be placed in Washington DC.

During this time, in 2017, I suffered the loss of my friend, national homeless advocate Michael Stoops, who will never be forgotten.

I traveled with Eric in 2018 to witness the intentional flooding of indigenous people to create surface water. After 40 years at Legal Aid, I semi-retired at age 69. Before leaving, I created a 3-inch-thick operations manual so that Legal Aid for the Homeless could carry on without me. It was typed by my friend and legal secretary, Karen Gilbert, and four copies were made. One copy is being submitted to the Austin History Museum. I then began the emotionally painful task of disassembling parts of the nonprofit, House the Homeless, that I created in 1989, shoring up other parts so it can continue. I stepped down as President and became the National Education Director, NED.

In 2019, Sylvia (best ever special education teacher) and I made a major move. We sold the Austin home that we had lived in for 30 years and moved to Weddington, NC, to be near our daughter Colleen. Here, we bought ourselves another home plus a house for Sylvia's parents. Since then, I...

- made over 400 face masks, starting in early March of 2020, with my wonderful Sylvia, for anyone who would wear them.
- designed a Horticultural Tree Plan to plant trees throughout Community First! Village so that everyone can claim a part in building this National Best Practice Community.
- drove with Sylvia 8 times to and from Washington DC looking for a second statue location.
- connected with one of only 4 makers of the ceramic tiles on which a Q.R. Code can be printed. Now while standing in front of the statue, you can use the app on your smartphone and get the backstory of the statue characters at Community First! Village.
- submitted an application and complete workup regarding the Universal Living Wage Campaign and Calculator for consideration and publication with Wikipedia. This remains pending. On May 10, 2021 I received an acceptance letter of the 2nd Home Coming statue by the Catholic Church on July 1, 2021 Sylvia and I drive to Washington DC to complete the process (hopefully) with a

successful vote from the United States Conference of Bishops and make arrangements for ground installation of the statue at the Basilica of the National Shrine of the Immaculate Conception.

Then, I wrote this book.

Why does any of this matter? My story is not here to toot my own whistle. It is to tell you I've been up close and personal with homelessness. I've been homeless and struggled to claw my way out. I have a home now. But my struggles and determination put me in the position to know how homelessness comes to be and how we can generate solutions to end it. There is no doubt that I have been blessed. And to me, to have been blessed means that I have a responsibility to give back to others. I/we must share our experiences, the good and the bad. That is now my charge, to tell my story, my whole story, and by so doing, to help others with real solutions.

And, this matters because you can help. There are many things you can do, both small and large. Every small kindness and every conscious action does help. The final chapter is devoted to you: How You Can Help to End Homelessness.

Note: A few of the stories in my first book are retold in this book, in slightly more detail. Each of these represents a significant moment in my life. It is my sincere hope that every life that was touched along the way has been enhanced. I know that mine was, and I thank each and every one of you and Jesus who pulled me back from the brink...so many times.

3 Executive Summary
by Richard R. Troxell

This book outlines basic, pragmatic steps for ending and preventing homelessness in the nation. It opens with a framing preface from the brilliant Professor Edgar Cahn, who, among many other remarkable accomplishments, is credited with the creation of civil legal services for the poor in America. Dr. Cahn opens his remarks with a refreshing perspective and his vision to value all human contributions and the need to identify those contributions as a form of work.

The book also contains an insightful overview of the most recent wave of homelessness in America by the indefatigable Sue Watlov Phillips,

M.A. retired licensed Psychologist, Independent Clinical Social Worker, Marriage and Family Therapist, Certified Sports Psychologist, currently Executive Director, MICAH (Metropolitan Interfaith Council on Affordable Housing), political activist (1965-current), current President of the National Coalition for the Homeless, and friend.

The book shares a brief view of current approaches used to combat homelessness. However, combating homelessness is *not* preventing homelessness, and so, we delve into other approaches to end and prevent homelessness.

First, we suggest a permanent fix of the **Federal Minimum Wage**, FMW, with my formula that ensures that if a person works 40 hours in a week, they will be able to afford basic food, clothing, shelter, phone, and public transportation, wherever that work is done throughout the nation. This will end homelessness for over 1 million people and prevent economic homelessness for all minimum wage workers.

We suggest another approach for those who cannot work—fixing the Supplemental Security Income, SSI program from a state or national perspective. This will stop the current practice of placing non-sustaining disability checks into the hands of our nation's people who are coping with disabilities. Due to these limited economic funds, these folks will eventually find themselves living on the streets of America with those pitifully small checks crumpled and shoved deep into their pockets.

The book blends the history of recent American homelessness with my approach and formula of using existing government guidelines to successfully tackle our institutional Federal Minimum Wage and set it on a permanent course to ensure housing for any full-time minimum wage worker, and I then go on to do the same for all people struggling to cope with disabilities. Together, these two concepts affecting those who can work and those who cannot work are forged into the concept of Livable Incomes for all.

We then have the opportunity to merge this with the concept of recognizing human value as defined by Professor Cahn and blend it all together.

Realizing that at no time do we know as much about an individual's needs as when they have entered one of our major institutions, I propose an ethical standard and methodology for our institutions to devise and then execute their own blueprint to "Discharge No One into Homelessness," preferably into homes but certainly not onto the street.

Along the way, we stop to say goodbye to Michael Stoops, an icon, role model, a dear friend, and true champion of all folks experiencing homelessness across the entire nation.

Next, we look at a successful effort to forge change for the better, as we watch House the Homeless, Inc. engage the very folks who have been beaten and arrested while they were down and living on our streets. We see them rise up and knock down a damning local (Austin, TX) ordinance, No Sit/No Lie, just like Lech Walesa in Poland when he climbed that fence on the workers' dock and smashed that foreman square in the jaw. He had been spreading word-poison and messing with the worker's pay in an effort to crush their spirit, instead of simply paying a fair wage, for a fair day's work.

After more than a decade of work, we unveil *The Home Coming* statue: its origin, present, and future. That led us to Community First! Village that epitomizes National Best Practices for re-envisioning community for our nation's folks experiencing homelessness with disabilities.

We then examine Traumatic Brain Injuries—a major cause of homelessness. Our warrior heroes, America's veterans, unite behind Dr. Gordon's medical protocol, rise up, and prepare to finally come home in peace.

Since so many people experiencing homelessness are affected by the devastating problem of alcoholism, we focus on identifying a funding mechanism for treatment without blame by looking through the lens of *product liability*.

Finally, we answer the question, "How can you help end and prevent homelessness?" With an array of action items to choose from, you can be sure that you'll find one that fits you.

*All of these components encompassing: economics, healthcare, political struggle, the power of art, struggles with addiction, finding ones' shared voice, and taking action to achieve our goals, all add up to the struggle to end our nation's homelessness with love, compassion, honor, dignity, and fairness.

40

Author's Comment: Speaking of Flushing out Viruses, Here's Suds in Your Eye!

In 1983, The Ku Klux Klan came to Austin in their complete clown outfits. The Austin citizenry mooned them and serenaded them with a mooning song. I was not there; I did not arrive in Austin until 1989. On January 16, 1993, they returned to decry the birthday of the Reverend Doctor Martin Luther King, Jr. I was out of town. I am told that 50 of these people waddled in their clown outfits to the new Austin City Hall, stood on the newly built speaker's platform, and desecrated it by spewing their vile hatred. It was on the news. I returned to Austin the next day, Sunday, January 17th. When I learned what they had done, I gathered six of my closest homeless friends, and we met at the platform with buckets, brushes, and soap. For the next two hours, we scrubbed that 20' by 20' square of sacred ground until it was immaculate and free of filth.

Similarly, like our response to the KKK, the only way to end homelessness is to draw attention to it and then *take action*!

Richard R. Troxell
In Unity There Is Strength

4 Livable Incomes: Homelessness Solved!

To end and prevent economic homelessness, people working at and earning a Federal Minimum Wage need *Livable Incomes*. Period. Full stop. For those who *can* work, we need a Universal Living Wage, and for those who *cannot*, we need to fix the SSI stipend, otherwise known as Supplemental Security Income.

The Universal Living Wage information found in this chapter first appeared (in part) in the white paper: "Prevent Homelessness at its Core, the Universal Living Wage for Dramatic Business Savings". It has been updated with current calculations and 2022 Fair Market Rents to display current wage values. However, the principles and examples remain valid.

Our approach that solves the income problem for minimum wageworkers, when combined with the income problem solution for our nation's disabled, will end and prevent economic homelessness in the form of Livable Incomes. A national economic stimulus (the Universal Living Wage) answers several hard-core American problems when it comes to homelessness prevention. It is good for business, good for the taxpayer, and good for the American worker.

Preventing Economic Homelessness

This discusses some primary methods of ending and preventing homelessness, along with other less impactful methods. Principal solutions:
1. The Universal Living Wage
2. Fix all income support programs, e.g., the federal Supplemental Social Security Income (SSI), so it is a livable income
   2a. Fix the state SSI stipend
3. The combination of all: Livable Incomes
4. Discharge No One Into Homelessness

A Brief Look at Current Practices to Address Homelessness

If you come to this discussion with any preconceptions and prejudices about people experiencing homelessness and their worthiness, let's be clear right from the beginning. No doubt there are those who suffer drug and alcohol addiction or mental health concerns, including traumatic brain injuries or developmental disorders. Still, you will need to realize that, by far, the vast majority of the conditions referred to in this book are the direct result of a glitch in the American Dream that results in *income inequality*. The Federal Minimum Wage no longer works as intended.

Since our beginnings as a nation, we have referred to America as the "land of opportunity," but for so many, it is now the lack of economic opportunity that has rendered them homeless.

An often-used method of assisting someone who has run into financial trouble is to provide the individual with a handout to help that person bridge the economic gap in rental or mortgage arrears. These are usually one-time, limited assistance supports that will temporarily hold off eviction or mortgage foreclosure. This support usually ranges from $25.00 to $200.00 (COVID-19 response aside). Programs providing these funds, such as churches, and governmental entities, rarely ever follow up on the long-term success of their investments because dollars are scarce to begin with, and any kind of follow-up monitoring is quite costly. While possibly helpful at the moment of issuance, this is a superficial response to arrearage, and it doesn't address the core problem: basic income doesn't cover basic expenses.

Another fairly popular prevention program is known as the Federal Housing and Urban Development, HUD, **Section 8 Program**. This is a simple yet complicated preventative program. It enables people to rent housing that their budgets could otherwise not afford. Here is a simplified example. The landlord owns several properties in an area, but the populace in that area cannot afford the $1,200 a month rent that the landlord wants to charge for each property. There are two needs to be met here. The landlord needs his/her asking rental price to continue operating his/her properties. The tenant needs to find affordable housing. So, to achieve both desires, the federal government steps in and writes a check of around $200. This brings down the rent to an affordable level of $1,000 for the tenant, and the landlord gets his/her asking rental amount of $1,200.

This symbiotic relationship works well on a limited basis. Its success is limited to the amount of existing housing stock and the limited number of landlords willing to involve themselves with government programs requiring additional paperwork and with inherently economically unstable tenants. However, the program can only help a limited number of people. Still, it prevents at least some households from deteriorating into a homeless situation. This is basically a subsidy program for renters that also simultaneously benefits the landlords.

Another tax-supported, federally funded housing program is known as **Permanent Supportive Housing**. It is designed to respond to the condition of homelessness for people who have persistent problems with substance abuse, addiction or alcoholism, or a diagnosis of mental illness or a developmental disorder. This program is no doubt expensive and clearly a responsive, after-the-fact program for people experiencing homelessness, but it can act to end the condition of homelessness. This program, however, does not prevent the condition of homelessness. Rather, it *manages* and attacks personal control over ones life.

The **HUD-Veterans Supportive Housing Program** (HUD-VASH) basically provides the same kind of rental assistance for homeless veterans, coupled with case management and clinical services provided by the Department of Veterans Affairs.

Again, it is reactive, not proactive, certainly not preventative, and it again accommodates homelessness while disempowering the Vet.

Another very successful taxpayer-based assistance program is known as the **HUD Mortgage Assignment Program** of the 1980s. When the homeowner of a federally backed mortgage fell behind in their payments, "due to circumstances beyond their control," the federal government would step in and temporarily or permanently take "assignment" of the note from the original note holder.

Circumstances beyond one's control might include long-term illness, serious injury, and loss of income. At this point, the nature of the "assignment" could take on many forms. For example, if the borrower, now facing foreclosure, had already recovered from the financially disruptive event and was now able to continue with regular monthly payments, HUD might amortize the arrearage, spreading it out over an 18-month or 2-year period. By increasing the monthly payment by a reasonable amount, the arrearage is paid off, and the monthly payment eventually returns to the original level. This situation often results from the general trend toward encouraging people to "buy more home than they could afford."

The HUD Mortgage Assignment Program worked so well that mortgage foreclosure preventionists, as advocates, created a similar mortgage foreclosure prevention program in Pennsylvania to deal with the 1980s recession. The then Sheriff of Philadelphia County characterized it as a time when "more foreclosures occurred than during the Great Depression."

Coincidentally, the onset of modern-day homelessness in this country in the 20th century was reflected in the creation of these two programs. They all came as a result of the end of the Vietnam War with tens of thousands of returning veterans, double-digit inflation, and inflated gas prices with gas lines stretching for blocks. Mental health facilities closed, and seriously ill individuals were abandoned with nowhere to live and no out-patient care. Today, 40% of adults experiencing homelessness suffer from severe mental health problems, and around 30% are veterans. (Some studies are reporting that this has reduced significantly for veterans since 2000.) The promised community-based facilities were never funded at a level necessary to assist the folks de-institutionalized or new folks, dealing with significant mental health issues.

The federal government decided to stop warehousing its poor citizens in high-rise apartments and reduced its funding in this area by 75%. This resulted in the transfer of poverty relief responsibilities to our nation's municipalities.

The extreme increase in homelessness has been attributed to the vision of President Ronald Reagan (with permission from Republicans and Democrats in Congress) and his "trickle-down theory" or "voodoo economics" as it came to be known. The result almost cost him his presidency. However, the damage mostly came to rest on the backs of the minimum wage workers, many of whom became "the homeless."

According to the National Coalition for the Homeless and the National Law Center on Homelessness and Poverty, at least 3.5 million people will experience homelessness during this year, 2021. The people who will become homeless include single men and women from unemployment, underemployment, insufficient wages (including college graduates who can't find work), women and men from failed marriages/relationships, single women/men with children, whole families, youth aging out of foster care, and senior citizens. Other future homeless people have drug or alcohol problems or have been released from correctional or mental health facilities. Returning veterans suffering traumatic brain injuries are also in this group. The list is long and more groups are constantly being added. Despite the existence of some impromptu financial safeguards, an estimated 30 to 40 million Americans could be evicted because of the COVID-19 pandemic.

Historically, our nation's limited response has been to address homelessness by categories (e.g., President Obama's initiative to end homelessness for veterans). Battered women's shelters have garnered a significant share of "homeless" dollars. Previously, our nation has simply responded inadequately to the condition of homelessness; however, in viewing the experience of homelessness as an issue of poverty, we should now stand back and re-think our entire approach to this phenomenon. This chapter will examine poverty prevention and its positive effects on business, economic growth, and the people suffering homelessness.

Presently, the American taxpayer bears the brunt of our current response to this phenomenon of homelessness. As homelessness has found its way into our cities, churches serving sandwiches soon found themselves struggling to help the burgeoning problem. Well-intentioned but ill-equipped to deal with the scope and depth of the problem, they stretched their limits to respond. Some set up family rotation programs where beleaguered homeless families would be passed every two weeks from one church to the next, exhausting everyone.

Municipal ten-year plans promoted by the George W. Bush White House and the National Alliance to End Homelessness addressed the symptoms and had only a superficial effect. In part, this was true because *none of the plans had an economic component of any kind that addressed the root causes of homelessness* or established prevention methodologies.

The San Antonio Story

In 2012, representatives from San Antonio, Texas, came to Austin to tout their success in dealing with homelessness. Thanks to the benefactor of the Chapman Project, they refurbished 18 buildings and built four others to house the Haven for Hope program, composed of a single point of entry. Mr. Chapman later died and left an endowment to carry the project forward.

At the presentation, I learned that their annual operating budget was 47 million dollars! Audience comments made it clear that they were shocked to learn that this budget did not include any transitional housing or supportive housing programs. The room was full of dignitaries, including numerous city council members and homeless advocates, who were stunned. I asked the lead presenter to share what must now be their single greatest focus? What steps were they taking to end homelessness through prevention? At first, he looked like a deer caught in the headlights. Then he shared a story of repeated recidivism by a man suffering from alcoholism. He finished by saying that people just needed to commit to ending their own homelessness. The room became stone silent. I simply backed away from the microphone.

The Bigger Picture

What we need to look at is what would cause an individual to go through the excruciating pain and humiliation of withdrawal, only to repeat the act repeatedly for over 20 years of addiction. Could it be a lack of economic opportunity and conditions that lead to despair for which alcohol or drug abuse provide only temporary solace?

As our nation transformed itself from an agrarian society to an industrial and now a technological one, our workforce migrated from rural America to urban America seeking jobs. During the Urban Renewal of the 1960s through 1980s, we destroyed the residential hotels, single room occupancy, SRO units and did not replace housing for working poor and folks on fixed incomes. Since the 1970s, jobless workers have come to congregate in our cities, looking for jobs and places to live. The 1980s brought President Reagan and Congress's 75% reduction in the nation's Housing Authorities. Many became homeless and remained, still looking for work, dependent on limited charity resources or throw-away items, and approaching people to ask them directly for help ("panhandling").

All across America, downtown businesses have been feeling besieged by this ever-growing, ever more desperate population of needy individuals. Consequently, they developed Business Improvement Districts that allowed them to raise money and push laws to criminalize the behavior of people experiencing homelessness. Enforcement is provided by "Joe the cop," who is caught in the middle when directed by "Bob the business owner" to remove the people they perceive as affecting their bottom line, namely, the business's profits.

So, the shopkeepers and restaurant owners post signs saying "Restrooms for Patrons Only," and the city makes laws against urinating in public. As a result, people are often arrested for exposing themselves, which can come with a lifetime of being treated as a sex offender. Other laws including no camping, no panhandling, no solicitation or no aggressive solicitation (which is open to interpretation), no loitering, no sitting, and no lying down, have been passed all across the nation. Business owners say that they are merely coming after the "condition" of homelessness with their laws. But after decades, the nation's business community has done almost nothing to address the causes of homelessness, including paying living wages. Note—Between 1997 and 2007, and between 2010 past 2021, Congress compounded the homeless problem by failing to raise the Federal Minimum Wage at all.

Reluctantly, America's urban entrepreneurs have been swept up in the dynamic of homelessness. These business people are simply trying to live the American dream of raising a family, attaining homeownership, and sending their kids to college. However, with people experiencing homelessness literally coming up to their patrons on a Saturday night, confronting them, and asking for help, business owners feel overwhelmed and have gotten laws passed that they call "Quality of Life" ordinances.

This sends a message that people experiencing homelessness are sub-human and worthy only of contempt—in short, that *their* quality of life does not matter at all.

Today, people experiencing homelessness comprise the single largest target of hate crimes in the nation. These physical attacks range from clubbing with baseball bats (Florida) to zapping individuals with 50,000 volts of electricity from a stun gun while they sleep on a park bench (Ohio), to immolation (Texas), to decapitation for gang initiation (Colorado). The cost of homelessness to American businesses, our institutions, and the taxpayers is astronomical. Costs include:

- constructing and maintaining emergency homeless shelters all across the nation,
- the misuse of emergency rooms in our public hospitals as if they were health clinics,

- misdirected use of police officers nationwide to enforce the "quality of life" ordinances,
- Community Courts to prosecute homeless folks for violation of "quality of life" ordinances,
- for sleeping, loitering, and asking for help (panhandling), etc.,
- creation and maintenance of the temporary fix known as transitional housing facilities,
- creation and maintenance of nationwide community care health facilities in our emergency homeless shelters,
- Homeless Management Information Systems HMIS, used to identify and track people experiencing homelessness, and
- creation and maintenance of permanent supportive housing units.

The U.S. budgeted 3.1 billion on homelessness in 2021 without even beginning to solve the problem of homelessness.

Combating Homelessness is NOT Preventing Homelessness

While inundated businesses scream for help and pass laws seeking relief, they fail to realize and/or acknowledge that businesses are a huge part of the problem. The federal government has set a wage standard; the Federal Minimum Wage (FMW) is so low that according to the last several United States Conference of Mayors reports, a full-time 40-hour-a-week worker cannot keep basic rental housing. The amazing thing about that statistic is that everyone knows that the most expensive item in every American's budget, be it home ownership or rental, is their housing costs. At the same time, although the FMW relates to no part of the reality of poverty economics, its wage standard is repeatedly plucked out of the air by members of Congress and presented as an irrefutable fact. We have briefly looked at the framing of homelessness and the different human factions making up the population of homelessness. We suggest that we now think of people experiencing homelessness as fitting into two major categories: Those who *can* work and those who *cannot* work (and, of course, those who can work only some of the time).

The Yardstick

Imagine our society as a horizontal yardstick divided into 3 lengths of 1 foot each. The yardstick represents our socio-economic structure. In the section on the right, my beautiful daughter, Colleen is represented. When she and her friends were in school, they were simply tasked with learning. That was their job. They were not expected to make any financial contribution to society at that stage of their lives. In fact, from the day they entered kindergarten until they turn 18, they cost us, as taxpayers, a considerable amount of money. We construct and maintain learning institutions so that they and the multitude of students behind them will be equipped to complete their task of being good students, and ultimately, good productive workers. Loving my daughter as I do, I was more than okay with Colleen not financially contributing anything to the system. That was not her job. In my mind, her job was to major in art, minor in business, learn French, and tell me who to write the checks to.

On the left side of the yardstick is another one-foot section, representative of Colleen's grandparents. They are in their mid and late 80s and have earned their right to retire. They have worked hard all their lives, and for their remaining years, they will reap the fruits of their labors. They have stopped working and now rely on their savings and Social Security for the rest of their lives. People in this sector are no longer expected to make substantial financial contributions to the system. That, too, is okay.

But this leaves only the middle section—the "worker foot"—to sustain not only itself but also the two other sections. That is a tremendous financial responsibility. Moreover, starting in the 2000s and continuing for the next 20 or 30 years, a dramatic shift will occur, and an exceptional number of people will leave that productive, bills-paying segment as "baby boomers" continue to move into retirement. Regardless, the "worker foot" will continue to be expected to sustain both the "student foot" and the "retirement foot," in addition to themselves.

The "worker foot" contains 10.1 million minimum wage workers plus an estimated 10 million undocumented workers. These 20 million people are working for anywhere between $2.13 per hour to slightly above the federal minimum hourly wage of $7.25. (Now, with the *15 and Fight* campaign, there is a smattering of other breakout wages.)

These wages are insufficient for them to get into and keep basic rental housing as individuals. The National Homelessness Law Center and the National Coalition for the Homeless point to this and state that 3.5 million people are expected to experience homelessness again in 2021. Folks are working but don't make enough to sustain them in housing. Therefore, hard-working minimum wage earners are falling out of the "worker foot" and instead experience homelessness. This does not bode well for our society as a whole. Between the aging workers shifting to the "retirement foot" and good working people falling out of the "worker foot," there is a tremendous strain on each end of our yardstick. Some say the stick could break.

Others say that it has already snapped, and the evidence is the unbridled immigration that has occurred in this country in recent years and an overwhelming worker response in our urban areas where some wages have been blindly re-set in some cities at $15.00 per hour.

50

The Federal Poverty Guideline

In 1963, the U.S. Government established the Federal Poverty Guidelines. President Johnson was from the South and had seen the face of poverty. Social engineers (social workers) spoke out about hunger in Appalachia, the impoverished region within the Blue Ridge Mountains. The television airwaves beamed out pictures of starving children.

The "War on Poverty" commenced. As the "breadbasket of the world," we declared that it was unacceptable for anyone to go to bed hungry in America.

Of course, it was important to know how poor you had to be in order to be considered impoverished, so a standard was created. At the Social Security Administration, Mrs. Molly Orshanski took a small basket and filled it with the "staples of life." She placed meat, bread, and potatoes into the basket. She used a multiplier of three and then multiplied this by the number of people in the household. Voilà! They had created the first of the Federal Poverty Guidelines. Remarkably, this same standard is still in use today! How relevant was or is the standard in reality? In 1963, food made up 23% of the monthly family budget. Housing, at that time, made up 29% of the monthly family budget. Today, food makes up only 16% of the monthly family budget, whereas housing makes up 37% to 50% or even more. Obviously, the costliest item that we all share is *housing*, not food. Logic dictates that if in our society, our lives are centered around housing, and the majority of our living expenses are for housing, and lack of housing results in homelessness, then the goal should be to make basic wages relate to our ability to afford basic rental housing.

The Federal Minimum Wage

In 1938, both halves of Congress established the Federal Minimum Wage (FMW). The FMW was created in response to the millions of men who wandered our country during the Depression in search of work with a living wage. There were over 14 million people unemployed. The government determined that the minimum wage needed to be set at about fifty cents. So, of course, it was set at twenty-five cents.[1] Despite starting a little light in the pocketbook, the minimum wage served this country fairly well until 1973, when double-digit inflation struck concurrent with the energy crisis. In the early 1970s, a young man willing to work could walk onto a construction site, embellish his capabilities, get hired, strap on a hammer, work a full, hard day at $1.60 per hour, and walk away with enough money to rent a room at the YMCA, stash his stuff, get clean and rested, and return to do it all over again the next day.

However, in the 1990s Reaganomics, tax law changes in 1987 took tax breaks away from mom-and-pop landlords, and the high-tech boom had hit America head-on. The cost of everything inflated again. When the dust finally settled, the cost of everything settled back close to its original amount, except *housing*. Commercial realtors let properties sit fallow for years rather than reduce the rental price. Also, landlords have offered to let people move in for $ 1.00, waive security deposits, give away microwaves, etc. They offer anything to get you to sign a lease—everything but lower rents. As a result, the cost of rental housing in urban areas has soared well out of reach of minimum wage workers. When Congress debates an increase in the FMW, which they usually do every 4 or 5 years, they start by plucking a number out of the air. They usually start by discussing an hourly raise of $1 or $1.50, to be implemented gradually over a period of several years. They wrangle over this for a year, and in the end, settle on less than asked for or at any rate, certainly less than a living wage. This amount relates to nothing. It is not based on need or affordability but is totally arbitrary. Also, remember that Congress failed to ever link the Federal Minimum Wage to the local cost of living and even failed to raise the FMW during two separate decades.

Housing

Clearly, housing is the antithesis of homelessness. We as a capitalist society do not enjoy a society in which the taxpayer is bearing the housing bill for our nation's working poor, but we do so for the homeowners through tax subsidies. Because both halves of Congress have already determined that FMW is the law of the land, legislators say, "Why not just simply, periodically, adjust the base wage amount slightly?" However, what needs to occur is to *make the Federal Minimum Wage relate to the local cost of housing throughout the United States*. This would provide an incentive to work. As the cost of housing rises, so would wages. In this fashion, no matter how high the rent rises, if the worker puts in their 40-hour week, the worker would be able to afford basic rental housing.

Workers could be assured of housing affordability, and the economy would be stimulated by the construction jobs provided by filling the need for housing that minimum wage working people could then afford. In fact, they would once again be positioned to chase the American dream of homeownership.

52

5 Livable Incomes Foundation: The Universal Living Wage

Group picture with bilingual banner

In 1997, as president of House the Homeless, I devised a single national formula, using existing government guidelines. It ensures that, if a person works 40-hour a week, be it from one job or more, then the wage they earn would enable them to afford basic rental housing, food, clothing, phone, public transportation, and shelter, wherever the work is done throughout the United States. This is called The Universal Living Wage.

Economic homelessness is a term for when someone does everything society expects—specifically, holds a job—and still can't afford rent. House the Homeless Inc. *conservatively* estimates that the Universal Living Wage will end homelessness for over 1,000,000 people and prevent economic homelessness for all 20 million minimum wage workers.

Who can disagree with this approach? Besides, what is the alternative? People are going to survive, and they will do it any way they can. In this society, money dictates everything. People will sell whatever they can to get by. Of course, at the lowest economic level, with minimally adequate wages not in the picture, there are only three things readily available to sell: drugs, guns, and other people. This is not my vision for America, and it doesn't have to remain our reality. We need to choose a viable wage alternative instead.

America is the greatest nation on earth. It is the land of milk and honey. It is the land of opportunity, but not for all people working and living within the system. The system is failing the people at the bottom and squeezing them out. It is forcing people to make bad ethical decisions just to survive. The system is robbing them of their dignity and their self-respect. It is driving them off the tax rolls and onto the tax dole, or worse. Why would anyone work at a minimum wage job 40 hours a week when it will not even get him or her into housing? With the "worker foot" shrinking, does it make any sense that we allow 3.5 million people to experience homelessness in our country every year? Remember, the federal government says that 42% of the people experiencing homelessness are working at some point during the week! The work ethic is there; however, the wage is not.

When the Universal Living Wage is passed, there will be a huge stream of income available for housing. Once the ULW goes into effect, we will put the difference between the FMW ($7.25 per hour) and its new level in any Fair Market Rent region throughout the United States, into the pockets of millions of minimum wage workers; all of whom need the same thing, housing. For the first time, millions of people will have the financial ability to afford basic rental housing. Today, in 2021, that housing stock does not exist. There has been no financial incentive to build it. There will be plenty of financial incentives when the ULW is passed. The soundness of our logic is reflected in the endorsement of the ULW by a national construction company, HSR Construction, which resulted from informal discussions. Additionally, the federal government and the U.S military have followed our lead and now offer a "locality pay" that ensures that the wages they pay enables their people to afford the basics of life.

Some people have wrongly suggested that, upon the passage of the ULW, housing costs will soar beyond the reach of renters and cause unbridled inflation. This is problematic but not exactly accurate. First, the cost of everything else has already been inflated. The FMW has not kept up. Because the ULW is indexed to the local cost of housing, anyone willing and able to work 40 hours will be able to afford basic rental housing regardless of how expensive basic rents become. Second, we believe that once established; the free market would continue to respond to this enormous pool of new money with the *creation* of additional local housing. Furthermore, for the first time, there will be an incentive in the market to keep rental prices in check. Failing that, because the federal government is already monitoring and establishing Fair Market Rents, it will be in position to respond to any unscrupulous market gougers appropriately.

U.S. Fair Labor Standards Act of 1938 and the ULW Effect on the Economy and Business

According to statistical surveys, minimum wage workers have spent almost 100% of past wage increases right back into the economy, thus creating quick economic growth and job creation.[2] As seen with the passage of the U.S. Fair Labor Standards Act in 1938[3] in response to the Great Depression, establishing a living wage similarly stimulates the overall demand for goods and services in the economy. Families become dramatically more creditworthy and can avail themselves of more goods and more services.[4] The overall demand for goods and services will increase demand for low-wage workers as industry responds to this demand and stimulation.[5] Paying a living wage will create new business as new revenue promotes commerce. Businesses do not like high employee turnover because of the costs associated with recruitment, training, supervisory time, and administrative paperwork. Many economists argue that higher pay results in increased productivity by making jobs more desirable to both get and keep. Paying a living wage is good for the local economy because small local businesses rely on local dollars. Obviously, more money for city dwellers will mean more customers for municipal businesses.

To a lesser extent, the same is true in rural America. It has been suggested that paying living wages would cause businesses to relocate from one or another specific district based solely on wage levels. However, because the ULW is uniform nationwide and will affect people equally on a relative basis, that won't occur. It creates a level playing field. Additionally, businesses choose locations in large part because of quality-of-life issues and governmental considerations. A 1998 study issued by ICF Kaiser Economic Strategy Group states: "To maintain Austin Texas's economic success and high standard of livability, the region should focus on the business already here as opposed to attracting new business." The report cited three elements of a "Sustainable Advantage Economy," including the need for "a long-term commitment to improve quality of life and to address social disparity issues as the economy develops."[6]

Others Affected by the ULW

According to the report, "The Sky Hasn't Fallen," the last minimum wage raise did increase earnings of low-wage workers, and this increase "primarily benefited low-income families." Additionally, according to the report, "America's Well Targeted Raise," also released by the Economic Policy Institute, 57% of the gains from the increase went to working families in the bottom 40% of the income scale.[7]

Job Loss

Some argue that the wage increase will lead to job loss. Once again, the national wage increased in 1997 did not lead to job loss. In fact, the conclusion of 'The Sky Hasn't Fallen" report ends with this: "given the statistically and economically insignificant (and mostly positive) employment effects of the change, it might be more useful if the next debate spends less time focusing on the cost of the increase and more on the benefits to low-income families." The report was supported by grants from the Rockefeller Foundation, and the Charles Steward Mott Foundation, and the U.S. Department of Labor.[8]

Ben Bernanke, in his first month of serving as the newly appointed Federal Reserve Chairman, February 1, 2006-January 31, 2014, testified before the House Financial Services Committee. Congressman Bernie Sanders asked Mr. Bernanke if Congress should raise the federal minimum wage "so that every worker in America who works 40 hours a week escapes poverty?" Mr. Bernanke responded, "On the minimum wage, it is actually a very controversial issue among economists. Clearly, if you raise the minimum wage, then those workers who retain their jobs will get higher income, and therefore it helps them. The concerns that some economists have raised about the minimum wage are first: Is it as well targeted as it should be? Is this related to how much of the increase will go to teenage children of suburban families, for example? And secondly, does it have any employment effects? That is, do higher wages lower employment of low-wage workers?" Mr. Bernanke then definitively declared, "My response is that I think it doesn't lower employment."[9] Following a minimum wage increase, we may see unemployment numbers rise. But authors Robert Pollin and Stephanie Luce point out that a minimum wage increase inspires many low-income people who have stopped looking for work to get back in the game.

Unemployment numbers swell, giving the false impression that there is an increase in the number of unemployed. In reality, they are just returning to the "official" ranks of job seekers, where they are again counted.[10]

Outsourcing

If we raise wages, will the low-wage jobs become more vulnerable to being outsourced to countries where the labor is cheaper? In reality, service jobs cannot be outsourced. Minimum wage jobs are service jobs that are required to support the local community. While so many other blue and white-collar jobs are vulnerable to outsourcing, low-wage jobs will remain in this country. Someone must stand in that cafeteria line and prepare and serve the food. Someone has to be present to wash the windows. Someone has to be here to pick up the toilet brush to clean the urinals. Ditch digging is local. Laying rebar on a construction site is local. Selling retail and flipping burgers are all local. These jobs cannot be outsourced to India, China, Mexico, or anywhere else. Unlike in the past, when minimum wage jobs were stepping-stones to the next better-paying jobs, people are now remaining in these low-wage jobs for ten years and longer.[11] As Professor Pollin and Dr. Luce pointed out; we have a "minimum wage family" in this country. If people are going to remain in these jobs long-term, and these jobs cannot be outsourced, then indeed we must ensure that every eligible minimum wage worker is being paid a Universal Living Wage.

Inflation

One of the great fears about increasing the Federal Minimum Wage is that it will cause the price of everything to go up. In reality, wages are just one of many economic factors that make up the cost of an item. The others are manufacturing, transportation, equipment, rent, warehousing, advertising, business location, income demographics of the community, employee recruitment, training expenses, maintenance and more. Clearly, the cost of goods does not automatically have to rise just because one small portion of their make-up increases. An example of the non-inflationary relationship between wages and the cost of goods can be found in the 1996 survey report, "Think Again: A Wage and Price Survey of Denver Area Fast Food Restaurants." This survey focused on four national fast-food chains: Arby's, Burger King, McDonald's, and Taco Bell. All are major employers of entry-level, low-wage workers. Overall, the study clearly showed that just because wages rise, there is not and does not have to be a corresponding increase in prices. In fact, "survey results indicated that higher starting salaries are coupled with only slightly higher, identical, and in many cases lower prices than those in stores that paid a lower starting wage." For example, the lowest-paid Arby's employees were found at a franchise charging the second-highest price for a meal. Conversely, a Taco Bell store paying $1.50 per hour above other restaurants for starting wages simultaneously had the lowest food prices among the twelve other Taco Bell restaurants surveyed.

It would appear that the rise in pricing is more a question of what the market will bear or of what the consumer will tolerate. There may still be economic pressures of an inflationary nature. In some cases, meeting the bare minimum amount necessary to afford basic food, clothing, shelter, and public transportation might substantially increase the minimum wage. Large employers may need to realize a little less profit. Similarly, small employers will need to learn to grow at a much more reasonable rate. At the same time, increased demand for goods will protect the business's bottom line.

Let the "Free Economy" Be Free

Over and over again, a select few businesses repeat that a "free economy" should decide the wage rate. I am more than a little bit concerned about a "free economy" that, for the most part, is based on the taxpayer subsidizing business with several subsidies: the Supplemental Nutrition Assistance Program, SNAP or "food stamps"; Temporary Aid to Needy Families, TANF; the HUD Housing Choice Voucher, formerly known as Section 8 housing subsidy; the Earned Income Tax Credit; General Assistance; and tips, etc. Patrons of the restaurant industry and many other businesses are expected to bring the minimum wage of $2.13 per hour up to $7.25 per hour by paying tips.

Count them, at least six major subsidies, all paid by the taxpayers and patrons because business has not been asked to value its workers on the same level as it values the other components of doing business. Why don't we respect work value?

During the 10 years that followed 1997 with no further minimum wage increase, there were dramatic changes in the marketplace, including the high-tech boom and bust. Housing costs skyrocketed in our urban centers and continued to climb. Congress abandoned both the business community and low-wage workers by not making an adjustment until 2009. The earning power of the minimum wage worker dropped to its lowest level since 1962. Without Congressional guidance on the FMW, the market had been very "free," that is, free-falling. Many employers felt the pressures of market forces and responded by paying $8.00 or even $9.00 an hour to minimum wage workers—but this apparent progress was canceled out by occurring in cities where life-sustaining costs were double what our own government standards had established as minimum.[12]

Nevertheless, employers did not respond appropriately. They did not ask their employees, "Gee, Sally, are you able to pay all of your bills? Are you stealing to get by, Sam? Are you doubled up with strangers, Margaret? Are you selling drugs to make ends meet?" No, that did not occur. For the most part, without the appropriate guidance from Congress, business failed its employees and, as a result, left itself in a destabilized condition. Then, outdoing its previous inaction by doing more of nothing, Congress failed for a second decade, 2010-2021, to raise the Federal Minimum Wage! (Oddly enough, I don't remember Congress's salary taking a dip...ever!)

As a result, business continued to face retraining costs and an unacceptable failure rate. The workforce's response to wholly inadequate wages was explosive! Fifteen and Fight! Starting in 2012 in the big cities, demands for higher wages skyrocketed as workers sprinted to the picket line and the television screens. Major concessions came, and they came fast! The demand for $15.00 an hour became the hue and cry of the streets. Within three years, a dozen major businesses were forced to provide between $10.00 and $15.00 per hour, and others promised to do it within three more years. Wow! The campaign continues in 2022. Talk about market forces.

But the Federal Minimum Wage is a national standard, and these were city area increases. At this point in time, $15.00 is well below the minimum amount to pay for minimum standards (food, clothing, shelter, phone, and public transportation). In some cities, the FMW (as calculated, using the Universal Living Wage formula in 2022) would be in the range of $10-$40 per hour. For example: in New York City, the FMW would be $33.60. In Santa Cruz-Watsonville, CA, the wage would be $40.10. In Denver, CO, it would be $23.77. In Boston, MA, $31.88. So, by only seeking $15.00 per hour, the protesters undershot their mark.

For rural America, there is a concern that paying employees $15.00 an hour will put small businesses out of business. Fortunately, the main characteristic of the Universal Living Wage is flexibility. In Iberville Parish, LA, the new FMW in 2022 would be just $11.62. Amarillo, TX would only need $11.94 per hour. Hattiesburg, MS would be looking at 11.10. In Union County, SC is just $10.06.

So, how did jumping to a one-size-fits-all higher number help the workers, the businesses, and the mom-and-pop shops across the nation? $15/hour proved to be too low in a third of the cities and too high in another third of the cities. Consequential and devastating to truly small businesses in those cities. But—had they chosen to promote the Universal Living Wage, which is indexed to the local cost of housing—it would have turned out to be just right for the workers and the employers and the small businesses.

Sounds like a trifecta!

One Size Does Not Fit All

We live in a consumer-driven society. Everyone is exposed to the televised version of the number of cars, resort homes, and sailboats that the successful person is expected to own. We have come to believe that if we open a business and employ people, all of the successful trappings of business should instantly be ours. Perhaps, we will have to learn that it is not all instant success. Operating a small business is hard work. According to The National Small Business Administration, there is a 64% failure rate of all small businesses after only 4 years and a 90% failure rate after 5 years. This may be related to the fact that we continue to create destabilized workforces by paying our workers less than the minimum amount needed to afford the necessities of life. If we are to have a more stable business community, if more businesses are to succeed, if our full-time minimum wage workers are to sustain themselves without government help, then businesses will need to try harder to become fully engaged community partners. Also, we, as consumers, will need to pay a share that is closer to fair. We must talk together, work together and collaborate together in order to prosper together.

Effect of the ULW on Housing

The ULW Ten Year Plan supports the 2022 *Bringing America Home Now!* Campaign, that through a series of bills calls for the right to 1) Housing, 2) Health Care, 3) Livable Incomes, 4) Education and Training opportunities, 5) Civil Rights, and 6) Racial Equity. That third prong includes the ULW for people who can work and fixing the SSI stipend for people who are unable to work.

As a society, we must raise the economic floor of the minimum wage workers to a level that allows them to afford basic rental housing, and we can argue from a moral perspective that people who are too disabled to work should be supported with income that allows them to afford and maintain housing without risk of becoming homeless. Passing the ULW will provide a fair wage for a fair day's work. On the other hand, stipends and supports place the responsibility, both moral and economic, for the disabled among us, fully on the shoulders of the American taxpayer (as it should).

The Effect on Business

When workers make more money, they also have more money to spend. In fact, minimum wage workers have spent almost 98% of past wage increases right back into the economy. Increased personal income inevitably promotes commerce and stimulates local and nationwide economies. By protecting and stabilizing the very foundation of all businesses (the employees themselves), we can equally protect and stabilize businesses everywhere.

In the 1920s, automobile production was exploding, and competition in the industry was fierce. Mr. Henry Ford was desperate to find a better way to shave dollars and produce cheaper cars. His Model T was on top but seemingly not for long. His competition was hiring his workers out from under him. Thinking creatively, he reviewed his budget's expense column and realized that he was facing astronomical *retraining costs* due to high employee turnover. He calculated that he had to *refill the position of every employee four times a year.* He also recognized that *absenteeism* generally was also costing him what he considered an unacceptable amount. He realized that when a worker did not show up, he needed to keep the assembly line moving, so more time and money was again spent on temporarily hiring and training a replacement. Realizing that money could be the stabilizing factor, he almost doubled the wage to $5.00 a day. The result was immediate and dynamic:

He saw a significant *reduction in employee turnover*, significant *reduction in retraining costs*, and a significant *reduction in absenteeism*.

Unexpectedly, he found a *vast reduction in internal theft* (about 50% of internal retail theft is committed by a business's employees, according to *The Living Wage: Building a Fair Economy* by Robert Pollin and Stephanie Luce.)

Ford employees were also placed in a financial position *to buy the very product that they were making*. This further stimulated his business and the will of his employees to make a better product.

The bottom line is that Mr. Ford showed that by paying a living wage, he stabilized not only his business but also the lives of his employees.

6 Livable Incomes Solution 1: The Universal Living Wage Formula

The ULW mathematical formula is three-pronged. Let's take a brief look at the concepts behind each prong.

1) Work a 40-Hour Week

First, we are talking about wages and the standard government work week (40 hours). While we speak in terms of being able to afford housing on a monthly basis, it is important to understand that just as the FMW is an hourly wage, the ULW would also be an hourly wage. If a worker puts 40 units of work wage together, that wage would be sufficient for a person to afford basic food, clothing, rental housing, phone, and public transportation no matter where that person works throughout the United States. This may require a worker to take a second or even a third job. An employer who chops up jobs into part-time gigs does not have to pay the benefits legally due to full-time employees. So, plenty of part-time work is available. Clearly, this is not ideal. But it does provide an opportunity for an aggressive worker to join the struggle for housing.

2) Spend No More Than 30% of One's Income on Housing

If you were to apply to purchase a home, and if the bank determined that in so doing, you would be spending more than 30% of your monthly household budget on your mortgage payments, they would not assign you a note or give you a mortgage. This provides what is seen to be a reasonable margin of financial safety for both the renter and homeowner.

Not surprisingly, whether a person buys a house or applies for housing assistance, America's banking institutions and HUD's Section 8 Housing Choice Voucher program both use the same guideline, the 30% standard. This federal voucher program subsidizes landlords and even finds some people places to live.

As explained previously, let's imagine that a one-bedroom apartment rents for $600.00 per month in your area, but no prospective tenant can afford to pay more than $400.00. The federal government steps in and provides a $200.00 housing voucher that the tenant passes along to the landlord. The landlord gets his asking rental price, and the tenant gets her housing. However, the taxpayer is required to pick up the $200 subsidy.

3) Index the Minimum Wage to the Local Cost of Housing

The federal government based the Federal Poverty Guidelines on food costs. Food, however, is a flexible commodity. Housing is a *durable* commodity, making housing, or the need for it, the true target required to attack poverty. The most basic rental housing available is the efficiency apartment, a single room that serves as kitchen, living room, and bedroom that might allow for a "Murphy" foldout bed or a couch. You might find space for a hot plate, and you might share a bathroom down the hall. Sparse conditions, but better than the streets.

To determine what value to attach to its vouchers, HUD created a program called Fair Market Rents. It conducts research nationwide to determine the rent amounts for an efficiency, a one bedroom, a two-bedroom, a three bedroom, and a four bedroom apartment in any particular area.[13] HUD uses a sophisticated formula to review these amounts yearly, although it does not necessarily make annual adjustments. HUD Fair Market Rent Areas are approximately the size of counties and are often exactly that, counties. It also uses "metropolitan statistical" areas to represent large clusters of people.

Fair Market Rent Standard

FMRs are gross rent estimates that include the cost of both shelter and utilities, *except telephone*. HUD sets FMRs to assure that a sufficient supply of rental housing is available to program participants. FMRs must be high enough to permit a selection of units and neighborhoods and low enough to serve as many families as possible. The level at which FMRs are set is expressed as a percentile point within the rent distribution of standard quality rental housing units. As of April 2020, the current definition used is the 40th percentile of standard quality rental housing units that are rented. These percentiles are drawn from the distribution of rents of units that are occupied by recent movers (renter households who moved into their units within the past 15 months). Newly built units less than two years old are excluded, and adjustments have been made to correct the below-market rents of public housing units included in the database.

This is how HUD determines the uniform local cost of housing. The standard and formula are really well thought out.

The Universal Living Wage Formula

Richard with 100-old supporter, Ava Adams

We combined the three existing government guidelines:
1. Work 40 hours in a week;
2. Spend no more than 30% of one's income on housing;
3. Index (link) the minimum wage to the local cost of housing by using the HUD Fair Market Rent standard.

We created a mathematical formula, which ensures that if a person works 40-hour a week, their earnings would be enough for them to afford basic rental housing wherever that work is done throughout the United States. We have stated that we want a full-time worker to be able to afford basic rental housing, food, clothing, phone, and public transportation. This will stabilize him/her so that they are positioned to escape poverty and pursue the American Dream.

Living Wage Formula

HUD STANDARD: No more than 30% of a person's gross income should be spent on housing.

HUD Fair Market Rent $_____ (Efficiency Apartment, in _____).

TOTAL MONTHLY INCOME: $_____ ÷ .3 = $_____ monthly gross income necessary to afford basic housing.

PREMISE: Anyone working 40 hours/week should be able to get housing and get off the streets.*

WORK HOURS: 40 hours/week @ _____ weeks month = _____ work hours/month, _____ work hours x 12 months = 2080 hours/year.

Total Gross monthly
    Income of $_____ x 12 months = $ _____
    $_____ ÷ 2080 Hours/year = $_____ /hour
        NEW HOURLY WAGE in Any City, USA.

Total Monthly Expenditures:
    $_____ Total Gross Monthly Income
    −$_____ Fed. taxes, Soc. Sec., Medicare**
    −$_____ Housing Costs
    $_____ Remaining for: Medical, Clothing, Food,
            Transportation, Telephone

------

* Whether a person works 4 hours per week or 40 hours per week, they should be paid at the full 40-hour rate. A full hour's work deserves a full hour's wage.
** Minus $_____ for Federal Income Tax, $_____ for Social Security, and $_____ for Medicare. The Federal Income tax rate (15%) is based on the monthly deductions outlined in the Internal Revenue Circular E, Employer's Tax guide (Rev. Jan. 2002, Social Security is 6.2% of gross monthly income, and Medicare is 1.45% of gross monthly income (Total equals $_____)

Sample Living Wage Formula (Fiscal Year 2022)

For Minneapolis-St. Paul-Bloomington, MN

HUD STANDARD: No more than 30% of a person's gross income should be spent on housing.

HUD Fair Market Rent $ 932 (Efficiency Apartment, in Minneapolis–St. Paul-Bloomington, MN)

TOTAL MONTHLY INCOME: $ 932 ÷ .3 = $ 3,106.60 monthly gross income necessary to afford basic housing.

PREMISE: Anyone working 40 hours/week should be able to get housing and get off the streets.

WORK HOURS: 40 hours/week @ **4.33** weeks month = **173.33** work hours/ month, 173.33 work hours x 12 months = 2080 hours/year.

Total Gross monthly
    Income of $ 3,106.60 x 12 months = $37,279.20
    $ 37,279.20 ÷ 2080 hours/year = $ 17.92 /hour
    NEW HOURLY WAGE needed in Minneapolis-St. Paul-
        Bloomington, MN for an efficiency apartment as of 2021.

Total Monthly Expenditures:
    $_____ Total Gross Monthly Income
    –$_____ Fed. taxes, Soc. Sec., Medicare**
    –$_____ Housing Costs
    $_____ Remaining for: Medical, Clothing, Food,
                    Transportation, Telephone

To get the current values for a Fair Market Rent area, email EMAD-HQ.gov or go to UniversalLivingWage.org and click on Wage Calculator at: http://www.universallivingwage.org/wagecalculator.html

One Size Does Not Fit All

In advocating for fixing the Federal Minimum Wage, the existing methodology selects a single hourly wage amount, like $7.25, $9.00, $10.00 or $15.00or any imaginable number that Congress might choose for the entire country. Currently, the federal government similarly ignores the fact that we are a nation of more than a thousand economies. HUD Section 8 figures show that an efficiency apartment in New York City in 2022 costs approximately $1747 per month. Under the ULW formula, we can see that the tenant would need to earn an hourly wage of $33.60. In Amarillo, TX, efficiency apartments rent for $621.00 per month and would require a wage of only $11.94 per hour.

As previously pointed out, with a single national wage amount of $15.00 per hour, we would not have gotten one minimum wage worker off the streets of New York City. At the same time, we would have destroyed small businesses in Amarillo, TX, when an individual there only needs $11.94 per hour to be housed, fed, clothed, make phone calls, and catch the bus to work. One size does not fit all.

The fact that Congress is stuck with decreeing only one national amount may explain their paralysis when it comes to ever getting around to a Federal Minimum Wage increase.

Established Practice

Many U.S. military bases are surrounded by rental housing for individuals and families who do not have quarters on the base itself. Since 1998, the government provides service members with accurate and equitable housing compensation that takes into account local housing costs. The Basic Allowance for Housing (BAH) is based on the person's geographic duty location, pay grade, and number of dependents.

The previous system had been unable to keep up with rising housing costs, and service members who lived off-base were paying too much out-of-pocket from what was supposed to be their discretionary income. But BAH, with increases indexed to local housing cost growth, protects service members from erosion of their housing benefits. In other words, the federal government thinks it's a good idea to pay its workers a little more in places where the rent is higher and make up the difference in places where the cost of living is lower. That's exactly what we said, but we said it first.

Local Wage Versus State Wage, Fair Market Rents

It is appropriate to use rental calculations relative to local housing costs in areas about the size of counties, the HUD Fair Market Rent areas. In the 1990s, we entered the high-tech boom and, while the entire country did not benefit from the success, many urban areas did. Financial success caused the cost of housing to soar. Today, in 2022, an efficiency apartment in Austin, Texas rents for $1092. This requires a living wage of $21.00 per hour. At the same time, in Abilene, Texas, unaffected by high-tech growth, to rent a comparable apartment would cost only $637 per month and require a living wage of only $12.25 hourly. Even within one state, there is a dramatic difference in rental costs, which this formula can handle without damaging any businesses because *the wage is linked to the local cost of housing.*

ULW Demonstration in Washington, DC

National Formula Versus Local Initiatives

There have been well over 100 local living wage campaigns at this point. According to the Brennan Center for Justice, several have successfully increased the minimum wage (130 ordinances passed as of 2007, according to the Brennan Center for Justice). In 2013, ten cities raised their minimum wage rates, but once again, they fell well short of providing living wages. But what about the scores of communities that cannot spearhead campaigns to fight economic forces that stand in opposition? What about America's rural communities? Do these workers not also deserve a roof over their heads? Recently, in May 2021, Heidi Shierholz, believing she was advocating for the nation's business community best interest as a spokesperson for Economic Policy Institute, EPI, suggested that a regional approach..."would lock in low wage conditions in certain regions that are the result of historic racism." On the contrary, our approach creates a uniform playing field nationwide while ensuring the total affordability of housing for every worker. Most local living wage campaigns benefit city workers, county workers, and sometimes those that contract with them. However, if we doubled, tripled, or even quadrupled all of the workers affected under these campaigns, we would not see income equity reached in 2000 years. Even in Louisiana and Texas, where several thousand workers may be affected, the numbers pale in comparison to the need. Factor in that according to the National Coalition for the Homeless, there are 3.5 million people experiencing homelessness. Thus, we conservatively estimate there to be over 10 million minimum wage workers nationwide. This is consistent with the 2000 Census. But by employing the ULW formula, we can begin to move all of these workers along a wage continuum that approaches self-reliance.

Local initiatives are vulnerable to attacks and repeal. For example, in 1996, the Houston, TX, Living Wage effort to raise the minimum wage to $6.50 per hour was stopped cold in the last week of the campaign. Moneyed interests who poured over a million dollars into creating misinformation handily defeated the initiative. There are serious concerns in the business community about local living wage campaigns. Local campaigns that draw circles around geographic areas are potentially damaging to small businesses. In fact, this was the basis of resistance to a living wage initiative in San Antonio, TX. Fears are that large businesses could and would pull up stakes and relocate just outside of the newly proposed wage boundary or even leave the region. The President of the San Antonio Restaurant Association was quoted as saying, "We need to work with businesses to get businesses in San Antonio. Let us say, for instance, that Houston does not have a living wage, and San Antonio does, and the PGA (Professional Golf Association) says, 'I can go to Houston and get these incentives to come, and I'm not forced to pay this living wage.' So, what is going to happen? Where are they going to go? They are going to go to Houston.

On the other hand, the Federal Minimum Wage (like the Universal Living Wage) establishes a balance. It is all industries. It is nationwide. So, there's a balance..."[14] But what this business leader is trying to say is that he can deal with a level playing field where all wages are raised relative to their local economies. What he sees as untenable is a situation where a local/isolated wage increase allows a business to simply cross a boundary line and operate at an unfair advantage.

Just as federal law overrules state law, state law preempts local law—except when it doesn't, which keeps judges and lawyers very busy. There have been successful efforts to create state laws that would forbid paying more than the FMW!

At least ten states in recent years have tried to ban local minimum wage laws, including Louisiana, Arizona, Colorado, Florida, Georgia, Missouri, South Carolina, Oregon, Utah, and Texas. Oregon and Florida have passed legislation to increase their minimum wage while both still have laws that prohibit "political subdivisions" from passing wage-related laws.

ULW Relationship Between the Worker and Employers

Between workers and employers, there exists a symbiotic relationship bordered by a delicate framework. The employer needs the employee for their labor, and the employee needs to make at least a minimal decent living through the employment. While the need is mutual, the power balance is not, and therefore, workers must demand that the employer embrace the principles of the Universal Living Wage formula. If an employee works a standard number of hours, they should be able to afford basic life-sustaining necessities (food, clothing, shelter, phone, public transportation, and access to healthcare). This is consistent with the United Nations document, the Universal Declaration of Human Rights, which identifies these life-sustaining necessities as "definitive components of the right to a minimum standard-of-living and dignity for every (nation) state."

Living Wages Are Good for Business

Paying living wages is good for business. Every business should explore this exciting new business practice. When workers make more money, they have more to spend. In the past, every minimum wage increase has resulted in spending 98% of that increase right back into the economy. By protecting and stabilizing the very foundation of businesses (the employees themselves), we also protect and stabilize businesses everywhere. Approximately 20 million minimum wage workers provide support for our "principal" businesses. This pool of minimum wage, low-paying jobs includes restaurant workers, construction laborers, daycare aides, hotel workers, janitors, bank tellers, theatre attendants, farm workers, receptionists, nurses' aides, maids, poultry processors, child care workers, home care aides, garage attendants, retail salespeople, car washers, manicurists, ambulance drivers, cash-register attendants, landscapers, data-entry keyers, elder-care aides, security guards, and infant caretakers.

Again, none of these jobs can be outsourced because you have to be on-site to wash windows, serve our children food in the school cafeterias, change the sheets on hotel beds, etc. Clearly, business is dependent on these minimum workers to both drive their businesses and prosper.

Today, the Universal Living Wage formula (www.UniversalLivingWage.org) will similarly provide a stimulus where workers will spend money for the single most expensive item in the budget of every American: housing. Unfortunately, in recent years, the cost of housing has skyrocketed not just in Austin but all over America. Presently, no one working a full-time 40-hour a week job can afford even an efficiency apartment. In fact, they cannot get housing without having either tax subsidies or two jobs.

Should employers take our ethical challenge and begin paying living wages, local and national construction industries, learning that this money is available will scramble to create the rental housing necessary for all 3.5 million homeless minimum wage workers.

The ULW formula links the federal minimum wage to the local cost of housing. At the end of the week, every full-time minimum wage worker should be able to afford a roof over their head (other than a bridge) by working one job, and the taxpayers should not have to pay for it.

So that is the plan to help those who are homeless and who can work (52%). For those who cannot work, 47% (the disabled), we can use the same ULW formula to link their SSI Disability Stipend to the local cost of housing. This proposal can now be seen as providing Livable Incomes for all people experiencing homelessness. Now with our businesses and our taxpayers pulling together and equally pulling half the load, we clear the path to house all of our homeless people both in Austin and nationwide.

Support Workers

Our nation's labor pool contains 10.1 million minimum wage workers in support jobs. They support principal businesses whose higher-ranked employees make much more than minimum wage. Top chefs make more than restaurant servers. Architects make more than construction laborers. Hospitals make more than the people who clean the rooms and launder the sheets. The minimum wage businesses are not villains. They have to satisfy the demands for support and service at the least possible price, or the principal businesses will find cheaper subcontractors.

If MegaBigCorp moves to town, it does not make the decision based on minimum wage salary scales because it does not generally employ workers at that low wage level. When MegaBigCorp builds its offices, it may contract employees such as construction laborers and landscapers who are minimum wage "support" workers. Once the facility is built, the core business will also need laundry services, restaurants, janitors, receptionists, etc.

Remember, the pool of minimum wage workers includes:

- Restaurant Workers
- Theater Attendants
- Construction Laborers
- Farm Workers
- Dry Cleaner Operators
- Receptionists
- Janitors
- Nurse's Aides
- Day Care Aides
- Maids
- Store Clerks
- Poultry Processors
- Landscape Workers
- Garage Attendants
- Home Care Aides
- Hotel Workers
- Bank Tellers
- Data Processors
- Car Washers
- Elder Care Aides
- Manicurists
- Security Guards

Also remember that none of these jobs can be outsourced. One must be on-site to wash the windows and make the hotel beds. A child care worker must be present to change the diaper, etc. As stated previously, each of these workers must receive a wage sufficient to secure basic food, clothing, shelter, and public transportation to get to that work. As Henry Ford noted, absence of an adequate wage results in high employee turnover, increased absenteeism, and an increase in internal employee theft, none of which is good for business.

Work Opportunity Tax Credit

To help the food industry replace employees and train replacements, Congress provides $2,400 per employee under a law called the Work Opportunity Tax Credit. Every time an employee leaves a business, that business can claim a *retraining stipend*, and this can be repeated as often as every 400 hours per replaced employee.[15]

If an employee were to quit, the business can then go out and hire a replacement worker. The business claims an amazing $2,400 bonus to show this new person the ropes. But it gets even better. What if the employer has transformed the cash register from a numbered instrument

73

to a *pictured* instrument so that the new employee can push a picture of a hamburger or French fries rather than having to key in data? For teaching the new hire how to do that, along with some other important facts like when to call the police on a rowdy customer, the employer gets $2,400. In Travis County, TX, one person in five astonishingly cannot read or write. The implication of this pictured system is that the employee base for cash register operators just increased dramatically, and the employer's profits just took off.

In 1997, this federal program paid $385 million. Potential savings are significant: If you take 2,080 hours (number of hours worked in a year by an employee working 40 hours per week) and divide that by 400 hours (the minimum work hours for a single employee necessary for the business to be eligible for the subsidy), this will equal a 5.2 potential turnover rate (Henry Ford was facing a turnover rate of only 4.0 when he felt compelled to almost double the wage for his employees). In modern times, this is the same turnover rate experienced at the Greeley Beef Slaughter House supplying ConAgra.[16] Potential benefit to businesses 5.2 x $2,400 retraining subsidy = $12,480 per employee slot per year. $12,480 x 4.5 million minimum wage workers in the fast-food industry[17] equals a potential savings of $56,160,000,000. Of course, this is a projection and a worst-case scenario. If treating employees well and paying living wages reduces the turn-over rate, then there is significant potential savings to the American taxpayer.

On the other hand, as stated, I can think of at least one major employer that uses a picture register approach and seems to make working there harder as their employees close in on the 400-hour mark.

Stability Leads to Better Financing for Business and Families

New small businesses are more likely to receive bank loans and support from the Small Business Association (SBA) if they produce solid business plans showing how they provide adequate budgeting to support all aspects of their business in a sustainable fashion. This includes manufacturing, advertisement, geographic considerations, warehousing, transportation, employee training, and wages.

According to Professor Robert Pollin and Dr. Stephanie Luce in the analytical book, *The Living Wage–Building a Fair Economy*, "Family reliance on non-health-related subsidies will fall by 16.1%, and the family will become dramatically more creditworthy...thus being able to avail themselves of more goods and services, which, in turn, will serve to stimulate the local economy when earning a living wage."[18] Furthermore, according to Beth Schulman, author of *The Betrayal of Work: How Low-Wage Jobs Fail 30 Million Americans and Their Families*, these minimum wage jobs are no longer the employment/economic stepping stone of the past, but rather the economic job plateau at which people/families are stagnating for as many as ten years.[19]

According to the report, "The Sky Hasn't Fallen,"[20] the 1997 minimum wage raise did increase earnings of low-wage workers, and this increase primarily benefited low-income families. Additionally, according to the report, "America's Well Targeted Raise," also released by the Economic Policy Institute, 57% of the gains from the increase went to working families in the bottom 40% of the income scale.

Tax Savings

Where businesses have fallen short in paying a wage sufficient to cover the costs of life's basic necessities, individuals are being forced to fortify their incomes with subsidies such as food stamps, TANF, EITC, general assistance, and tips. If businesses paid fair living wages, the tax burden shouldered by taxpayers would be dramatically reduced.

While we tend to think of minimum wage workers as individuals, they are often attempting to sustain more than just themselves. In his book, *The Living Wage/Building a Fair Economy*, economics professor Robert Pollin suggests that there exists a prototypical U.S. minimum wage family comprising four people: two children and two adults, one of whom is working at the minimum wage.[21] Because the minimum wage falls short of economic sustainability, a significant amount of government subsidies are required to support this family. With the enactment of the ULW, it is conservatively estimated that potential national tax savings of billions per year could be realized.

Roughly 60 percent of all workers in the bottom decile of wage earners (those paid less than $7.42 per hour) receive some form of government-provided assistance.[22]

Why should we as taxpayers pay this subsidy if **business** is *benefitting from the employees' labor?*

Self-Sufficiency Models and the Dynamic Nature of the ULW

There is an approach to economic family stability that determines basic living costs by calculating one light bulb and one roll of toilet paper at a time. Using this data, proponents calculate how much a worker must earn per hour in order to afford their household items and expenses. This is the Self-Sufficiency Standard, devised by Wider Opportunities for Women (WOW). The Standard sets out precisely how much money working adults require to meet all basic needs without governmental subsidies. The Self-Sufficiency Standard assumes that all adults in the household are working and includes the costs associated with working full-time. As of 2020, thirty-nine states have completed calculations, including Texas, which was tabulated in 1996.

The Universal Living Wage can be seen as an economic mechanism for achieving this Self-Sufficiency Standard. However, not only does the ULW establish *a pathway* to achieve the Standard, it does so through *incremental steps* using existing *governmental guidelines*. Similar to this WOW Standard, the ULW assumes full-time workers in the calculation. Also, similar to the Standard, the ULW considers local housing costs. The WOW Standard then painstakingly looks at a plethora of other ancillary costs and takes into account that their costs inflate at various rates. The ULW also takes into account these other costs. Two-thirds of the total wage is available to meet monthly budgets beyond housing costs.

The ULW formula sets the Federal Minimum Wage level so that individual workers will be able to afford an efficiency apartment. This will prevent economic-based homelessness for all of our nation's 10.1 million minimum wage workers. Then, because the formula is "dynamic," members within each Fair Market Rent area can (at prescribed times) vote to move the community along the formula continuum. In other words, every full-time worker is initially assured of reaching economic viability at an efficiency apartment level. Subsequently, with the ULW formula, each community (through local elections) will have the ability to extend that economic viability to the next housing level. For example, by using the same ULW formula and then by merely substituting the HUD Fair Market Rent amount for a one-bedroom apartment instead of the efficiency apartment, we then produce a wage that provides economic viability for all workers who need a one-bedroom apartment. This would be appropriate where a community has determined that a single working mother/father with a child should not be allowed to remain homeless due to inadequate wages. There are federal restrictions for certain financial support programs that prevent a person with a child from living in an efficiency apartment.

The ULW formula produces similar economic levels to those of the Self-Sufficiency Standard. However, the ULW identifies the *vehicle* (the Federal Minimum Wage) and lays out the staged *pathway* (over ten years, and the *methodology* (formula) for actually reaching economic viability.

Comparing Three Living Wage Standards

The Living Wage standards presented here come from three different groups. They attempt to arrive at a better method of measuring the basic needs of families and individuals. The comparisons were created by the Delaware Housing Coalition in 2001-2002. This stellar statewide organization researches and fights for safe, decent, affordable housing for all people in the state of Delaware. The three standards compared include one promoted by the National Priorities Project, the Economic Policy Institute, and the Universal Living Wage.

Standard 1: National Priorities Project

The National Priorities Project developed a conservative family budget from a detailed methodology obtained from the organization. The NPP Living Wage in Delaware is $14.38 for a family of three and $15.88 for a family of four.

Standard 2: Economic Policy Institute

The Economic Policy Institute's living wage information for Delaware is even more detailed and painstaking, with adjustments made for variations in cost by county, as well as the age and sex of family members. The methodology was developed and applied in their publications How Much is Enough? and Hardships in America. Delaware's EPI living wage standard is the highest of the three, with a living wage for a family of three ranging from $15.23 to $15.92. The range for a family of four goes from $17.56 to $20.74.

Standard 3: House the Homeless, Inc. (Universal Living Wage Standard)

The final living wage standard is based on the HUD Fair Market Rents. It comes up with a range from $11.71 to $13.98 in Delaware, assuming the family of four would be able to live in a two-bedroom unit. (Including the very real possibility of needing a three-bedroom unit for the family of four increased the upper range of the living wage to $18.96).

Conclusion of Delaware Housing Coalition's search for the best formula for determining a living wage: [23], from DHC Executive Director Ken Smith:

"The Universal Living Wage makes a simple and powerful argument. Housing is the heaviest household burden, and the poorest people in a community should be able to make enough working full-time to afford the very cheapest housing. The advocates of a Universal Living Wage promote the passage of a new federal minimum wage based on, at the very least, the efficiency apartment FMR. This argument has the appeal of being a wage that is not tied to any particular sector of the labor force (e.g., public employees), and it takes as its primary consideration: the homeless of our community."

Endorsers of the Universal Living Wage Campaign

1,700 plus businesses, unions, non-profits, and faith-based organizations beginning in 2001, were presented with a synopsis of the Universal Living Wage and asked to sign and return a letter of endorsement. The fruit of that campaign can be found in the Appendix.

Summary

Looking at Core Needs Facing Homeless Folks:
- Affordable Housing and Livable Incomes
  We define Livable Incomes as having 3 parts: for those who can work as Living Wage Jobs. We call this the Universal Living Wage, ULW. Our ULW formula uses the Section 8 Fair Market Rents to Fix the Federal Minimum Wage by linking the wage to the local cost of housing and ensuring that anyone working 40 hours in a week, (be it from one job or more), workers will be able to afford basic food, clothing, shelter and public transportation to get to that job.
- For those who cannot work, (folks coping with disabilities) we must raise the SSI check so folks can afford basic housing and life's necessities.
- And for the third group it has been suggested something called a Guaranteed Basic Income. This would provide a support stipend for alternative workers. This concept provides tax payer funds for individuals who want to use their funds in creative ways such as art or invention or whatever. There would be no actual work requirements. This is not part of the Universal Living Wage campaign.

Post Script

As the deadline to get this manuscript to my publisher fast approaches, I face pressure of a greater level. After more than 20 years with only one small increase in the Federal Minimum Wage, "Progressive" Democrats press for a long overdue and desperately needed increase to the FMW. Again, it is a number plucked from out of thin air, but this time, it is a substantial number. It is again one-size-fits-all for our entire diverse nation, and it is $15.00 per hour. Lord knows we need a massive wage increase. But what we don't need is a wage that hurts or even devastates small mom-and-pop businesses in rural America simultaneously being an insufficient hourly amount to get homeless folks off our streets and into housing in our big cities.

The pressure comes from the fact that the number of Democrat Senators and Republican Senators are tied, and only a vote from Vice

President Harris can break that tie. Democrat Joe Manchin, a Democrat from West Virginia sees this as an opportunity to make political gains. I have previously written him and methodically pointed out the problem with the Democratic approach for the installment of a $15 wage will indeed force West Virginia small businesses to pay several more dollars *per hour* to each minimum wage worker than is needed to afford housing in any city in his state of West Virginia.

The "Progressive" Democrats realize that changes to big partisan issues only tend to be achievable in the first 2 years of a new administration. We are now hundreds of days into that countdown. They also believe that the only way of assuring a successful wage vote is to do away with the filibuster and the rule calling for a 60% winning vote in the Senate. President Biden is pushing back and seeking a bi-partisan compromise instead. But if he decides that the only way he can only get his much sought-after trillion-dollar infrastructure bill (now signed) and the Build Back Better America bill through Congress is to do away with the filibuster rule, he will do it.

If this happens, the "Progressive" Democrats will rush to beat the sunrise to pass the $15.00 per hour wage raise.

This is my deadline. My plan is to send each member of Congress and every Governor an individualized letter comparing the $15.00 and Fight Campaign and the Universal Living Wage Formula. Using our Universal Living Wage calculator, I present the benefits of this approach and the very negative consequences of the approach of the Democrats. That amounts to 587 hand-crafted letters plus one each to President Biden and Vice President Harris. My goal is to interject some common sense into the discussion before it is too late. Below is one sample letter.

bridge the economic gap
UniversalLiving Wage

(National Locality Wage) An Initiative of House the Homeless, Inc.

P.O. Box 2312 ■ Austin, Texas 78768-2312 ■ 512.796.4366

■www.UniversalLivingWage.org info@UniversalLivingWage.org

National Coalition *for the* **Homeless**

Bringing America Home

June 18, 2021

President Joseph Biden
1600 Pennsylvania Ave
Washington, DC NW 20500

Honorable Joseph Biden:

 Respectfully, I am writing this follow up letter on the subject of the Universal Living Wage (ULW) (National Locality Wage). I have written all members of Congress and Governors, contrasting the one-size-fits-all approach of the Federal Minimum Wage, (FMW) and the reality that we are a nation comprised of over a thousand economies, tailoring each letter to the local cost of housing for each leader. Most all of us have traveled from our hometowns to Washington, D.C. and throughout the U.S. and seen differences in the cost of living. The ULW formula *fixes* the Federal Minimum Wage. It uses *existing government guidelines*: 1) work a 40-hour work week, 2) spend no more than 30% of one's monthly household budget on housing, and 3) use the HUD Section 8 Fair Market Rents, FMRs, as key components. The ULW, (National Locality Wage), ensures that anyone working 40 hours in a week, (from one or more jobs), **can afford basic, food, clothing, shelter** (an efficiency apartment), **and transportation**...*wherever* that work is done. Note, in 1938, following the Great Depression we learned that local control of wage rates unevenly considered businesses verses the individual. We realized we must create a balance between the worker and business as it is a fragile symbiotic relationship where *both* must be supported on an equal basis. In an unsuccessful attempt to create fairness for all, our nation uses a single federal standard (FMW) of which people of color are overly represented as recepients. Supporters of the ULW, (National Locality Wage) are now tweaking the standard to create the highest level of equity & fairness for all. See: *Looking Up at the Bottom Line: The Struggle for the Living Wage* (https://tinyurl.com/y4clowk8.). See Chapter 6, pages 193-231.

 I came to this common-sense, ethical approach, while working on solutions to the economics of homelessness. The inclusion of the HUD, Section 8 formula allows us to *index* the FMW to the *local cost of housing* across America, because *housing* is the single most expensive item in the budget of every *single* American, and the cost as you know, is different depending on where people live. The use of the Federal HUD Section 8 formula, allows us to know the cost of apartments in various localities. See- http://www.universallivingwage.org/wagecalculator.html to explore the wage calculator.

 The FMW has been upgraded by Congress 23 times. This is because Congress has never *indexed* the wage to the cost of living or better yet, to the *local cost of housing*.

 Once the FMW is indexed to the local cost of housing by using the ULW, the local/national construction industry will benefit from consumers who *all* need the same thing-**housing**- who will finally have the funds for housing. Businesses will quickly work to respond to that financial opportunity and build suitable housing across the U.S. Businesses will then benefit by having economically **stable** minimum wage **workforces.**

 The *Fight for $15* movement to gain pay equity is a poor response to Congress's efforts to keep the FMW aligned with the rising cost of housing. Remember, from 1997-2007, (one decade) the U.S. Congress did not raise the FMW by even a penny. This was also repeated in 2009 on up through today (another decade plus.) It is now clear that a **$15/hour wage may *devastate small businesses* in rural and small-town America.**

By the government-based ULW formula, it is clear that it requires more earnings per hour in Washington, DC $27.21 than in San Antonio, TX $13.23; Pittsburgh, PA $12.44; Flint, MI $9.31; Butler Co., KY $8.92; Boon WV $7.98; etc. In fact, many small cities are in the $8-$9 range. **Clearly, the short-coming of the Fight for $15 campaign is that it puts an undue burden on small, "mom and pop," businesses throughout rural America.** Why in heavens name would we raise the wage *several* dollars *per hour* above what is needed to get by in *more than half* of America?! **The wage should be indexed to the local cost of housing!** Again, housing is the single most expensive item in the budget of every American.

Strikingly, GA, TX, SD, ND, NC, SC, PA, MD, ME, FL, WY, WI, WA, VA, UT, TN, RI, OR, NE, DE, MS, MI, NV, MN, MT, MO, MA, LA, KY, CO, AR, AL, WV, VA, AZ, AK, IA, OH, IL, KS, CA, CT, NM, NH, NY, & IN are not alone in this economic divide. Even *within* states, *most* of America is rural. We must re-think our wage system and let it work for the worker <u>and</u> the businesses. That is what the ULW formula does.

At the same time, the <u>*one size fits all*</u> $15.00 per hour push, falls *short of helping* minimum wage workers (who often serve others) afford housing etc. in cities like, Midland, TX $20.38; Seattle, WA $27.23; or San Francisco, CA $35.04; etc. As the $15.00 per hour hurts small businesses in rural America, it won't pay enough to get a single minimum wage worker out of poverty...or even meet their rent. In these cities, and many other cities, a $15.00 wage hike won't get one poor person off the streets. Across America 3.5 million people are experiencing homelessness off and on due mostly to insufficient income. This should and can end now!

One answer to the wage inequality problem is to simply embrace the ULW formula. See: www.UniversalLivingWage.org (National Locality Wage) as both the *U.S. military* and the Federal Government now use **"locality pay,"** starting 1 year after the ULW formula release. Both gov. entities mirror the ULW to ensure that the salary paid their employees will ***automatically rise*** with the <u>local</u> **cost of housing** wherever the work is done. This will begin to erase poor wage practices and national economic scars of slavery.

Recently, Heidi Shierholz -Economic Policy Institute, suggested that a regional approach... "would lock in low wage conditions in certain regions that are the result of historic racism." On the contrary, our approach creates a uniform playing field <u>nationwide</u> while ensuring the total affordability of housing for every worker.

The National Coalition for the Homeless, NCH, is spearheading the launch: **Bring America Home Now! A Comprehensive Grassroots Campaign to End Homelessness in the U.S.** We focus on the passage of multiple pieces of federal legislation aimed at addressing the interconnected solutions to the decades-long epidemic of homelessness in the United States. Our major policy areas include: 1) Housing, 2) Health Care, 3) Livable Incomes, 4) Education and Training, and 5) Civil Rights and Antiracism. This approach will help restore opportunity for all.

Again, let's ***index the wage*** to the ***local cost of housing***. If we don't, *inflation* and *time* will <u>again</u> consume all wage gains. Over 20 years of outreach tells us that 1800 businesses, faith-based organizations, unions, nonprofits all agree with the ULW approach. See Appendix page 262 in *Looking Up at the Bottom Line*... for organizations in support.

Thank you,

Richard R. Troxell
NCH Board Member since 1997
National Education Director & Founder House the Homeless, Inc.
National Chairman ULW Campaign (National Locality Wage)
rrtroxell@aol.com (512) 796-4366

Sue Watlov Phillips
NCH President

7 Livable Incomes Solution 2: National Approach—Fixing the Federal Supplemental Security Income, SSI

There is nothing except shortsightedness to prevent us from guaranteeing an annual minimum—and livable—income for every American family.
Reverend Dr. Martin Luther King

Since the early 1980s, I have worked for The Legal Services Corporation as a mortgage Foreclosure Preventionist and as Director of Legal Aid for the Homeless through 2019. I helped homeless folks coping with their disability apply for and secure disability benefits. The process can take up to 18 months. Once someone has been judged to be 100% disabled and expected to remain that way for at least a year, and unable to perform "*substantial gainful activity.*" The Social Security Administration must determine the level of the stipend that will be provided.

If the person struggling to cope with a disability cannot produce a work history, the federal government will provide a monthly support check. In 2021, the amount is $783.00 per month for any individual anywhere in the United States. This is based on the Federal Benefits Rate, about half of the current Federal Minimum Wage of $7.25 per hour, which itself has been found wholly inadequate in the last several U.S. Conference of Mayors Reports. It is not enough for a full-time worker to rent a one-bedroom apartment anywhere in America.

House the Homeless contends that the failed government standards, SSI and FMW, are the two greatest reasons for the perpetuation of economic homelessness in this nation.

The intention of Congress with the enactment of the SSI may or may not have been to house our nation's citizens coping with disabilities, but surely, this should be the moral standard for our nation. As a taxpayer, I am willing to help these workers coping with disabilities, but businesses must also participate. Business benefits from the labor of our nation's workers, and as a good community partner, they should pay living wages to prevent their workers from becoming homeless. If businesses are willing to embrace the correct moral and ethical posture and take responsibility to pay fair living wages (that will also act to stabilize their businesses and reduce retraining costs), then as a taxpayer, I am willing to pay a disability stipend that will similarly prevent homelessness due to failed economics. A House the Homeless health survey showed that 48% of the people experiencing homelessness were so disabled that they could not work.[24] While over 90% of all surveyed understandably expressed a desire to work, only 52% expressed having the ability to work.[25] Let's assume that business agrees to pay its minimum wage employees living wages that are indexed to the local cost of housing throughout the United States. It would seem appropriate to prevent homelessness by similarly indexing the SSI stipend to the same HUD, Fair Market Rent standard used to make up the ULW formula.

This approach would end and prevent economic homelessness for all minimum wage workers and all SSI recipients struggling with disability throughout the United States.

8 Livable Incomes Solution 3: State Approach—Fixing the SSI Stipend

Another approach to the same problem could be addressed at a *state* level. Presently, California and several other states, including NY, MI, DE, ME, MA, PA, RI, VT, NJ, and WA, fully recognize that the cost of living and the federal SSI program are not aligned and partially close the gap by providing an additional stipend.

House the Homeless, Inc. is proposing that states be encouraged to raise their subsidy amount to a level that would enable these benefit recipients to engage competitively in the general housing rental market. This would result in:

1) the housing of people with disabilities and

2) stimulation of the local housing construction industry.

Concerned that these additional funds might cause the individual's SSI payment to be reduced, we've learned that in accordance with Social Security regulations, as long as the money comes through a "voucher" program and is "based on need," the goal can be accomplished without financial benefit reduction.

House the Homeless again suggests that the SSI stipend be sufficient to afford individuals coping with disabilities an efficiency apartment, wherever that person seeks housing.

9 Solution 4: Federal and State Governments —Sharing Fiscal Responsibility

Alternatively, the federal government and state governments could equally share this fiscal responsibility, just as the federal Medicaid program is a cost-shared arrangement between the federal government and the states.

Looking at Core Needs Facing Homeless Folks: Housing and Livable Incomes

We define Livable Incomes as having two parts: for those who can work as Living Wage Jobs. We call this the Universal Living Wage, ULW. Our ULW formula uses the Section 8 Fair Market Rents to Fix the Federal Minimum Wage by linking the wage to the local cost of housing and ensuring that anyone working 40 hours in a week (be it from one job or more) will be able to afford basic food, clothing, shelter, phone, and public transportation to get to that job.

For those who cannot work (folks coping with disabilities), we must raise the SSI check so they can afford basic housing and life's necessities.

- Realize that living wage jobs require the involvement of businesses.
- Businesses benefit from the labor of the worker. They need to be at the discussion and decision table.
- Paying Living Wages is good for business:
- Creates significant reduction in employee turnover,
- Creates significant reduction in retraining costs,
- Creates significant reduction in unscheduled absenteeism,
- Almost completely stops all internal theft

Living Wages create a true economic stimulus as employees can buy more goods as 97% of wage increases are immediately spent right back into the economy.

Creating this new, affordable housing (as the building construction industry will build new housing stock) will remove folks from the streets! Removing folks from the streets will:

- Stop hate crimes against these folks,
- Stop civil rights violations against these good folks,
- Stop criminalization of homeless folks: (No Sit /No Lie, No Camping, No Panhandling, No Loitering, No Soliciting ordinances, etc.) will all become moot and stop.

So, let's put our resources and energy into creating livable incomes!

10 Solution 5—Discharge No One Into Homelessness

The Americans with Disabilities Act (ADA) of 1990 states that no one who qualifies with a disability shall, "by reason of such disability, be denied from participating in a public entity's services, program, or activities." One of the regulations, now referred to as the "integration regulation," requires that people with disabilities be released into the most appropriate (meaning least restrictive) setting that suits their needs. The decision was based on two women suffering from schizophrenia. It was determined that they would be best served in a community-based treatment program. This was reviewed by the U.S. Supreme Court in *Olmstead vs. L.C.* 1999. The Court ruled that undue institutionalization is discriminatory in nature.

In 2009, President Obama initiated the "Year of Community Living" in an effort to enforce the Olmstead decision and ensure that people with disabilities receive appropriate care in the most integrated setting possible. Our organization, House the Homeless, Inc., has begun to focus on the relationship between reintegration and homelessness prevention. What if we focused on the people leaving our institutions!

Here is the key concept. **At no time do we know as much about an individual as we do when they have entered one of our institutions.** This is true of youth aging out of foster care, individuals released from incarceration, patients leaving hospitals or mental health facilities, people leaving homeless shelters, and discharged military veterans.

Already, our society has stationed social workers at all these points. By garnering *appropriate* resources and focusing our energies around this concept, we can go a long way toward preventing homelessness. Our simple tenet is to: discharge no one into homelessness but rather into a safe housing environment immediately. When a person is admitted to a hospital, their insurance status becomes known, and so should their housing status. If we immediately begin to plan for their discharge, we have a better chance to find stable housing for them.

While our tenet "Discharge no one into homelessness" is simple, the task is not. More resources are needed. However, if we immediately embrace this concept, we can assess our service needs and costs and shape future plans. All of these institutions operate quite differently, and not wanting to micro-manage any of these facilities or these responders; we urge them to begin this prevention process by pledging to "Discharge No One into Homelessness. Rather, we need to discharge them only into a safe housing environment on their original out date."

Examining Prisons as an Institutional Example of Discharging No One Into Homelessness

Again, at no time do we know as much about an individual as when they enter one of our institutions.

This is a brief examination of the prison institution in Texas regarding healthcare relating to financial and human costs as seen in part by those experiencing the prison system first hand.

Small planned changes can have a significant positive impact on current outcomes that are financial in nature and contribute to the benefit of the prisoners and the community as a whole. Collectively, these changes can help to prevent homelessness as people transition out of prison settings. It is imperative that we first understand the prison healthcare system just prior to discharge.

Looking at California, we know that failure to address healthcare issues resulted in the ordered releases of 40,000 prisoners in 2010. The cost to Californians has already been in the billions of dollars as a result of inadequate/poor healthcare planning.

What is also clear is that by examining the prison population and culling its numbers by paroling the elderly and infirm who fall into the non-violent category, we can create dramatic savings to this institution and the community at large while adding human value (life without incarceration) to the lives of all affected.

For background, this section relies on the research of the Texas Civil Rights Project Prisoners' Rights Program as found in its 2011 report *A Thin Line–The Texas Prison Health Care Crisis*–https://www. prisonlegalnews.org/news/publications/texas-civil-rights-project-the-texas-prison-healthcare-crisis-and-the-secret-death-penalty-2011/. They based their findings on prisoner complaints, evaluations of prison operations produced by the Texas Legislature Sunset Advisory Commission, major newspapers, and criminal justice experts.

Prisoner participation is paramount to gathering all of the essential information and perspectives necessary in making that shift. We must ask, "What do you think you will need to be successful in exiting prison? What do you need to keep you from coming back here?"

In Estelle v. Gamble, the U.S. Supreme Court prohibits the "unnecessary and wanton infliction of pain," according to the Eighth Amendment.[26] Basically, anyone denying or delaying medical treatment has interfered with a prisoner's constitutional rights. Following a barrage of prisoner complaints, the U.S. Fifth Circuit ruled in Ruiz vs. Estelle. The Judge ordered the Texas Department of Criminal Justice (TDCJ) to "prepare and file with the [c]ourt a plan which will assure that prisoners receive necessary medical, dental and psychiatric care from the moment of their arrival in the Texas Department of Criminal Justice."[27] The Court then laid out a comprehensive list of requirements to protect their constitutional rights. In response, the Texas prison system created a Managed Health Care program in its prison system. Note. This case became the most far-reaching lawsuit on the conditions of prison incarceration in American history.

Recommendations: The report *A Thin Line* makes numerous recommendations. Among them are:

- A call for "amendments to the Public Information Act to make information about prison conditions public."
- The use of "best practices" to "foster more humane attitude toward prisoners."
- Expand the use of telemedicine[28] that allows doctors to hear about and address the medical needs of prisoners over an electronic video system.
- Establish a universally available records system to enhance communication among medical providers.
- Create a quick response to medical needs to keep costs down, health up.

Shortcomings of Board of Pardons and Parole

According to the report, *A Thin Line*, overcrowding can also be directly attributed to the failure of the Board of Pardons and Parole. In 2008, 65% of the 139,134 TDCJ inmates were eligible for parole. However, only 36% of eligible inmates received parole.[29] Why? As of 2007, 17 of the 19 voting members of the board had professional backgrounds in law enforcement or criminal justice, 30 with no defense-side or social work backgrounds to provide another view." Additionally, the Board is not required to explain why the inmate was refused parole, thus denying them an opportunity to alter their behavior or address undisclosed errors in inmate records.

Simply releasing inmates over 55 who are receiving prison medical care and who have not committed a violent crime could save $20.2 million yearly in medical costs alone. [30]

In 2005, the system was saddled with low-risk prisoners who made up only 5.4% of the prison population yet accounted for 25% of the hospital costs.

A person with end-stage cancer, for instance, might be eligible for Medically Recommended Intensive Supervision (MRIS) with a medical recommendation from the appropriate authority. But, without proper advocacy, only about 1 in 10 eligible inmates are released.[31]

Recommendations

- Hire and retain qualified security and medical staff.
- Expand the Board of Pardons & Review Board, and hold them accountable.
- Allow prisoners access to their records and Parole Board decisions.
- Increase MRIS approval rates.

Prisoners Suffering Mental Illness

27.25% of Texas prisoners (42,556) are or have been diagnosed with mental illness.[32] The cost to Texas taxpayers of treating *repeat*, mentally ill prisoners is $682 million per year.[33] But according to A *Thin Line.* that treatment in a community-based facility would cost only $92 million per year.[34]

The mental illness diagnosis includes 11,388 individuals diagnosed with major depression, bipolar disorder, and schizophrenia.[35] Other inmates not falling under a mental health category include violent crime perpetrators, chronic drug users, and sex offenders. Some members of these groups will one day be released, and the civilian population will be best served if they receive mental health counseling.

Recommendations from *A Thin Line*

Create a statewide plan for persons with mental health conditions, including prevention, diversion, and discharge elements for community placement.

Expand the use of telepsychiatry and telemedicine.

Regularly assess the general prison population for mental health concerns.

Increase the number of mental health workers and social workers.

Infectious Diseases

Due to close quarters, response time, unsanitary conditions, and the reluctance of the community to see prisoners receive what is often perceived as preferential treatment, prisons are incubators for infectious diseases. Drug-resistant diseases can develop and be carried out into the civilian population. COVID-19, which is *highly contagious*, is of great concern. Variants such as the Delta variant are 6 times more contagious than the original virus.

The Hepatitis C virus found at a level of only 1.8% in the general population), is over-represented in the nation's prisons at 40%! Improperly treated or untreated, it can result in the need for a $400,000 liver transplant.

Another contagious disease, tuberculosis, clarifies that failure to properly and thoroughly treat TB puts both the prisoner and the community-at-large in very real medical danger.

Texas prisoners are infected with HIV/AIDS at five times the rate of the general populace. The medical treatment costs over a lifetime are currently estimated at $300,000 per individual. According to A *Thin Line.* post-prison HIV care is a health condition that Texas must place at the top of its critical care lists.

Similarly, MRSA, a staph infection, is another drug-resistant disease. The prison environment, hospitals, and homeless shelters are ideal breeding grounds for staph infections. Obvious signs of infection can be diagnosed for as little as $28.00, while treatment can cost as much as $40,000.

A *Thin Line* points out that 95% of prisoners eventually return to the community, so it would be advisable to pay more attention to the problems they carry back into the world. Their physical health and especially their possible infectious status should be assessed when they enter the system and also when they are released. Inside institutions, sanitary conditions need improvement. No court sentenced anyone to a case of TB. They shouldn't be getting it and *definitely shouldn't be leaving with it.* To prevent the spread of sexually transmitted diseases, there is a need for education and condoms. Even the former inmates who catch a habit again do not deserve to die from a disease worse than the one they already have. Making clean needles available is something a civilized society would do. So is helping former inmates figure out how to stay healthy and earn a living. Before release, they need information about available resources to bridge the gap between incarceration and full self-sufficiency.

As advocates for a better world, we must focus on areas where our nation's homeless population is the most heavily concentrated, our prisons, hospitals, and shelters of all types. We must advocate to change the conditions of these institutions. We must then recognize that there is a great fluidity with people entering, leaving, and re-entering these institutions. With this fluidity, there is disease and potential epidemic transference at its highest level. Limited income or the lack of sufficient, sustaining income will lead to further exacerbation of homelessness. Economic stability can lead to better health responses that in and of itself leads to the prevention of homelessness.

Societal Re-Entry Involving Co-Production

As we ask institutions to explore innovative approaches to discharging no one into homelessness, we must think expansively, "outside of the box," and we must find ways to involve those most immediately affected by these changes.

In the report "Coming Home,"[36] we find such an approach. It is subtitled "Asset-Based Approach to Transforming Self and Community...a report on societal Re-Entry" (post-prison)." It says, "In 2006, more than 7.2 million people were on probation, in jail, in prison, or on parole."[37] Within two years, over 70% of people being released from prison will be returned to prison. This is shocking in terms of the cost and waste in human potential. This paints a stark picture of failure to achieve good "quality of life" outcomes for over 650,000 exiting prisoners in America every year.

As a nation, we spend $60 billion on prisons and corrections every year.[38] From the very beginning of the report, the clarion call is for the involvement of former inmates to be partners and promote the concept Dr. Edgar Cahn calls Co-Production. It means involving the individuals who are most directly affected with professionals/experts in the field in an effort to create cohesive and integrated solutions for re-entry success. To enable self-motivated behavior modification, this must begin *before* release by allowing inmates access to the information considered by the Hearings and Parole Boards.

They feel that they must also shed the stigma of demeaning terms such as con, ex-con, lifer, etc. The term "homecomers" was chosen to bring civility to their status while crystallizing an image of what they are undergoing: **societal re-entry**. Critical to their success, homecomers have now rightfully been identified as a major untapped resource in the re-entry process. Finally, these re-entrants are to be considered part of a cohesive, interactive national team and part of a local community effort to restore family, hope, functionality, and personal will to succeed. To that end, a team of interested professional experts and these directly affected individuals joined forces to identify six priority areas of focus: 1) "Economic security, 2) change in the language and image, 3) mental health, 4) supportive and supported community, 5) new roles with children and families, and 6) systems change in the criminal justice system."

They determined that their activity/advocacy must occur simultaneously on two fronts; at the grassroots/community level and the policy and systems level.

The result of the team's brainstorming gave rise to the concept that a National Societal Re-entry Academy would be necessary to make the kind of broad-based systemic system changes that they seek. The committee decided that there will need to be "a network of projects" promoting the principle of co-production, a process for nominating and funding individuals, and a Board of Regents to act as the voice for the entire process. The Board of Regents' charge will also include new approaches to re-entry and keeping the program's vision strong locally and nationally. The vision embraces the idea that given the opportunity to succeed and actually succeeding promotes the feeling within those homecomers of wanting others to succeed.

To carry out the vision, there needs to be...

- creation of micro-enterprises that pay living wages,
- access to accredited education,
- financial assistance,
- creation of work for re-entry that pays living wages,
- replicable strategies,
- mental image of the re-entry model,
- positive interaction that, through education, favorably assists families and communities in building economically viable neighborhoods with the return of "homecomers."[39]

We need to create housing and employment opportunities that do not discriminate/prohibit people with correctional issues. If you have resources, own a business, a home, one does not typically face homelessness when released. If you have no resources or a home, you are at a high risk of homelessness.

This framework outlines just one approach for accomplishing the result. I focused on the prison system and suggested just one possibility of how it might be achieved. I believe it to be a viable option. It is an approach that includes what the author of this paper believes is an essential element in formulating any plan to prevent homelessness. The proposal requires that we always *involve the individual* at risk of becoming homeless prior to and upon discharge.

In researching the concept of Co-Production, I contacted Professor Edgar Cahn, and in addition to Co-Production, we discussed his involvement in devising *Time banking*, a system of bartering using one's labor-time as a unit of measuring its value. Time banking can be considered a form of community currency. We talked about it in terms of Community First! Village. He emphasized that everyone can be viewed as a commodity that they can market. He mentioned that every villager at Community First! Village has value as a human being, and they can provide a service that is bankable, whether it's "teaching the ABCs to a small child or turning over soil in the community garden or having a conversation with a senior citizen who hasn't had a conversation with another human being in two weeks." The folks at CF!V get this, and everyone is allowed to contribute at their own pace. Think about all the practical applications of integrating bartering human value into society on a daily basis, especially when so many folks are discharging from an institution and needing to reintegrate into society. Professor Cahn graciously invited me to share his words and concepts here so others might benefit.

Solving Homelessness Summary

Currently, several of the top homeless programs merely respond to the condition of homelessness. They are simply reactive in nature and offer limited help at best.

With an eye toward the prevention of homelessness, we embrace a new perspective. In a new light, we clearly see people experiencing homelessness through an economic lens and one that values not only the perspectives of the affected individual but also his or her contribution, whatever that may be. Furthermore, this approach will have a significant positive impact on the nation's business economy and save additional billions of dollars for taxpayers all across America.

These responses are bold, pragmatic, proactive, common-sense steps designed to prevent homelessness. All will yield billions of dollars in savings to taxpayers and increased revenue for business in the long run. Finally, they will help us change the face of poverty, homelessness, and healthcare in America and our role as human beings.

Conclusion

Modern-day homelessness in this nation is not new. In our fifth decade of growing homelessness, it is the longest episode since colonial days. It has manifested as Hoovervilles, recognized in the bodies of hobos and the creation of workhouses. Now, it has been brought about by numerous social changes, with soldiers returning from the Vietnam War, the retraction of federal funding of our national housing authorities by 75%, insufficient wages, and ineffective responses toward the growing problem in general. I have outlined how the responses have been reactive, not proactive or preventative.

By fixing our Federal Minimum Wage and indexing it to be the local cost of housing, we can prevent economic homelessness for 20 million minimum wage workers. We can simultaneously stabilize small businesses coupled with millions of dollars saved in retraining costs. We can avoid spending millions of other dollars of taxpayer money on supports.

By fixing the Supplemental Social Security Income stipend, and similarly, indexing it to the local cost of housing, and sharing the financial responsibility from a state or national or combined perspective, we can ensure that the elderly, and mentally and physically disabled citizens do not end up in dire economic straights and homeless on our streets with an insufficient government check in their pockets.

We can, and we must, "Discharge No One Into Homelessness." By asking each of our institutions and shelters to begin pragmatic, comprehensive, and *expansive planning* for the discharge of their consumers *on the very day that they enter the facility*, we can prevent their recidivism, realize billions of dollars in savings, and avoid incalculable human suffering.

As Dr. Cahn suggests, we must find a way to attribute a negotiable value to the contributions of every human being, whether they are employed in traditional work, non-traditional work, or simply engaged in human interaction. No one deserves to be homeless. It is preventable. But we can also love and care for those that need it. Just Look to Community First! Village in Austin, Texas, and feel free to draw on the chalkboard; it's a blank slate.

Group with ULW banner

Resolution—A Call to Action!

WHEREAS, our nation's Municipalities are facing untold millions of dollars of taxpayer costs to address and respond to homelessness that includes constructing emergency shelters, daytime drop-in facilities, transitional housing units, single room occupancy units, case management at various levels, the use of hospital emergency rooms as if they were health clinics, creation, and maintenance of parallel homeless court systems and police involvement to deal with "quality of life" ordinances, e.g., No Sit/No Lie, No Panhandling, No Feeding, No Loitering, No Camping, etc., ordinances including the creation and enforcement of drug courts, detoxification, treatment facilities, excess reliance on food stamps (SNAP), excess reliance on general assistance, on Temporarily Aid to Needy Families, TANF, Earned Income Tax Credits, EITC, and

WHEREAS, our parks and wooded areas have become occupied with people experiencing homelessness, thus changing and affecting their intended use for general recreational purposes and

WHEREAS, multiple studies have shown that while 90% of people experiencing homelessness are desirous of work but half of all of these persons are so disabled that they cannot work or even access housing with the federal government stipend (Supplemental Security Income), SSI, presently set nationwide at $794.00 per month or about $5.00 per hour and

WHEREAS, multiple studies have shown that the other half of all people experiencing homelessness who are capable of work are unable to obtain and retain basic housing even by working 40 hours a week at the current Federal Minimum Wage presently set nationwide at $7.25 per hour and

WHEREAS, several U.S. Conference of Mayors reports have indicated that a full 40-hour a week minimum wage worker cannot get into and keep basic rental housing and

WHEREAS, both the Federal Minimum Wage and the Supplemental Security Income, SSI stipend, are set by a governmental standard outside of the jurisdiction of the nation's Municipalities, and yet the outcome of these standards create the financial conditions and burden as described above, and

WHEREAS, the antithesis of housing is homelessness, and the antithesis of homelessness is housing.

THEREFORE, BE IT RESOLVED, that the US Conference of Mayors is urged to bring this matter to the attention of the United States House of Representatives and the United States Senate and call upon them to address the Federal Minimum Wage and SSI Standards, and all income supports and the enactment of the change occur over a ten (10) year period that indexes both the FMW and the SSI to the local cost of housing using the US Department of Housing and Urban Development, HUD Section 8 Fair Market Rents, thus ensuring that 40-hour a week minimum-wage worker can afford basic food, clothing, shelter (including utilities), phone, and public transportation wherever that work is done throughout the US and that any person found to be disabled by the Federal Social Security Administration receives a stipend that ensures that they can afford basic food, clothing, shelter (utilities included), phone and transportation relative to where they live. http://bit.ly/UniversalLivingWage2020

And

All US institutions such as the US military, or where our Youth are aging out of Foster Care, or people are leaving our jails or prisons, hospitals, mental health institutions, etc., should access discharge needs and immediately design plans for the eventual discharge of any user into a safe decent, accessible, and affordable housing environment rather than discharging them into homelessness.

Mayor _____ for the City of _____
in the great state of _____

Note: Complete this form.
- Send it to each of your Congressional Leaders.
- Send a copy to your mayor
- Send a copy to House the Homeless, PO Box 2312, Austin, Texas 78768-2312
- Call 1-202-225-3121 to get contact information for your Congressional Representative and your Senator.

Thank you, Richard R. Troxell rrtroxell@aol.com
www.HouseTheHomeless.org
www.UniversalLivingWage.org

11 Michael Stoops: A National Treasure

Michael Stoops: May 1, 1950 - May 1, 1917

I was there as an invited guest. Michael Stoops, the National Coalition for the Homeless national organizer, had come to Austin, Texas, talked to the people on the streets, and nominated me for the Beverly "Ma" Curtis Award for homeless advocacy. The true honor was being recognized by Michael in an NCH Board of Director's meeting of 60 like-minded homeless advocates, most of whom he had personally gathered to break the bonds that bind our people to the streets of America.

Among those we serve, he is a legend. Michael was the heart and soul of NCH. He championed the cause of people experiencing homelessness as the nation's field organizer for millions of people. Clearly, he had broad shoulders.

A Champion

Michael was born in the farming community of Milan, Indiana. He came from farming stock that was community-based and that had roots well beyond his immediate family. In fact, driving through the outskirts of town, you'll come across Stoops Road. At age 11, his young eyes saw drink lead his grandfather to fall into homelessness. But Michael was a rare bird. At age 9, he had already declared to his sister, Lisa, and his mother, that he knew how he would spend his life. He would help people who are homeless.

His social advocacy influence was clearly his grandmother, who in the Great Depression had fed hobos from the farm's back porch. Growing up, he both developed and nourished a defiantly strong sense of justice. Michael spoke in mild, dulcet tones with an almost flat affect, in rare moments punctuating the conversation with a wry smile and elfish excitement. Like Philip Roth's character in "Everyman," he could easily slip into and out of a room without being detected, even if you were looking for him. Even those who know him often remained just outside his secret society of one. In advocate mode, Michael was laser-focused. Professor Brian Levin, hate crimes statics analyst and NCH Board Member at California State University, recalls getting calls like, "I helped arrange for you to go to Texas next week to testify at their statehouse, and I know you'll do great!" Or, "Come right away to DC to present our data to the Senate." Levin says, "He was always there to elevate all of us into his orbit, without even a drop of pretense."

Michael attended Ball State University in Muncie, Indiana. At some point, he became a Quaker. At another point, he was a uniformed, tam-wearing Guardian Angel in Portland, OR. He burned his draft card in 1974 on the steps of City Hall. He was a member of the Peace Corps and served on an American Indian reservation in South Dakota. He later became an AmeriCorpVISTA supervisor.

Michael often worked with young folks, knowing that any hope of change depends upon them. He became involved with the late Mitch Snyder in the 70s and 80s when he slept outside on a grate. Michael fasted with Mitch in a protest to demand passage of the landmark McKinney-Vento Homeless Assistance Act and the creation of the federal/city shelter, Community for Creative Non-Violence, CCNV in Washington, DC.

As the National Coalition for the Homeless came into being, Michael became the Director of Community Organizing. He recognized the power of the written word and recognized the need to directly empower the people experiencing homelessness on our streets. He helped homeless newspapers get their footing in this country, encouraging NCH to become a fiscal agent for California's Street Sense. For example, our House the Homeless street newspaper in Austin, *Notes from the Blues Box*, got some guidance from Michael around voting rights for people experiencing homelessness. He also shed light on the fact that people experiencing homelessness are the targets of hate crimes. There were random beatings, burnings, and beheadings that were said to be gang initiations. I was honored to work with him on broadening the definition of hate crimes to include the targeting of victims based on their economic status. In fact, Michael urged me to craft the original Homeless Protected Class Resolution, which was passed three times by the NCH, precursor to the Homeless Bill of Rights being passed by state legislators across the country today. See appendix for Homeless Protected Class Resolution.

Michael brought national attention to the purveyors of hate who created the Bum Fights videos. These exploiters, these human leeches, offer pocket change or a beer to homeless folks to injure themselves or each other for the camera. In one video, a guy runs, pushing his buddy in a shopping cart, and intentionally plows it headfirst into a brick wall. Videotapes were manufactured and sold in stores and on the internet. In Austin, House the Homeless, Inc. protested against Best Buy retail stores for selling these hate videos. For the powerful story, see my book, *Looking Up at the Bottom Line*.

Michael created the Faces of Homelessness Speakers' Bureau, which arranged for homeless and formerly homeless individuals to talk at churches, schools, and universities.

He took a page from George Orwell's 1933 book, *Down and Out in Paris and London*, and breathed life into the concept of the Urban Plunge. Amazingly, he persuaded college students from all over the nation to forego their spring beach vacations for the life experience of spending days or weeks living on the streets.

After all, what's more exciting to an adolescent, testosterone-crazed young man than working with an elderly downtrodden woman wearing two coats and three sweaters, rather than vibrant young women in wet t-shirts? This Stoops guy must be the next Svengali! His goal of course, must have been to cultivate in the young a sense of empathy for the plight of people experiencing homelessness. He also cajoled more than a few politicians into sharing this eye-opening experience. That's how we thought of Michael Stoops—dynamic, powerful, a leader, an educator.

Suddenly, the homeless community was stunned.

We had received word that Michael had suffered a devastating stroke causing severe brain damage.

On that dreadful day in 2015, we held our collective breath as he lay, stricken, in a hospital bed. No longer sedated, he still had not regained consciousness. When asked to squeeze a hand, Michael was unresponsive. The hospital had to ask the well-wishers to please stop coming. They were inudated. Michael was placed on a feeding tube. His devoted friends kept each other updated. Emails and calls poured in from all over the nation urging prayers and announcing prayer groups. Tireless advocate and past NCH Board President Anita Beaty was at the time Executive Director of the Metro Atlanta Task Force for the Homeless. She wrote from its shelter, "We prayed hard for Michael yesterday at Peachtree-Pine." Rev. Stephen E. Braddock, Ph.D., President, and CEO of the Florida Keys Outreach Coalition, sent a classic photo of Michael grasping a microphone and speaking to a group about civil rights causes facing homeless folks. Messages of love and support just kept coming.

When I visited him, I couldn't help but think that Michael and I were the same age, and when I looked at him, I saw myself as if in his image for the first time ever. I knew it could have just as easily been me lying there. We did not look good. His legs were all twisted up in the sheets, for he was restless in his sleep. From the look on his face, he was having anguishing nightmares. I knew the dreams. I shared them with him, but he had stood on one side of the Washington Monument, and I was on the other. We had both fought for America, but Michael had fought for peace, and I had just fought. The war and the nightmares never end, and the sheets never smooth out.

On August 6, 2015, the Department of Justice filed a 27-page brief and issued the following statement to address the criminalization of Homelessness. This embodies so much of what Michael had been fighting to achieve. This is the synopsis:

Department of Justice Brief

FOR IMMEDIATE RELEASE CRT
THURSDAY, AUGUST 6, 2015   (202) 514-2007
www.justice.gov TTY (866) 544-5309
JUSTICE DEPARTMENT FILES BRIEF TO ADDRESS THE
CRIMINALIZATION OF HOMELESSNESS
WASHINGTON—The Department of Justice filed a statement of interest today arguing that making it a crime for people who are homeless to sleep in public places when there is insufficient shelter space in a city unconstitutionally punishes them for being homeless. The statement of interest was filed in federal district court in Idaho in Bell v. City of Boise et al., a case brought by homeless plaintiffs who were convicted under Boise ordinances that criminalize sleeping or camping in public.

As stated by the Justice Department in its filing, "[i]t should be uncontroversial that punishing conduct that is a universal and unavoidable consequence of being human violates the Eighth Amendment...Sleeping is a life-sustaining activity—i.e., it must occur at some time in some place. If a person literally has nowhere else to go, then enforcement of the anti-camping ordinance against that person criminalizes her for being homeless."

"Many homeless individuals are unable to secure shelter space because city shelters are over capacity or inaccessible to people with disabilities," said Principal Deputy Assistant Attorney General Vanita Gupta, head of the Civil Rights Division. "Criminally prosecuting those individuals for something as innocent as sleeping, when they have no safe, legal place to go, violates their constitutional rights. Moreover, enforcing these ordinances is poor public policy. Needlessly, pushing homeless individuals into the criminal justice system does nothing to break the cycle of poverty or prevent homelessness in the future. Instead, it imposes further burdens on scarce judicial and correctional resources, and it can have long-lasting and devastating effects on individuals' lives."

"No one wants people to sleep on sidewalks or in parks, particularly not our veterans, or young people, or people with mental illness," said Director Lisa Foster of the Office for Access to Justice. "But the answer is not to criminalize homelessness. Instead, we need to work with our local government partners to provide the services people need, including legal services, to obtain permanent and stable housing."

In this case, the plaintiffs allege that enforcement of the city of Boise ordinances prohibiting sleeping or camping in public outdoor places, on nights when there is insufficient shelter space in Boise to accommodate the homeless population, amounts to cruel and unusual punishment in violation of the Eighth Amendment. In its filing, the United States does not take a position on the factual accuracy of the plaintiffs' claims but instead addresses the appropriate legal framework for analyzing their claims. The statement of interest advocates for the application of the analysis set forth in Jones v. City of Los Angeles, a Ninth Circuit decision that was subsequently vacated pursuant to a settlement. In Jones, the court considered whether the city of Los Angeles provided sufficient shelter space to accommodate the homeless population. The court found that on nights when individuals are unable to secure shelter space, enforcement of anti-camping ordinances violated their constitutional rights. The parties in Bell v. City of Boise disagree about whether the Jones court's analysis was correct, reflecting the longstanding disagreement among courts analyzing the constitutionality of anti-camping ordinances. The statement of interest was filed to address this currently unsettled area of law.

Bell v. City of Boise et al. was filed in the District of Idaho in 2009. This statement was pure Michael. He could have written it himself;

In fact, I'm sure he had a heavy hand in it.

As time moved forward, Michael regained his ability to walk and talk. In Barb Anderson's last report in the online newsletter, she mentioned the loss of his wry grin. He was smiling openly with a face full of teeth. No longer reserved, he hugged and kissed our people. As more and more time slipped away, it became clear that the old Michael was not coming back.

My Michael Moment

For me, my Michael moment was simply when he'd silence the world's din in a crowded auditorium with a gentle penetrating comment or observation and share a secret with me. Standing next to me, he'd turn his body slightly sideways. As he leaned in, he'd turn his shoulders inward as if to embrace me. He would partially cover his mouth with his right hand with two bent fingers that would just barely tap his lips. His voice would go low, and he'd look me in the eye. He'd speak to me in a slightly raspy voice displaying an almost indistinguishable stutter that emphasized the importance of his thought. He'd tuck his head down, and in almost a whisper, that drew me in and made me listen even harder, he'd make some off-the-cuff remark about events, speakers, or activities happening at that very moment. I'd feel like he'd raised his invisibility cloak shrouding us both in secrecy. Then I'd make an acknowledging comment in kind. His eyes would light up with real joy, and he'd quickly respond with, "Yeah, yeah..." while emphatically nodding his head in affirmation and pointing the two bent fingers in the air for emphasis. In that instant, just the two of us bonded over that seemingly critical comment that birthed some new found mutual perspective. For just an instant, the moment would seem to transcend time.

Then suddenly, the sounds of the external room would accelerate and catch up to my frozen moment, and things fast-forwarded and raced to reach their normal speed once more. In an instant, the words were gone. They simply evaporated into insignificance, unable to be captured, not needing to be captured.

I suddenly felt a loss. Indeed, I felt a pang of hunger, hoping for the moment's return. But in its place, I felt good, special, even enriched. I imagine he had the same effect on everyone.

But that moment that I had shared with Michael, the feeling that I and my opinion really mattered, lingered with me like a wisp of magic. I can't think of a greater gift that one person can give to another. Thank you, Michael.

Michael passed away on May Day 2017.

Final Note

Recognizing Michael's decades of tireless work for America's homeless, some called him the American Mother Teresa. Professor Brian Levin wrote in an email, "He was our brother, our friend, and our unassuming leader, and he would believe each of us were all blessed if we were to roll up our sleeves every morning and go fight every day to ensure that every person experiencing homelessness has a home where they can live with dignity, fairness, and a Livable Income until we have taken our very last breath on the very last day of our lives, just as he did."

12 The No Sit/ No Lie Ordinance

The No Sit/No Lie Ordinance is one of the "quality of life" ordinances mentioned in my previous book, *Looking Up at the Bottom Line: The Struggle for the Living Wage*, which basically outlaws the condition of homelessness. Other ordinances in this vein make it illegal to loiter (stand), panhandle (ask people for help), camp (find outside lodging), etc. These ordinances are class C misdemeanors, *criminal offenses*. For that reason, these tickets, just by themselves, become barriers to escaping homelessness. For example, if you, as a landlord, could choose between John who has no such offenses, or Jack, who has 13 such charges on his police record, who would you choose to rent to? You'd choose John every time. So, would I! Similarly, if as an employer, you could choose between Betty who had 7 such criminal charges, or Lawanda, who is just as ready and equally capable but has no such charges, who would you choose? You'd hire Lawanda.

That is why, when House the Homeless fought the no-camping ordinance for 5 years, our signs asked the "powers that be" to "Forgive us for being Criminal Sleepers." However, no one would.

The No Sit/No Lie Ordinance, like the others, carries a fine of between $200 and $500! Any person experiencing homelessness might say, "We clearly do not have the funds to pay the fine, or we would have been staying in a damned motel."

When you can't pay the ticket, "it goes to warrant." Then, you can be *picked up on the warrant* and taken to jail for at least three days. Who says there's no debtors' prison?

I was President and founder of House the Homeless, created in 1989. Around that same time, I created Legal Aid for the Homeless, an outreach office of Texas Rio Grande Legal Aid. For over 30 years, I left my morning office about mid-day and drove to the public parking lot across from the homeless shelter at the time. The last 15 years or so it was the Austin Resource Center for the Homeless (ARCH), where the men's shelter is located.

One day, with books and magazines I had gathered for the guys, I headed for the front entrance of the shelter. From the alleyway between the Salvation Army and the ARCH, snaked the same long line of people I had seen for the previous three days. The difference was that this time, two police officers were "working the line." I walked over to Dave, who every day occupies pretty much the same 3' by 3' space where the sidewalk would have been, had there been one. Dave is a beautiful Black man in his late twenties. He has relaxed, thick, yet semi-curly black hair that every woman I know would kill for. He looks like a dandy with pointy black shoes, black slacks, and a jet-black vest. He is mild-mannered, uses few words, and is very much into his own thoughts, as he suffers from schizophrenia. It took the two of us about a year to connect with one another beyond grunts.

I asked what was going on with the cops and the line. He just responded with, "Tickets." I asked, "What for?" He said, "Sittin." I remember pressing, "And the line?" Without looking at me, still focused on the line, he said, "Health clinic." Taken aback, I asked, "They're sick?" He kind of froze. Then slowly, very slowly, Dave turned and looked at me dead in the eye and paused before he said, "Yeah." Without seeing his lips move, I was sure I heard him say, *Yeah, they're in line, they're sick, been sitting down cause they're too sick to stand, and the cops are writing tickets because that's what cops do...dumb ass.*" But like I said, I'm not sure I ever saw his lips move. "Damn it," was my not too sophisticated response.

I put down my books, magazines, and backpack and cautiously approached one of the police officers. "Excuse me, sir, may I ask what the tickets are for?" "Sitting down," came the retort. "Aren't they sick?" came my naïve question. The next thing out of the officer's mouth was, "You want to go to jail?" My head flooded with Lynyrd Skynyrd singing..."Steps, give me three steps Mister, give me three steps for the door..." "Not particularly," was my response as I scooped up my belongings and beat feet. After dropping my stuff inside, I returned with my cell phone in hand. Click, click, click, I'm taking photos. The same cop yells, "Hey!" and in slow motion turns to me.

I suddenly remember a momma bear I once met who was sunning herself with her two cubs sprawled on a high rock shelf that jutted above a valley in western Pennsylvania. I had stupidly traversed the area ignoring some signs of danger, and brought myself and my traveling buddy Eric into quite a predicament. The momma bear, like the cop, had instantly shifted into high gear. Just like the momma bear, our young peace officer launched himself in my direction with similar blazing-red precision-laser eyes. Instantly, my brain flooded with the second part of the refrain, "Steps, give me three steps Mister...and I won't be back no more."

After capturing some shots in a flash in that Austin alley, I was back in my truck and gone. The destination was a trusted business, Miller Blueprint. It was probably one of the last years old man Miller was still alive. He was a great guy, really hands-on, who had run a very professional architectural blueprint/art supply business since the beginning of time. He made you feel like you were in his living room and welcome there. Within 20 minutes, they had enlarged the best photo of my new best cop friend, handing out tickets to enforce the No Sit/No Lie Ordinance on poor homeless folks who were too sick to stand in line for three hours. Are you kidding me?

Although the City Council had passed the ordinance in 1992, the police were just getting around to enforcing it, happy to have discovered one more arrow in their quiver to help them fight the crime of being homeless. This was the sort of justification they repeated to each other often to feel good about themselves.

It was now 2010, and *Looking Up at the Bottom Line* had finally been published, which added to my reputation as someone who might know what I was talking about. I took my 20" by 30" photo and stood before the Austin City Council and asked, "Is this the kind of city we want to live in... where sick people, who have lost everything, are ticketed for sitting down? This is unconscionable. At the very least, there needs to be exceptions!"

I scanned the room to be met with blank stares. Afterward, I met with Council member Mike Martinez. Mike was my kind of guy. When he was President of the local Firefighters Association, it became the first firefighters' association to endorse our national campaign to create the Universal Living Wage.

Without hesitation, he said, "The ordinance is too harsh; you're right; there needs to be medical exceptions." So, Mike agreed to carry the legislation saying, "We should be able to get this done in a couple of months." I raised an eyebrow as I left his office.

Naturally, a history was involved. A couple of years before this, there was a movement to get benches installed around ARCH. House the Homeless gathered several hundred signatures endorsing the idea, and I presented those signatures to Council member Lee Leffingwell. Predictably, there was pushback, notably from ARCH Executive Director Helen Varty, who wanted no part of it, fearing that the presence of benches would lead to drug sales. Leffingwell backed away from the project, as did we, in hopes of "living to fight another day." Would it be too much to hope that this might now be that "other day"? Because meanwhile, Lee Leffingwell had become Austin's mayor.

So here I was, two weeks after that meeting with Mike Martinez, again standing before the City Council, seeking to have the No Sit/No Lie Ordinance pay deference to folks with disabilities.

I shared some statistics. HtH held annual events, and this years' Thermal Underwear Party had drawn 650 guests, the single largest gathering of homeless folks in the state. 501 people had honored us with their trust enough to fill out the survey, which this year covered health issues.

House the Homeless Health Survey Results 2010

Check ALL that apply.
Do you have?..   High blood pressure 204
  Mental Illness 175   What Type? Schizophrenia 16   Bi-Polar 86
  Diabetes 84   Shots 16   Panic Attacks 70
  Arthritis 123   HIV/AIDS 10   Seizures 45
Are you a regular illegal drug user? Yes–59
Do you believe you are an alcoholic? Yes–92
Have you ever had a brain injury? Yes–83
Do you have cancer? Yes–83   Remarkably, 12 different types of cancer
were divulged.

As a result of this data, I called for and provided a list of exceptions to the No Sit/ No Lie Ordinance. The ordinance needed to pay deference to people experiencing homelessness while struggling to cope with their disabilities. The inclusion of the exceptions would bring the ordinance into compliance with the federal law: The Americans with Disabilities Act.

The list of Exceptions: Any Person:

- with a mobility-impaired bus pass
- with documentation of hospital care within the previous two weeks
- with documentation of food stamp work exception (for health issues)
- with an award letter from the Social Security Administration for disability
- with documentation of recuperative care within the previous two weeks
- with a doctor's note of disability
- with a letter of disability from the Department of Assistive and Rehabilitative Services
- with a letter of participation from the David Powell Health Clinic (AIDS/HIV)
- with a letter of participation from the Community Court for a court-ordered substance abuse treatment program
- with a letter of participation from the Austin Recovery Center's Substance Abuse Treatment Center
- with evidence of participation in a physical or occupational therapy program
- in line for any health clinic
- using canes, crutches, walkers, or other assistive devices
- with documentation that they have applied to the Veterans Administration for disability benefits
- with official documentation that they have applied to the Social Security Administration for disability benefits

- with an award letter of disability from the Veterans Administration
- taking Psychotropic medications
- who is obese
- who is pregnant
- when an area heat or smog advisory has been issued.

Interestingly, just before the vote, Mayor Lee Leffingwell, who had previously backed away from the idea of letting people sit near ARCH, remarked, "I would like the concept of benches to be explored." Mike Martinez had been right about one thing; the vote was unanimous. *However*, rather than simply grant the exemptions, the Council unanimously decided that a Health and Human Services Committee should "examine" the issue and make recommendations. But that first resolution had set the tone for the guys. Not only was it ours, but it had also been passed unanimously, and it said,

"Whereas, a recent survey by House the Homeless Inc. found a range of medical conditions that could be considered for exemption similar to disability that requires the use of a wheelchair or similar device; and..."

So, right there, in the middle of the ordinance, it referred to House the Homeless. This was awesome! We couldn't believe it. For the first time that any of us could remember in all our years of struggle, someone had listened to us. Sure, we had gotten press before, but this was different. This was respect. We didn't even have to raise our collective voice to a shrill pitch to get attention or state our case. We simply told the absolute truth and then...

"The City Manager is directed to work with homeless advocates and stakeholders, including House the Homeless, to consider additional possible medical exceptions to 9-4-14 of the City Code within 60 days." The Resolution went on to identify the possible exemptions, including:
- when in possession of official documentation from local, state, or federal agencies stating disability;
- official documentation from a doctor or hospital stating disability;
- waiting in line for health clinics; or
- utilization of other mobility aids besides wheelchairs (e.g., canes, crutches, or walkers).

This was everything we had argued to the Council that we needed!

Wow! We were in charge (sort of) and definitely on our way! None of us could believe what was happening. I kept trying to tell the guys we needed to go slowly and just work through it. After all, it was right there in black and white. The City Council had passed it unanimously. We were named in the resolution. All of our reasonable demands were clearly presented right there in an official city document that called for final recommendations within 60 days. Maybe Mike Martinez was right, and we could knock this out in a couple of months.

The First Wave

This was "not my first rodeo," as they say. So, I thought about being strategic in our meeting before the Health and Human Services subcommittee and how best to involve our homeless guys. I talked to folks in small groups of three and larger groups of 50 by going to the ARCH. I made sure everyone understood what we were fighting for and told them over and over, "We can do this." Not everyone shared my belief in our success. However, as Director of Legal Aid for the Homeless, I had literally helped over a thousand folks get disability checks. I had gotten them involved in flying banners for the Universal Living Wage and fought the no-camping ordinance for five years, so we had a working relationship built on loyalty and mutual respect.

Someone wheezing uncontrollably in response to congestive heart failure needs to sit down. So does someone who feels faint or who needs to elevate their diabetes-bloated feet. Everyone knows this, and that is how we would sell our message: as plain fact, acknowledged by any decent human. We were not making demands but stating obvious, unquestionable truths, with the full and calm expectation of being validated. Also, being what many people categorized as the unworthy, undeserving poor—the homeless—we were in no position to make demands.

I learned a decade before from the late great Max Weiner that we needed a clear message, singular and pointed. "Please help" and "Thank you" are compelling requests and words that hopefully would move the soul. We chose: "Thank you." That's it. That's all. We would psych them out by assuming that they recognized the justness of our request and thank them in advance for doing their part, which was simply to mold it into a resolution.

Max had taught me to paint block words on 20" by 30" individual sheets of white poster board. And so, we got together, and with one-inch-wide paint brushes, using black tempera paint, we crafted our message.

I contracted my buddy, Wade, from Hyde Park Baptist School. For $75.00, anyone could rent a 38-seat school bus for a round trip ride to a local event. This was tactical. While we were only going to travel about 10 city blocks, I wanted us to present a visible, identifiable united front, different from those who hadn't joined us. They could be our cheerleaders.

A couple of days before, I hung a clipboard and a sign-up sheet on the ARCH bulletin board. It pictured a big yellow school bus with lots of folks waving out of the windows with massive ear-to-ear smiles, headed to City Hall. "Sit on the bus so we can stand up for our rights!"

Alan Graham, Founder of Mobile Loaves and Fishes, and "my brother-from-another-mother," as he likes to say, provided food support for our action. Each rider received a sack lunch and a bottle of water, even though

112

the hearing was at 10:00 AM and everyone had pretty much just eaten. People experiencing homelessness can always eat! It might be boredom, but more likely, it is due to the absolute uncertainty and insecurity of being homeless.

I had the bus arrive at the ARCH 45 minutes early so people could see it, could hear from us about the issue again, and be persuaded to join. Over the ARCH loudspeaker system, I announced, "Our bus is here." As people decided to join us, they piled into seats with all of their life's belongings. Fortunately, school buses have big, spacious seats. It was all quite festive. There was constant activity, boisterous talking, and not unexpectedly endless movement on and off the bus by folks who had second thoughts and mumbled excuses about laundry or medical appointments. Johnny, the driver, was a little nervous. We were not his typical passengers. He was not sure what to make of us. Half the guys had already snarfed down their peanut butter sandwich, apple, and cookie. I quieted them and again explained (partly to reassure the driver) that half of us were so disabled we could not work. As a result, the city needed to make allowances for our health needs and not ticket us for sitting or lying down when we absolutely needed to.

Many heads nodded in agreement. I explained that we had gotten a unanimous resolution that mentioned House the Homeless by name and that called for a city subcommittee to find a way to acknowledge and accommodate our disabilities. Some nodded and grunted in the affirmative; others applauded. Folks commented on their personal situations. From Sara, "I got COPD, and I can't breathe." From Jerome, "I got bad feet and can hardly walk." From Malcolm, "I take medicine for the voices, and the sun takes me down." Then there was a rising din of conversation with people talking about respect and rights. I felt good... real good.

We arrived at City Hall in about nine minutes. As we loudly piled out of the bus, I tried to get folks to take their lunch bag trash and organize a single street crossing. "Fiasco" best described the assemblage and crossing. Motorists were most kind. They could see people were struggling as they hobbled and limped across the intersection with all their possessions hanging from their arms, strapped to their backs, and clutched in their fists.

A white male approached me, and when I say white, I mean that in the truest street sense possible. He was at least 6'4", a bit gangly, in his late thirties. Introducing himself as Hugh Simonich, he said he knew of me and House the Homeless and added, "I'd like to join you." His speech was clear and deliberate, and I imagined a bumper sticker across his forehead reading "bureaucrat." But, never one to turn down a new recruit, I simply said, "Sure, why not." My philosophy: everybody is golden until they're not.

We staged outside of the City Hall entrance in the shade of some seriously large potted trees and the cool shadow of the north side of the building itself. (In Austin, it's always at least 100 degrees in the shade). It was a new multi-million dollar building whose roofline on the south side presents to the river with its huge copper armadillo head, and on the north side, a 15' long copper armadillo tail. Did I mention that Austin is in Texas?

At any rate, the guys rested outside the entrance while I conferred with Tom, who runs the metal detector. Normally, he probably gets 20 people an hour. We were to be a steady stream of at least fifty backpacking, shoulder sack-toting, somewhat odiferous "street people." There had been 38 of us, but our number had swelled to 50 when late-comers walked the ten blocks from their woods.

People would finally get through the metal detector but not without setting off every bell and whistle, which required Bob to join Tom and put his wand to good use as coins, knives, watches would be forgotten by their owners but not over-looked by the ever-watchful electric eyes. After setting off every bell and whistle, we finally got everybody through the metal detector.

I would then hand them each a sign. We gave them all out, all 50 signs. I spoke briefly one last time before we entered the sub-committee chambers. I asked, "Ready?" Subdued by the building's opulence, they sheepishly nodded, and I led them into the large square room, and we stood our disheveled selves around the edges. Not one of us sat in the spectator chairs or moved toward the front. At the business end of the room were tables and several chairs facing toward the room. In front of those were a speaker's podium and three more tables with up to six chairs, apparently for speakers and city staff members, which filled up quickly.

Present were several City Council members I knew, and the three I knew fairly well. Laura Morrison had always seemed very kind and compassionate toward House the Homeless and our causes. The subcommittee chair was Randi Shade. Senior Member Mike Martinez was, of course, carrying our issue. However, who really knows any politician or what they'll do? They certainly didn't know what we were about to do and seemed quietly apprehensive.

Austin is the most laid-back city I've ever lived in. Casual wear is the norm. Wearing a tie is the exception anymore, even at an official function like a public hearing. So, there we were, occupying the edges of the room in our ragamuffin clothes (a little casual even for Austin) with our filthy backpacks at our feet, wearing used shoes that might have been donated to homeless collection boxes by the council members themselves. They say that "man's greatest fear is the fear of the unknown." Being literally surrounded by us seemed to cause palpable tension, and we learned what the expression "deathly quiet" meant that day. In addition, this motley crew was led by someone—me—whose reputation for unpredictability was known by all the Council members. Randi Shade, for instance, had gone with me through Leadership Austin in 1998, an experience that Legal Aid director Regina Rogoff decided to spend $1,000 to put me through. I didn't fit well. For the final group project, I went off on my own and wrote my first book, *Striking a Balance*, about the coming gentrification of East Austin and steps that could and should be taken to mitigate its negative impact on its Black and Hispanic residents. East Austin was about to be invaded by monied White interests, and senior citizens would be driven out as prices, rents, and taxes would skyrocket.

The book was anything but balanced. Its one-sided perspective was mine, based on what I had seen in Philadelphia and many other cities. It was an alarm bell.

In the subcommittee room, I outlined our situation. According to the House the Homeless statistical survey, half of the homeless population is disabled. Out of the 501 individuals sampled, 27 had various types of cancer. No less than 86 of those surveyed had been diagnosed with bipolar disorder (many with psychotic features that included hearing voices and seeing visions). Sixteen people admitted being diagnosed with full-blown schizophrenia, which involves regimens of antipsychotic medications, whose side effects are often debilitating in their own right, and certainly worse in 100-degree heat. Maiming arthritis was reported by 123 people, and 45 experienced seizures that prevented them from driving or operating any type of equipment or machinery. The list went on. I would pause, now and again, as I thought of what a victory here might mean to the guys. It might mean that for the first time, it was shown in a government public hearing that *there is a medical reason for their homelessness.* That could bring about empathy and sympathy, and relief from the endless physical and mental abuse. We held our collective breath. Cameras silently recorded the event. All the while, our people stood there in stone silence until abruptly, Randi Shade cleared her throat and said, "There will be a Stakeholders meeting to review the material." (A stakeholder is pretty much anybody who "has a dog in the fight," who can claim that an issue confronting the city will impact their economic well-being or general quality of life.)

Shade went on, "Mr. Troxell will be notified of the time and place of the meeting. Now, moving to the next agenda item...."

Slightly stunned, I raised my arms upward in a sweeping motion, and very loudly, I called out, "Zou ba! (We go!)" I'm not sure why I chose that time to practice my Chinese; I truly only know a few words or phrases. It just seemed clear and commanding. We shuffled outside and into the waiting lenses of the media. Shelton Green, with KVUE News, shoved a microphone into my face. "So Richard, what do you think you accomplished here today?" My acquaintance with this sincere, affable, well-informed, African American gentleman went back many years to his arrival in Austin as a rookie reporter. His first TV interview assignment had been House the Homeless.

His story led with, "Homeless Advocates ask for Benches." and mentioned that we were asking for exceptions to the No Sit/ No Lie Ordinance. He quoted me as saying, "Think about being disabled, standing in line for healthcare and not being able to sit down or to be subject to a fine ($200-$500) while you were waiting." The article went on to mention some of our requested exceptions, "...which include a doctor's note of disability, a mobility-impaired bus pass, documentation of hospital care within the previous two weeks."

Lastly, Shelton quoted me with, "We all pay taxes, that means we're all citizens whether we like to think of ourselves as all citizens and all members of the same neighborhood or not, but we are! And if you don't think of it that way, simply think of these folks as human beings."

I gathered the guys as best I could, as many had started to leave and walk back to the shelter. Not knowing how long our event would be, Johnny, our bus driver, had left. Aside from that, I thought that everything had gone fairly well. No one had gotten arrested, and we got our message out. Despite my cautious enthusiasm, the guys affect continued to be mostly flat. It had been such an emotionally draining day. Perhaps their sedate dispositions were due to the exhausting amount of emotional and physical energy that had been consumed. Or perhaps, it was because they had seen it all before with failed outcomes in the end. I was reminded of a photo I had once seen of two old Black folks on the front steps of the state capitol building in Charleston, South Carolina. Their richly brown, gnarled faces were deeply creased, and they slumped, leaning on their picket signs. One simply said, "I'm tired of waiting for nothing."

City Staff/Stakeholders Meeting

The room where the stakeholders meeting was held contained mostly strange faces, which was a little odd since I had been a stakeholder in the battle to end homelessness in Austin since 1989. But some I did recognize. There were members of the East Sixth Street Community Association (ESSCA), representing businesses in the entertainment district.

The Downtown Austin Alliance (DAA) was represented by Charles Betts, who had once told me in private that "the homeless should be exterminated." That organization's only contribution to the government-funded, 8-million-dollar ARCH had been to *insist upon metal detectors* at the front door.

Someone was there from Caritas, a wonderful faith-based organization that has served poor individuals, poor families, and immigrants in Austin for decades. Trinity Center was represented on paper with an affirmative statement about benches, but no actual representative was present. There were others I didn't know and representatives from the ARCH. Hugh Simonich and I were there for House the Homeless.

City of Austin staff members conducted the meeting. The Chairwoman, Susan Gehring, was a city planner at the time. White, perhaps in her early 50s, pleasant to speak with and quick to smile, she reminded me of a snake oil salesperson. Several years before, she had expressed to me much enthusiasm for helping the homeless. But in the intervening years, there had been no sign of that sentiment being translated into action.

The meeting began with introductions, which, with 35 to 40 participants, took a considerable amount of time. Then, Ms. Gehring laid out the issue as she saw it. I was finally given an opportunity to give the House the Homeless perspective. When I read the list of proposed medical exemptions to the No Sit/No Lie Ordinance, the room fell silent. Ms. Gehring filled the void by saying that she was hearing no support for the exemptions other than House the Homeless.

This was not strictly accurate. Mental Health and Mental Retardation (MHMR) had sent a written letter of support for exemptions, which generally spoke about medications such as antipsychotics and anticholinergics that can result in deleterious responses when combined with excessive heat exposure. They wrote that "psychiatric patients had twice the risk of dying during a heat wave than the general population." Furthermore, the letter pointed out that the Center for Disease Control and Prevention warned that persons who are "physically ill, especially with heart disease or have high blood pressure, or who take medications such as for depression, insomnia, or poor circulation, may also be adversely affected by extreme heat." The letter was presented by my friend Greg Gibson who also cares deeply about justice and our friends who don't have any. Some of the attendees said that while they were sympathetic toward the medical needs of our people, "There should be no exemptions." We heard several versions of, "After all, we don't want people lying all over our city." I had reiterated the collective findings of the House the Homeless survey, which had shown that 50% of the people responding were so disabled that they could not work, and therefore, they needed to be shown deference in accordance with the Americans with Disabilities Act.

Silence. Nothing.

Suddenly, Ms. Gehring started to adjourn the meeting. Stunned, I felt like shouting but turned pale instead. "What about the Mayor?" I blurted. The Chairwoman didn't miss a beat. "What *about* the Mayor?" she replied, with a slightly different emphasis that translated to, "Are you kidding?"

Grasping at straws, I brought up Mayor Lee Leffingwell's verbal recommendation at the previous meeting that the city should explore the bench concept. It took a little encouragement, but Ms. Gehring picked a date for another meeting about a week away and asked us to return, having considered benches.

The Quest for Benches

Hugh, while a stranger to the social service world, is an even-mannered, intelligent gentleman with a contemplative nature. He had recently joined House the Homeless. We formed a mini-committee of 2 to explore the world of benches, starting with photos on the internet; I was looking for one style, in particular, the kind divided by a center arm. This distinctive feature helps people with certain disabilities, like ruined knees, who can't get up or down without something to hold onto. The design has a bonus value. Anti-bench advocates contended that people experiencing homelessness would abuse benches by treating them like beds. The center bar, which prevents lying down to sleep, would be a major selling point. They all assumed our guys couldn't slip under the bar and saw a log. Well, they were wrong.

As often is the case, it was my sweet wife, Sylvia, who stopped what she was doing, and, within minutes, found the perfect photo. Amazingly, outside the very City Hall where we were meeting were similar benches! How could anyone deny our request for benches now? We took photos from every possible angle.

Then Hugh and I moved on to the heart of the project. We set out to identify downtown locations where benches might be placed. The potential sites could not impede pedestrian traffic in any direction and had to be disability-accessible. A bench could not interfere with customers going in or out of businesses or with the delivery or pickup of goods to or from businesses. Benches anywhere near bus stops must not affect the loading and unloading of passengers. We limited our initial sampling to just a few downtown streets, starting in front of homeless service providers.

Second Stakeholders Meeting (Bench Presentation)

The group discussion of benches would be the second and supposedly final stakeholders meeting among city staff, business owners, downtown neighbors, downtown homeless non-profits, and homeless advocates (which at this point pretty much consisted of House the Homeless.) On June 7th, with high-definition photos of the perfect benches and our examples of appropriate locations, Hugh and I confidently returned to City Hall. We had done our homework.

We were very excited to see what proposals the others brought to the table. Would theirs be a simple duplication of our efforts? Or, would they suggest benches farther out to steer our people away from their precious downtown?

Once the room had filled, city employees droned intolerably in fluent bureaucratese for almost 15 minutes. Even the business people started to fidget. I presented the House the Homeless bench proposal with its photos and carefully-researched locations.

Bench in Austin, Texas

Possible Bench Locations

Possible bench locations pursuant to House the Homeless health survey and exposure of major health conditions relative to the No Sit/ No Lie Ordinance.

Location	Number of Benches
ARCH porch north wall	2
ARCH west wall	6
ARCH south wall	6
CARITAS west wall	2
CARITAS north wall	2
Salvation Army north wall	2
Salvation Army west wall	2
Trinity Center east side	3
Trinity Center south side	3
East 7th & Congress to I-35	8

Angel House		3
Congress 1st-9th	staggered/ E & W	9
Red River 4th-15th	" " "	11
University Methodist-Guadalupe		3
Guadalupe throughout the Drag		6
Main Library		4
Cesar Chavez, Congress to I-35 N & S sides-staggered		10
100 East 5thStreet & Congress North side		2
East 5th & San Jacinto NW side of 5th Bank of America		2
NE side San Jacinto @ 5th on corner		5
504 trinity on NE side Copper tank & Event Center		2
311 East 5th St & Trinity SW side		1
East 5th & San Jacinto SW side corner: 2 on San Jacinto side		
& 2 benches on 5th St side (322 Bus)		
108 East 5t St South side (apartments)		3
SW side of East 5th St. & Brazos (Barber shop)		2
SE side of East 5th & Brazos		1
SE side on 5th St.		2-3
South Side of 105 East 5th		2-3
South side 100 East 5th & Congress		3
N side of 6th St E & W e.g. 6th & Red River Bus Stop #4		2-3
Note. All sites listed here & below have an extended 16' walkway.		
NW side of 6th & Sabine		2-3
NE side of 6th & Sabine		1
N Side of 6th-West of Sabine at Alley		1
South side of 6th @723 6th Street		1
South side of 6th @709 6th		1-2
South side of 6th@ 701 6th		2
South side 6th West of Sabine @500 Block of Sabine		1
SE side of 6th and Red River		2
SW side of 6th and Red River		1
SE side of 6th and Neches		2
SW side of 6th and Neches @ 423 6th Street		2
SE side of 6th & Trinity		2
SE side of 6th and San Jacinto		1
SW side of Brazos &Congress @115 6th St.		1
NW side of Alley@ 106 6th St. @Louie's Bar		1
NE side of Alley @ 200 6th St.		1
NE side of 218 6th St.		1
NE side of 300 6th St. @ Malaja Bar		1
NW side of 422 6th St. @ Neches @ Nimos Bar		1

I closed with, "Additionally, it is recommended that a physical survey be conducted in the entire downtown area to determine the appropriate placement of *additional* benches."

Subcommittee Chairwoman Susan Gehring asked for other recommendations. A long pause ensued. There were no additional recommendations, *none*. Silence, as if the entire room were holding its collective breath. Then someone burst out, "No benches!" and everyone started talking at once. "We don't need benches...we have plenty! The homeless will take them over...sleep on them...set up camp on them!" Then this from—of all people—a representative of Front Steps, the non-profit, faith-based organization that runs the ARCH:

"We don't want benches. The benches will enable the homeless to use them as a base of operations for drug dealers to sell drugs to innocent people. The benches will prey upon the people." A representative from Caritas, another homeless service provider, supported the "benches are bad" position. I was stunned.

The Episcopal homeless service ministry, Trinity Center, is right downtown close to the ARCH, Caritas, and the Salvation Army. In her beautiful Israeli accent, Executive Director Irit Umani said, "The Trinity Center would like a bench; in fact, we'll take two." Bless you Irit.

I quickly gathered my thoughts and spoke again. The police stationed at the ARCH had already commandeered several offices on the second floor and established lookout posts, and put in video cameras on the sidewalks surrounding the men's shelter and the Salvation Army. They got in there in the first place on the promise of "community policing," In theory, the uniformed officers were to routinely pass among these people experiencing homelessness, converse with them, get to know them, and learn to move some along and intervene when appropriate.

Holding benches accountable for drug sales, I told them, was like tearing down a house because it had been the site of some massive drug sting. An inanimate bench could not be capable of buying and selling drugs. Only humans could do that. I went on, "The idea of not having benches in response to the need of people with disabilities to have a bench to sit down upon when they are having an asthma attack or when the neuropathy in their feet spikes and rises to the level of daggers in their soles is like destroying those drug houses when we have a national affordable housing crisis! It is insane!! It is bureaucracy and bigotry joining hands and running amuck. It is the definition of insanity." I paused. The room went stone silent. Then all at once, folks started speaking, and one voice rose above the din. "Yeah, no benches and no exemptions."

Well, there you had it. The people had spoken.

The Neighbors Speak

While we licked our wounds, gathered our thoughts, and regrouped, the city staff called another meeting. It appeared to be scheduled at the last minute, but the room that Hugh and I and several other House the Homeless members walked into held over 100 downtown citizens. A sea of intense, anxious faces all turned in our direction, and I imagined them all armed with torches and pitchforks.

In charge were city staff members I did not recognize. We had arrived at the appointed time, and yet clearly, there had been discussion already. Nothing fishy about that!

With deep scowls, the crowd looked like it wanted to arrest us for promoting "criminal sitting." Pointed questions were being asked, coupled with furtive looks in our direction.

Obviously, it was a setup. I turned to our people and said in a raspy, hushed voice, "We say nothing." The others registered disbelief. I repeated, "We say nothing...we can't win here." We spent the hour passively absorbing all the awful, hateful, toxic thoughts shared by the "citizens." I thought of the fire hoses being turned on the good folks in Selma on the Edmund Pettus Bridge and the dogs that attacked them. They didn't fight back. I thought of wave after wave of Hindus marching to the sea in their salt protest, where person after person was clubbed only to be systematically replaced by others willing to sacrifice their bodies to drive the British out of their lives. Standing in silence, listening to these shameless comments of hatred, was nothing compared to those events. And yet, I was sad. We were all so very sad. We had done nothing wrong. We had worked when we could, but the pitiful wages they paid failed to sustain us. And when we fell into disability, the stipend they paid was about half the amount of the pitiful wages and far too insufficient to place a roof over our heads... other than a bridge. The system really is broken, and the people have been taught to blame their fellow citizens.

Benny Sorrells

Benny with hat. Photo by Alan Pogue.

As we prepared to leave, I realized that my old friend Benny Sorrells was standing with us. That's the way it was with Benny. He always seemed to appear and disappear like a leprechaun. In fact, he was standing right next to me with a little, scruffy white beard made whiter next to his dark skin. As usual, he was looking up at me and mumbling something with a very intent look on his face, "Now see, here, what they mean criminal sleeping?" It always seemed that I'd catch Benny's first sentence, and then the mumble would become so severe that I couldn't follow along much past that point.

Benny, as best as I could tell, had moved to Texas from California. He had gotten into some legal trouble for looking at a white woman too long but swears that he didn't even do that. Sometimes he'd start to tell me about a "piece of land that these white men took from his family in east Texas." Then he'd trail off, and I couldn't follow along with that either. Benny was as sweet and gentle yet as intense as you could imagine. He survived on his God-given gift of art. He painted with such intensity and beauty that at the end of each year's "Art from the Streets" show, he would sell every single one of his paintings fast and for top dollar. Every year since 1993, my wife Sylvia and I would look for him. I'd almost always ask him to explain the painting that caught my eye. He'd start to tell me about some injustice that had occurred, and then I'd soon lose the thread as his mumbling would increase with the telling. It was always intense and always an accusation. As we all shuffled out of the hearing room, he grabbed the sleeve of my shirt, vice-grip tight, declaring that this "sleeping business was a crime all right, you can't lock a man up for sleeping...God makes you sleep..." And I didn't understand any more of what he was saying, but I knew he was right. We all did.

On July 22, 2011, the City Council's Health and Human Services subcommittee met again. Again, Randi Shade presided, accompanied by Laura Morrison and Mike Martinez. Also, present was Judge Michael Coffey of the Community Court, which was created for the sole purpose of convicting people experiencing homelessness who allegedly violated "quality of life" ordinances such as the No Sit/No Lie Ordinance, City Code 9-4-14.

Police Chief Art Acevedo had made some highly controversial statements in the proceedings that included: 1) the police *were not* ticketing people in line while waiting for services. Having personally witnessed this on several occasions, I could not let those words stand unchallenged. So, I did challenge the Chief directly. In fact, I had taken a picture of one such event. 2) the Chief stated that the police were not targeting homeless people with these tickets.

There were other homeless service providers downtown, but the major ones were ARCH, The Salvation Army, Caritas, Trinity Center, and First Baptist Church. Under the Open Records Act, Hugh Simonich and I obtained police records and checked out 2,729 No Sit/ No Lie citations issued between January and December of 2009. The next step was to compare each ticket against their addresses meticulously. By astonishing coincidence, 96% of the tickets had been issued to one of these five addresses! Here was absolute proof that homeless people were being targeted with these tickets! We also amassed photo after photo of university students sitting or lying down in line for Apple computers, iPads, Star Wars tickets, and the like. We have *Austin American Statesman* newspaper photos of parents sitting, lying down, and openly camping while waiting overnight to get school transfers for their children. In none of these instances were tickets handed out to any non-homeless violators of the No Sit/No Lie Ordinance.

Any police officer, elected official, or City Council member who thinks that this law has been applied to all citizens without discrimination either has no grasp on reality or is knowingly fabricating a falsehood. So, they are either fools or liars. Choose your labels. I no longer have patience or tolerance for either.

As we entered the subcommittee chambers that day, next to the sign-up list we saw a stack of documents. Each was five sheets thick, with large print and only a few bullet points on each page. In the upper left-hand corner was the official seal of the City of Austin. The title page read: "Recommendations Regarding the Sit/Lie Ordinance." Created by the city staff, it was dated July 22, 2010. My eyes did not want to focus on this crucial document that could make us or sink us.

The background page mentioned the passage of the original House the Homeless ordinance seeking medical exemptions. It acknowledged that the City Manager had been directed to return to the Health and Human Services sub-committee to explore possible exemptions in addition to exploring the possibility of benches in the downtown area.

Under Staff Recommendations, the first paragraph stated that the majority of the stakeholders, including the downtown homeless services agencies, were opposed to additional exemptions. (Ouch!) Paragraph two referenced the feedback from various demographics: stakeholders, the Austin Police Department, and Community Court. The ordinance was working fine for them anyway. They saw no reason to recommend additional exemptions. The final page brought back memories of the second stakeholders meeting when the Great Streets Project was mentioned. I was familiar with its publicity. The "one block at a time" game plan would make Austin a world-class city. It occurred to someone on the other side to assert that the Great Streets Project would include benches, so no need to worry our pretty little heads about that. Back at the office, I did the research. Great Streets included no wide-spread plan for benches, and in fact, there were absolutely zero dollars budgeted for any benches. It was a sham.

In the interval between that meeting and this one, it occurred to someone on the other side to quickly amend that budget. Now, the subcommittee gave it to us in black and white: Great Streets would provide benches downtown, but not anywhere near the social services providers. And it was their strong recommendation that no other group should place a bench where it would help anyone who really needed it. (Ouch and ouch again!)

City staffers made a brief presentation, and I made a brief comment, simply, "Your ordinance is singularly targeting people experiencing homelessness and, in my opinion, it is in violation of the Americans with Disabilities Act."

Time to Go to Work

From the very beginning, I had approached my friend and expert housing attorney, Fred Fuchs. I told him and attorney Tracey Whitley, one of my supervisors (and friend), what I was working on. Fred referred me to Mike Urena, an attorney in one of our other Texas Rio Grande Legal Aid offices. I called Mike immediately. Though a little skeptical at first, he was willing to hear me out. It took more than one conversation, but he responded by fully engaging; awesome! As lines of reasoning occurred to me, I relayed them to Mr. Urena to see if they could be shaped into valid legal arguments. Exhibit A: the survey conducted by House the Homeless and the appalling truths it revealed about the lives of people experiencing homelessness. When forbidden to sit or lie down, the disabled individuals (and that's almost half of them) suffer in degrees ranging from extreme discomfort to acute pain. Being forced to stand for long periods (or depending on the disability, even for short periods) puts them at risk.

They get dizzy, lose their balance, and sometimes fall. They sustain various injuries—road rash, concussion, cuts, and broken bones.

Many Americans, for some reason, assume that all other Americans have cars. Homeless individuals often do not have cars, especially if they are disabled. A lot of them have to walk everywhere they go, and the distances can be significant. But because of their disabilities, sometimes they need to sit. With a law like the No Sit/No Lie Ordinance, they literally can't help doing criminal acts. Is there a legal remedy for such injustice? Because if there isn't, there should be.

And harassing people who are standing in line. Does the housed and/ or employed American imagine that people stand in lines for the fun of it? They have no choice because they desperately need whatever it is at the front of that line, be it food, medical care, or help to obtain the disability compensation for which they are eligible. Waiting for an appointment about your SNAP benefits doesn't happen in a nice air-conditioned space with comfy chairs and a TV. No, it involves a lot of standing around, in the sun if necessary, and we're talking about people who are old, some of them, or physically disabled, which is very common, or mentally disabled. We know Mr. and Mrs. America don't want them there and take their word for it; they don't want to be there either.

So how about it, Mr. Mike Urena? How does that translate into actionable civil rights violations? Have we got a case?

There's a thing called Title II of the Americans with Disabilities Act (ADA) that requires public entities to make "reasonable accommodations"

125

so that disabled individuals can avail themselves of services or activities made available by that entity. And the City of Austin came under that heading.

I knew the law was on our side. But as the old saying goes, "That and two and a half bucks will get you a cup of coffee." It was not enough for the law to tell us we were right. We needed it to tell our opponents they were wrong. Mike wrote:

> Unless the City makes a reasonable accommodation to ensure that public sidewalks are 'readily accessible to homeless individuals with a disability, the No Sit/ No Lie "quality of life" ordinance, and thus the City, violates the ADA. It is important to understand that while first passed in 2005, it was seriously broadened and expanded later on. And now we are stretching the edge of the envelope once more.

He was prepared to argue that providing benches or allowing exemptions that would allow disabled individuals to sit on public sidewalks would be two ways of providing a reasonable accommodation.

To establish a prima facie (basic) case of discrimination under the ADA, a plaintiff must demonstrate:
- that he or she is a qualified individual with a disability within the meaning of the ADA;
- that he or she was excluded from participating or denied the benefits of the services, programs, activities for which the public entity is responsible, or was otherwise subject to discrimination by the public entity; and
- that such exclusion, denial of benefits, or discrimination was "by reason of his or her disability."

He cited the case/ruling that he felt supported such an argument and went on to cite another supporting case/ruling:

"[U]nder Title ii of the ADA, discrimination need not be the sole reason for the exclusion of or denial of benefits to the plaintiff." Bennett-Nelson V. Louisiana Rd. Of Regents, 431 F. 3d 448, 454 (5th Cir. 2005).

So basically, to be found eligible to sue under the ADA, you have to be both *disabled and denied services*. Attorney Urena went on to cite the "Preamble to Regulation on Nondiscrimination on the basis of Disability" https://www.law.cornell.edu/cfr/text/28/appendix-A_to_part_35
in state and local government services, which requires law enforcement to make changes in policies that result in discriminating arrests or abuse of individuals with disabilities.

So now, we have a law that says the police must change their policies and practices against our homeless folks—like the ones who got 96% of the No Sit/No Lie tickets.

Mike addressed the question of applying the ADA to Austin's quality of life ordinance as it relates to the use of sidewalks. He proposed that obviously, any person who is not traveling in a motor vehicle or bicycle is a "qualified individual" entitled to use public sidewalks. He argued that homeless individuals with disabilities are, therefore, "qualified individuals" entitled to use the public sidewalks and other related services in downtown Austin. Brilliant, Mike!

"However, they may not be able to stand for long periods of time *unless* there is a reasonable accommodation. He went on to further expand the argument." He asserted "that the public sidewalks and the public services those sidewalks that lead into and out of downtown Austin, may not be readily accessible to homeless individuals with a disability that limits their ability to walk long distances if no reasonable accommodation for their disability is provided. The argument is that these two classes of individuals may therefore have a legal, monetary claim against the City of Austin under the ADA."

Looking at case history, it became clear that an individual would need to inform a public officer that they had a disability that might not be visually apparent and a need to sit down. Why? Because to be fair to everyone, intentional discrimination can't happen unless there is express knowledge on the discriminator's part.

Conversely, if the police officer was told of the person's disability status and still denied them their right to sit down, it would be in violation of the ADA.

Finally, the placement of benches in appropriate places would also be reasonable accommodations since many individuals who cannot stand or walk for long periods "may also have difficulty standing up from sitting on the ground." All this went into the Memorandum of Law relating to City Code 9-4-14 that we submitted to the Health and Human Services subcommittee.

Response from City Attorney Cathie Childs

The response from Assistant City Attorney Cathie Childs was quite shocking and sadly laughable. Her memo read:

"Homeless" is not, in-and-of-itself, a "disability" under the ADA.

The City's public sidewalk program does not "provide services to the City's homeless population"; and,

The City's sidewalk program does not discriminate against the homeless receiving services based upon any alleged "disability".

Memorandum of Law—Response from Mike Urena, Texas Rio Grande Legal Aid Attorney

Mr. Urena began by quietly stating that Ms. Childs was incorrect that he had addressed any constitutional issues. He had only addressed issues as

127

they relate to accommodations under the Americans with Disabilities Act. He added, tongue-in-cheek, that he would be willing to explore, at another time, the possibility that the ordinance violates the equal protection clause of the U.S. Constitution.

Also, no one had stated that homelessness is a "disability." In fact, he had pointed out that the ADA requires an exemption to Austin City Code 9-4-14 for disabled individuals whether they are experiencing homelessness or not.

He asserted that the Childs memo only addresses "homeless individuals" and not homeless individuals with a disability that impairs their ability to walk or stand.

He made another very strong point, "Since 48% of the individuals experiencing homelessness surveyed have a disability, it is surprising that of the 2,729 citations received by the downtown Austin Community Court between January 2009 through December 31, 2009, only 2.3% were dismissed due to medical, mental health, or disability reasons by the court."

Mike and I both felt that the Childs memo displayed a blatant disregard for the rights of disabled persons who are experiencing homelessness.

My father, Captain Richard R. Troxell, USN, once said, paraphrasing Churchill, "When dealing with intellectual issues, it is unfair and even uncivilized to fight an unarmed man.' Mr. Urena reminded me, "It is clear that we were engaged in a desperate fight with people who were neither compassionate nor well informed. Together, that can be a lethal combination, and we should tread lightly."

During this time, I communicated with Randi Shade and tried to express some of the details that were being ignored and the nuances that were being overlooked. By expressing my conviction that, *"The whole thing was unfair,"* I had naively hoped to make it easy for her to ask, "What makes you say that?" or show at least some interest in what had placed the burr under my saddle. A lot of the alleged facts that were bandied about were simply not true. Take the 708 tickets resulting in No Sit/No Lie convictions that we had studied. These individuals were disabled every day, not just once a year, for a prank. Yes, some people had received multiple tickets. The Chief of Police, the City Attorney, and Judge Coffey had translated this into a "massive number of repeat perpetrators."People who had been at that meeting, including House the Homeless members and even reporters, were telling me they had smelled fear in that chamber. Perhaps this was because certain people deliberately, provocatively conflated this ordinance with the highly inflammatory issue of panhandling and knew they might get called out for trying this provocative ruse.

It was clear to me that our approach to a reasonable accommodation (benches and exemptions) had fallen on deaf ears. It was the no-camping ordinance battle all over again. Back then, having full control of the court system, the City had hit us with 12 pre-trial motions and dragged the matter through the court system for five agonizing years before we "won." And still, they couldn't let it be! Just a few weeks after Judge Jim Coronado's ruling that the no-camping ordinance was unconstitutional, the City rewrote the ordinance and came after our folks one more time! So now, faced with what looked like a replay of history, I was bound and determined that I would not permit that draining and wasteful process to happen again. I would write her a letter, reduce our intentions to the clearest possible sixth-grade level, and then hold my breath to see what might happen.

Through correspondence, I reminded Ms. Shade how the Police Chief's repeated definitive statements that his officers never ticketed people while they were in line for services were "blatantly untrue." I went on to paint a picture of how things seem from our perspective. I reminded her that people who are homeless and sitting down in response to their disability find themselves on a daily basis, looking up at a 6-foot-tall uniformed police officer with a gun strapped to his hip.

These people who have lost everything, their family, their work, their lives as they once knew them, all of their belongings, and their dignity, are now told what time to go to bed, what time to get up, what bathrooms they can and cannot use, etc. Laws have been made just for them that state where they can sit or stand or camp or travel. This sounds like the Jim Crow laws of the not-so-distant past. I asked if this kind of treatment of a class of people sounded vaguely reminiscent to her.

I closed with, "I realize that this is simply the process, but when all the power sits on one side of the room, and when we sit on the side of the street (not even on benches) ...it all seems pretty unfair."

Two days went by; nothing. Five days, then seven passed. Nothing. I called Ms. Shade to see if she had gotten my letter. I was conciliatory. I thanked her for her leadership over a very difficult issue. I could hear a softening in her voice. Proceeding to the call's purpose, I quietly said, "We are going to sue you and the City under the Americans with Disabilities Act. Your legal counsel may well be an idiot. They think this is out in left field. I realize this is a total stretch of the Act, but I believe our counsel can make a strong, reasonable argument, and we will win." Pause. I held my breath and mentally pictured Ms. Shade sitting at her desk with a certain piece of paper in her hand. That document was a memo, and she and the Health and Human Services Subcommittee were not the only recipients. Copies have also gone out to the Mayor, the City Council, Police Chief Art Acevedo, City Manager Marc Ott, and City Attorney Michael McDonald. The author of that memo was leading civil rights attorney Jim Harrington. Some time ago, he had gained my complete respect by suing the State of Texas for failure to allow access to convenience stores to people with disabilities in wheelchairs. Technically, law had already been made insisting that businesses be wheelchair-accessible, but it wasn't happening. Each curb cut would cost $2,500 to modify, and municipalities dragged their feet. To give disabled customers the access and freedom of mobility they had been denied, Harrington deployed the Americans with Disabilities Act enabling disabled folks to purchase lottery tickets to create tax dollars.

He won!!! Curbs got cut!

Jim Harrington's memo simply stated that he could use the ADA to make a case for the House the Homeless argument and that he "looked forward to litigating the issue." Sure, the other side might come up with some tricky legal maneuver, and we might lose. I pressed on, assuring Ms. Shade that even if that happened, we would win in the court of public opinion.

We will have shown ourselves to be sympathetic individuals who have lost everything and now find ourselves disabled and living on the streets. We will have shown ourselves to have been more than reasonable, offering over 16 possible exemptions backed by doctors, the United States Military (VA), the federal government (SSI & SSDI). We will have shown ourselves to have offered a completely reasonable accommodation that would have simultaneously offered a way out and to save face by installing benches that would benefit all citizens and moved the city in the direction of becoming a "world-class" city as it can now only purport to be. You and the city, on the other hand, will be rejecting all of these attempts at administrative remedy. Your staff, who thought they were steering the outcome of the stakeholder's meetings to achieve the outcomes that they thought you desired, will be exposed for having rejected all of these attempts at compromise, and we will win!"

The Phone Call—In the Room Where It Happened

Only half expecting Randi Shade to pick up the phone, I had called her from my truck in the ARCH parking lot. The windows were down, but there was no breeze, and it must have been 112 degrees in there. I was sweating profusely, and my head was starting to throb. I had thrown the Hail Mary, and now I held my breath.

Finally, she said, "Well, they shouldn't be ticketing anyone in a line...." We won! Right then and there, I knew we had won. I didn't even need to hear the rest of her thought. We had won!

Council Member Shade and I began to talk about the possible language that would address both of our concerns. When the Health and Human Service Subcommittee next met, there were substantial words. Not unexpectedly, someone from the city legal department had inserted the word "physical," making the ordinance read that anyone with a "physical disability" would be exempt under the ordinance. But that would mean anyone with a mental health disability would be subject to fines. *House the Homeless could not let that stand.* I asked for a meeting with Police Chief Art Acevedo and Council Member Laura Morrison.

Chief Acevedo said that he simply did not want disabled homeless people sitting and lying down all over the city. (Well, frankly, neither do we—the difference being, we want them housed, living healthy and productive lives.) The City seemed to want a disabled person to have some obvious problem, like a missing limb. But there are people whose disability does not show, like feeling dizzy due to high blood pressure and needing to sit for a spell. There are people with mentally based disabilities.

The bickering continued, so the next step was to work with Council Member Laura Morrison to include the definition of disability in the ordinance as outlined in the federal Americans with Disabilities Act, namely, "having a physical or mental impairment that substantially limits one or more major life activities."

Physical or Mental Impairment means any physiological disorder or condition, cosmetic disfigurement, or anatomical loss affecting one or more of the following body systems: neurological; musculoskeletal; special sense organs; respiratory, including speech organs, cardiovascular; reproductive; digestive; genitourinary; hemic and lymphatic; skin; and endocrine; *or any mental or psychological disorder*, such as mental retardation, organic brain syndrome, emotional or mental illness, and specific learning disabilities.

Major Life Activities means functions such as caring for oneself, performing manual tasks, walking, seeing, hearing, speaking, learning, breathing, and working.

This was a major victory, but it wasn't enough. I fought to add a specific requirement to a phrase in their draft so it would read like this: "It is a defense to prosecution if a person sits or lies down as the result of a physical manifestation of a disability, not limited to visual observation. This would protect someone with an invisible ailment, like a splitting migraine headache, from the heavy hand of the ordinance."

The Devil Is in the Details

However, Art Acevedo, Randi Shade, and their attorney were not done. They strategically inserted the word *"affirmative"* into the action phrase of the ordinance. So now it read: "A person wishing to avoid prosecution must "create an affirmative defense." So, the individual would have to prove not only that they were disabled, but also that they had been dizzy, weak, faint, nauseated, or in pain at the time when they committed the "offense" of sitting down.

Like many fellow Americans, Council Member Laura Morrison's husband Phillip suffered from diabetes. If he was out in public and needed to sit and rest, he could, theoretically, be ticketed. He could be required to prove that on that exact date, at that precise time, it was low blood-sugar that had caused him to feel woozy. If a blameless, housed citizen in clean clothes would be hard-pressed to come up with that proof, how much worse would the dilemma be for a mentally ill, disabled homeless person? How does a person prove retroactively that they felt so sick at a specific moment in the past that they were unable to stay on their feet? No one could answer that question. I asked them all. No one could tell us how to provide that affirmative defense.

In these negotiations, the subject of the Community Court, which dealt exclusively with people experiencing homelessness, came up. Randi Shade thought it was "a good process to get people with mental health concerns the help they need." Holders of this opinion tend to brush aside certain ethical questions, and when measured on an ethical scale, the concept of presenting people with $200-$500 fines for being homeless so you can get them into court so as to get them healthcare falls totally flat. We heard testimony from Greg Gibson of Austin Travis County Integral Care (ATCIC formerly MHMR) (who later became a board member of House the Homeless and continues in that capacity to the time of publishing.) Funding had been reduced, and further cuts had been announced. Referrals from Community Court would be fewer, and ATCIC would have to curtail the services it could offer to people in need of them.

I worked every day at the ARCH, where ATCIC had an outreach facility, and every day I saw people with serious mental illness. Far too many went untreated. The "ticket, to Community Court, to coerced care" pipeline was essentially a recruitment arm to bring in clients for already overburdened service providers. And involvement with any court always represents one step closer to potential incarceration.

First, the accused has to show up. Not everyone has a cell phone. Not everyone has a watch, a calendar, or an alarm clock. Sometimes, a person honestly does not know what day it is. To be somewhere at the prescribed time, on the right date, not everyone has what it takes. So, the ticket "goes to warrant," and the accused winds up in jail. A housed person might think, "What's wrong with that? There's food, and it's better than being out in the cold." (Yes, Austin gets cold in the winter.) A housed person might think jail sounds like a pretty good deal—after all, the prisoners get "three hots and a cot," as the old saying has it. Trouble is, that could mean a cold baloney sandwich three times a day and a mat on a crowded floor. It definitely means you're now "in the system," which is no small matter. Imagine the scenario with you in the starring role. If you thought finding a place to live or work was tough before, just try it with a criminal record! So, there you are, experiencing homelessness and schizophrenia and not particularly wanting to get locked up, which could still happen for a number of reasons, even though you appeared here as ordered. You understand that the person up there is a judge and that pleasing the judge would be good for you.

The only problem is, you can't make out what he's saying because the voices in your head are louder. Not to mention; the delusional thoughts and the occasional hallucination, you squint and try to focus. The judge wants a coherent explanation of something that happened when? Two weeks ago? All he requires is for you to affirmatively prove that on the way to the soup kitchen, you sat down because you were dizzy, dizzy from being hungry because yesterday you were too dizzy to make it to the soup kitchen either. The judge says, "Cool story, Bro, but where're the receipts?"

Wait, did he really say that? Can a judge do that? As it turns out, judges can pretty much do what they want.

Now, here is an interesting trivia fact. For class C cases, like the heinous crime of sitting on a bench, there is *no* Public Defender. People who are already traumatized, probably with one or more disabling conditions, are expected to represent themselves by preparing an "affirmative defense" that will stand up in court. What might such a defense consist of? How would a person fight the charge? We asked the folks on the subcommittee who had taken it upon themselves to write the law. They didn't have a clue. In front of a Community Court judge, forced to defend themselves, they could perform no better than a hapless PTSD-haunted dumpster diver. And yet, the City Council members have no idea how outrageously irresponsible and short-sighted their meddling is. The people they are messing with are taxpaying citizens who buy things in a sales-tax state. But, much more important, they are human beings who need to be treated with dignity and fairness.

Get Ready: We're Going to the Big Show—Focus

A week and a half before the hearing, I took the guys to face the dragon. We hiked the 10 blocks over to City Council Chambers. I got one of my guard buddies to open the doors and switch on the lights. Tiered seating made the chambers seem incredibly impressive. There had to be fifty questions asked, one for every person. Where do you stand to speak?

Can you be at each of the two microphones? How many council members are there? Can we speak to them? Will there be other issues discussed? How long will it take? They were so childlike but understandably so because this was the seat of power that had passed so many laws against their very existence. Finally, they just stood silent for the longest time. They were absorbing the room, breathing it in, so to speak, and maybe, just maybe, even envisioning victory. I could tell a couple of the guys had tears in their eyes. I addressed them, then I said, "We're coming back to this chamber, and we're going to win." And I challenged them. "Aren't we?" I repeated myself, "Aren't we?" My voice grew louder. They started to respond, and they too, grew louder. Finally, I filled the chamber with my voice and roared with clenched fists, "We will win!!" and roars came back, "yeah, yeah!" Clapping. We left the empty chamber owning it!

Bringing in the Big Guns—One Last Time

I reached out, yet again, to Jim Harrington with the Texas Civil Rights Project. We were headed toward the finish line, and I needed him to chime in one last time.

First of all, in a criminal case, requiring an "affirmative defense" is not appropriate. It puts the burden of proof on the defendant, not the accuser, and messes with basic principle of the presumption of innocence. Jim believed that the proposed ordinance would violate the Americans with Disability Act and Section 504 of the Rehabilitation Act. *Both the ADA and Section 504 require that the City accommodate people who have a known or apparent disability, whether mental or physical.* Not doing so is a violation of federal law.

Subjecting someone to criminal prosecution because of their disability is not an accommodation but a discriminatory act. Jim reminded the other side, "This is all the more since a person charged with a Class C misdemeanor is not entitled to an attorney." He also reminded them that he would be happy to litigate this issue.

He went on to state that the first apparent omission was that of mental disabilities or less than full coverage, as I had pointed out. Regardless, Jim went on to point to the affirmative defense in criminal cases as soundly inappropriate.

Get on the Bus

I had been doing my best to keep the guys informed during this fast-moving, year-long battle through flyers and small group discussions. But now, it was time to sit down with them again, roll up our sleeves and hash out the nuances. The guys were great! Once again, they asked more than a dozen questions and not too many wasted ones. Finally, I told them that even if we didn't get a single additional change, this would be a huge victory if we could get it passed through City Council. After all, behind the scenes, there was a tidal wave of pressure to defeat *any* changes to the ordinance.

134

I was pushing Randi Shade as hard as possible, and I intended to push harder. When I rolled out my strategy, the guys were all in. So, we painted our signs, rented our bus, lined up food support from Mobile Loaves and Fishes, and the day finally came.

Zou Ba! We go! And we mounted our bus and headed back to city hall. We had made that brief orientation visit but had never actually conducted business in the massive City Council Chambers itself. All of a sudden, it felt hardcore real. We were about to go face to face with *the man*. I got everyone to their seats. Tradition ensued. A local clergy member said a prayer and blessed the chamber, the Mayor and the Council Members, and their work. He asked God to watch over them and bless the citizens of Austin and guide them to make only good laws and protect *all* the people. Wow! Even if it was unintentional, we felt included in that blessing, and of course, we were.

There was so much business to conduct. Our members listened intently to neighborly property disputes, environmental issues, and the like. At first, the guys were mesmerized. But as the stream of issues flowed on and on, we began to fidget. The seats got harder, and several folks realized that they again needed to use the bathroom or maybe even slip out for a smoke. But when our agenda item was called, everything else was forgotten. I stood up and signaled the guys to take their prearranged positions. Reluctantly but determined to follow through, they formed a semicircle in front of the Council and unfurled their banners and handmade signs. The Council was shocked into silence. No more, thank you! Now our signs held demands.

Stop attacking the mentally ill! Obey the federal law!

Help the disabled, don't hurt us! Don't give Austin a black *eye!*

In our hard-fought, behind-the-scenes discussions, we had gained ground and did not intend to lose it. We were prepared to attack any business or nonprofit or city staffer or council member who might oppose us. I spoke to the chamber clearly and deliberately. Once again, I described how the ordinance was an attack on the poorest of the poor, the most downtrodden among us. It was an attack against people who had lost everything—family, jobs, hope—and who, on top of that, were now disabled, unable to hold a full-time job of any kind. Again, I recited the list from the House the Homeless disability survey. Brain injury, diabetes, congestive heart failure, heart murmurs, missing body parts, cancers— breast, stomach, pancreatic, liver, bone, testicular, throat. With every new disease, I would rap the podium with my knuckles for emphasis—arthritis, seizures, panic attacks, bipolar disorder, schizophrenia, stroke, GERD, glaucoma, scoliosis. I showed them no mercy—degenerative nerve disease, ulcers, osteoporosis, degenerative joint disease, arterial sclerosis. I grabbed the podium with both hands, squeezed it tightly, and took a massively deep breath. I slowly let it out with emphasis and deliberation and said, "Just like these folks, if you or I had one of these major ailments, we would need to sit down and rest for a moment or take a brief, 30-minute respite, if need be." I turned to the audience and empathically asked the crowd, "Right?" I then turned to the camera that sent the event into local homes and asked them as well, "Right?"

I attacked the requirement for the ticketed party to make an affirmative defense. They would never give it up because the city legal department, the police, and Community Court had all dug in. But I pressed on, using again the example of City Council Member Laura Morrison's husband, Phillip, with the low blood sugar. I hoped the compelling and personal nature of the argument would compel her to offer an amendment to strike the requirement from the ordinance. She did not. Nor was there support from any of the other Council Members. *But,* when I concluded, no one, I repeat, no one spoke in opposition to our changes to the ordinance. The Mayor called the vote; we held our collective breath. The vote was unanimously for us!! We burst into cheers and broad smiles and gushing "thank yous" to the Council.

VICTORY! We shook anybody's hand we could find!!

Our guys took half-steps toward the dais (a huge no-no) and thanked each of the council members, including the Mayor, who more or less scowled at such impropriety, although there was a glint in his eye.

We gathered in the lobby for a group picture and words with the media, who were there in full force. In a sustained sense of triumph, we walked back to the shelter, light-footed and glowing and loudly sharing our stories of glory. One small step for humankind! But I knew the task was not complete.

Epilogue—Police Procedures

What influence does City Council or anyone have over the police and how they design procedures and carry out the laws passed by City Council? Marti Bier, an aide to Randi Shade, felt that a city council "cannot change or dictate police procedures." Attorney Mike Urena researched the issue and double-checked with Legal Aid colleague, David Rojas, who had been on the city council in Eagle Pass, TX, for years.

In David's view, he said that the best that could be hoped for was "the city attorney to establish procedures to ensure that police officers inquire if any exemptions apply before issuing a citation for violation of the ordinance, but that the Council cannot dictate procedures. " Bloody Hell! Well, I was damned sure I was going to *suggest* procedures. I had a complete scenario worked out. I submitted my thoughts in writing to

Commander John Carter, an assistant police chief with whom I had a pretty good relationship.

The police did an excellent job of capturing House the Homeless recommendations. In fact, they used much of our exact language and paraphrased us in other places. They even went so far as to include the 30-minute respite and to list some of our examples of what would be acceptable exemptions to giving tickets. We were already quite pleasantly surprised, but they positively shocked us by adding that officers will take into consideration *extreme weather conditions* such as high temperatures before taking enforcement action. House the Homeless interprets this as 100°F or higher, which in Austin can mean half the year!

The No Sit/ No Lie—Disability Card

To get the word out, House the Homeless produced thousands of laminated, eight-paneled, folding, pocket-size guides in English *and* Spanish that describe what to expect under the No Sit/No Lie (NS/NL) Ordinance and how both the police and disabled individuals might act. We gladly share them with the police and all homeless folks. Below is a picture of the front and back of the card (see Spanish card in Appendix).

Benches

To this day, no new benches have been added to advance the City of Austin to the "world-class" city that it supposedly aspires to be.

While No Sit/ No Lie Ordinances are now common in America, unfortunately, neither the National Coalition for the Homeless nor the National Alliance to End Homelessness has spent the time or resources to attack this "quality of life" ordinance. House the Homeless remains "First in the Nation."

Four years after that landmark accomplishment, a small percentage of Austin's police continued to issue No Sit/No Lie tickets without warning or asking if the individual was too sick or unable to move immediately. The ARCH (Austin Resource Center for the Homeless), still the main shelter, took the exclusionary step of painting a three-foot perimeter around its walls. Given the choice, someone who sits on the ground prefers a wall to lean against. But anyone who felt sick enough to fall inside that line would not be given a choice.

We continued to pass out the NS/NL plasticized information cards quoting the precise language that brought local law into compliance with federal law, but with only a modicum of success. They should have gotten a better response; I just knew. Then it hit me. The cards were generated

House the Homeless, Inc.
P.O. Box 2312
Austin, TX 78768-2312
www.HouseTheHomeless.org

Starting May 1, 2011, the **No Sit/No Lie Ordinance** will be amended to protect people with **physical** and **mental** disabilities.

You can have a **30 minute rest** to "catch your breath" if you are disabled and you are feeling (but not limited to):

**weakness,
shortness of breath,
heart problems,
light headed,
pain
migraine headache, etc.**

So, if you need to sit or lie down because you are disabled... You **MUST** tell the police officer that you are disabled because you suffer from:

diabetes
congestive heart failure
schizophrenia
bipolar disorder
depression
cerebral palsy
or any other disability

If a police officer approaches you and asks why you are sitting down, Tell him you are disabled, "I have diabetes (etc)-**see above**, I'm feeling dizzy (or whatever-**see above**). I just need a minute or two." The officer should ask if you need emergency care and if not, he should tell you: "OK, I'll be back in about 30 minutes. (You may be issued a warning ticket at this point). If after the 30 minutes you're still there and having a problem, you'll again be checked for emergency medical care.

(over)

cont. from front.

If you don't need the emergency medical care, you'll be asked to move on, immediately. If you don't move, you'll be ticketed. If a ticket is issued, the case will go before a judge.

Documents you can show the police officer or use in court:

*Mobility Impaired Bus Pass
Social Security Disability Award Letter
Food Stamp Work Exemption
Any Letter from a Doctor or Hospital
Any Letter from MHMR/Integral Care
Letter from David Powell Clinic
V.A Disability card/letter
or other*

You should also **NOT** get a ticket if:

You are:

-viewing a parade, demonstration, rally or the like.

-in a bus stop area waiting to use transportation.

-in line waiting for goods, services or public event.

-on a chair or bench provided by a public agency or the abutting private property owner.

Or when Austin is experiencing *extreme weather* e.g. heat /cold/ Ozone Action Day etc.

If you get a ticket, immediately bring it to Richard R. Troxell at the ARCH.

English Disability Card

by House the Homeless, a circumstance the police could easily brush aside. Eureka!

Having realized the nature of the dynamic, I simply went back to the police procedures manual where I had captured the words on Police Manual letterhead. I photographed them for the next batch of information cards. Boom! Ticketing stopped. It stopped as soon as Wanda and Mitchell Kanarie showed up at Community Court before Judge Coffey with a ticket *and flyer* that pointedly attributed the rules to the police department's own rulebook while produced by House the Homeless. Officers could no longer claim "It wasn't part of my training."

Finally. In 2020. The Austin City Council narrowly voted to rescind *all* the "quality of life" ordinances. Let's see what the future holds for our people. Perhaps the city will simply House the Homeless.

13 The Home Coming

The Genesis

On a sunny Sunday afternoon, my beautiful, precocious daughter and I drove my pickup truck past a McMansion house being built. We lived about a mile south of the Colorado River that runs through the city of Austin. When we pulled up to the stop sign, Colleen, who was about 6 at the time, casually pointed at the house and said, "Look, daddy, when they're done, the homeless can live there." I was pleasantly surprised. As president of the non-profit House the Homeless and director of Legal Aid for the Homeless, I often thought about all the hatred directed toward these people. Here was my little girl clearly and simply stating, in effect, this is what they need—Housing. Let's give it to them because it's what good people do.

When she was just a baby, I would swaddle her tightly in her tiny, fluffy "blankie" and slip her into a harness so she would rest upon my chest and walk for miles and talk to her for hours. I had always tried to speak of things in a positive way and with enthusiasm.

Later, Colleen and I, among so many others, shared books like *The Chronicles of Narnia* by C.S. Lewis, which fostered flights of imagination, compassion, empathy, and adventure.

Over the years, we would talk about who was in this group we call the homeless. I would speak of the Veterans like me and the mothers and their children. We spoke of the daddies who had been broken away from their families. We even spoke of the people who had mental health issues and even the ones who suffered addictions. But of course, we first talked about the little girls who were just like her, because I knew she would want to know all about all the little girls and their dollies and what they eat and what books they read and what were their favorite colors and how did they wash their dresses when they got dirty.

Later on, Colleen and I talked about my time after the war when I had been homeless for several years and landed in North Philadelphia. I slipped into an abandoned house where I ran an electrical line from an adjoining property, plugged in a Bakelite radio, and listened to the great consumer advocate, Max Weiner, who would one day become my mentor and lead me into the world of economics appreciation and reframe the role it was already playing in my life. He was friends with Ralph Nader, and together they coined the phrase and concept of "consumer rights."

North Philadelphia was once an affluent, all-white neighborhood, but by the time I arrived, it was a semi-impoverished, working-class, all-Black neighborhood, except for me. Having just spent 3 years in the marines, I felt comfortable wherever I went and enjoyed this world immensely.

After being discovered occupying what seemed an abandoned house next door to a gas station, rather than throw me out or have me arrested, I was offered a job as an auto mechanic/apprentice. As a hard worker, I was accepted as part of the team/family soon enough.

I loved the people. The row houses' proximity to one another soon led me to make many friends, and I immersed myself in the neighborhood. I also quickly learned intimate details of the lives of those good people. There was one story that captivated my attention. It was the brief tale of Anateen Maxwell. When I knew her, she was a middle-aged, African American woman who had been married to her husband Garland for 22 years. She had mothered three children, two girls and a son: Shandra, Leticia, and Leroy. Leticia had died tragically years before in a car accident. Miss Anateen, as we all called her, lived on Glenwood Avenue in a small row home with Garland and her other two children. Leroy was arrested and sent to prison under questionable accusations. One day, Garland got laid off from his job of 12 years. He searched for work for 4 weeks. He was 53 and felt for sure no one would hire him as jobs were scarce. A few days later, he walked to the corner store and never returned. Shandra became so depressed about her daddy disappearing that she started running the streets and got hooked on crack cocaine.

Shortly thereafter, Miss Anateen became chronically depressed and with no real income, was unable to hold onto their home. They were renters, and the owner boarded it up. There was a rumor that she slipped into homelessness and wandered the streets of Philadelphia.

I shared these stories with Colleen because I wanted her to know about life and that bad things can happen beyond our control. Life is not predictable, and regardless of what she might hear, nobody *wants* to be homeless.

Colleen, who was 10 at the time, and her mother Sylvia found Ceramics Bayou, a do-it-yourself craft studio. Colleen made me a Universal Living Wage penholder and the usual coffee mug emblazoned with DAD and enhanced with a small ceramic rose. (I still have both.) Then, one Father's Day, she presented me with three unrecognizable piles of fired clay. She told me they were the Veteran daddy, his little girl, and Ms. Anateen..."all homeless," she told me. I was not sure what to make of it, but when she said, "They are taking care of each other." I was touched—deeply.

So, in reflection, it was not surprising when Colleen had become so animated when I said we should think about molding a little girl in clay

142

to tell her story. It was Colleen's idea to have the little girl posed with her daddy so she could be sure to take care of him after the war. Colleen gave the cutest little smile when I suggested we name the little girl Colleen.

The story of this little girl in this one family continued to evolve from all the other stories, of all the other little girls, and all the Veterans and all the daddies and all the mommies from all the other families whose lives have spun out of control.

Colleen saw our little girl as a tragic figure whose mommy was always working and was always way too tired. Then together, we talked about the daddy as a loving, doting father who had been laid off from his construction job. He was a Vietnam Veteran who sometimes struggled with his war memories. He had to take a job at a fast-food restaurant. It was about half his previous pay. He said that he didn't mind the work, but he felt the "step down" was degrading, his self-esteem took a severe blow, and money was "tight." The mother had been at home raising the little girl and taking in sewing jobs to help make ends meet.

The parent's relationship was always under a lot of pressure, and they fought about money a lot. Often in the middle of an argument, the mother would shout out, "This isn't what I signed up for. This isn't what I signed up for." He would try and calm her down with, "Baby, we'll just work a little harder. We'll just try harder." One day, he awoke to find a note on the kitchen table. It simply read, "This isn't what I signed up for. I'm sorry."

And just like that, the world of the little girl and her father, who we later named John, came crashing down. Try as he might, John couldn't get overtime work at the restaurant, and when the franchise owner cut everyone's time back to 28 hours a week rather than pay benefits to the employees, the father and daughter ultimately lost their apartment and ended up at the Salvation Army. This didn't happen right away. At first, he had borrowed money from a military buddy. But that didn't last long or go very far. He got some help from the Baptist church where he had been taking his daughter, but there was a limit per household. He went to the Veterans Administration but was told they weren't set up to help with that kind of situation. Finally, he got $200.00 from Travis County Health and Human Services and then applied for food stamps. He had also applied for TANF, Temporary Aid to Needy Families, but there had been some kind of problem with the paperwork, he had been unable to locate Colleen's birth certificate, and it would take almost two months to get a replacement from Saint Louis, Missouri, her place of birth. So, they had ended up at the Salvation Army. But this took special permission from the "Commander" and special arrangements because it's the mommies who usually came in with the children...not the daddies.

John would work as many hours as the restaurant would give him. Colleen was bused to a school and was returned in the afternoon when he would find her in the Salvation Army playground made for just such situations and scoop her up, kiss her face all over, and squeeze her, (perhaps a bit too hard sort of like when Jimmy Stewart kissed ZuZu in *It's a Wonderful Life*).

But they would spend a lot of time together, traveling on foot to wherever they could and getting various things to improve their situation. It seemed like they walked endlessly, but they would always talk as they went. They would constantly pass through hordes of single men who were always loud and raucous. John was so protective of her, and she felt secure in his arms.

In 2011, having published a book about homelessness that didn't inspire people to flock to the bookstore, I searched for a new medium, feeling the need to draw people in with a visual image and a visceral experience that could move them. Before I could jump into such a discussion, I should have captured people's attention. It occurred to me that I would need another medium, one that is first visual and tactile. I thought of Colleen's clay figures and our story and decided that bronze sculpting might just be the thing.

A Long Journey Toward a Statue

Picking up the phonebook, I set out to find someone who would teach me how to sculpt. After collecting several leads, I had a brief conversation with Steve Dubois, founder of the Atelier 3-D Sculpture Studio.

I was fairly familiar with East Austin, a partly residential area mixed with commercial properties and warehouses. Run-down but not uncared for, the neighborhood tends to attract artists, who often need spacious quarters where nobody worries about making a bit of a mess.

Steve's enormous warehouse was alive with art of all kinds, everywhere. There were plaster items, including numerous naked female figures of a most curious and interesting style. It was not so much their figures but rather the techniques that I found interesting. Glass and brass objects hung from the ceiling in various stages of completion. There were countless nude male figures in contemplative poses; they all shared a commonality. Each had its own individual flaw; this one's thighs were too large. This one had unusually knobby knees. Another had hands that more accurately resembled clubs that a Viking might have wielded centuries in the past.

A number of mechanical pieces drew my attention. They were composed of recycled, reclaimed industrial metal scraps and isolated machine parts, gears, sprockets, wedges, and the like; of all shapes and sizes. They fit my definition of good art: if you like it, if it causes a visceral effect on the observer, and if it gets people talking, then it's good art.

From somewhere in the back, the sound approached, of a hearty, joyful voice extending an almost lyrical welcome: "Would you like some wine?" It was very early evening, so I declined, but I certainly appreciated the offer.

It gave me a very relaxed feeling. Steve was white, 5'8" and wiry, apparently in his sixties, with several days of gray stubble covering his face. He had a warm, soft hand with long, purposeful fingers and a strong handshake. "So," he asked, "what did you have in mind?"

"I work with folks who are experiencing homelessness, and I want to change the way people think about them." I briefly recapped my career since the mid-1980s and mentioned that my recently published book described a mathematical formula that would fix the Federal Minimum Wage once and for all. I needed to start a conversation about homelessness that might interest new parties and bring them to the table, not just to read my book but also to join in the fight to end homelessness.

I unfolded the vision to Steve of three life-size figures who share a chance encounter at a crucial moment. Already in place are a military veteran and his young daughter. An elderly African American woman who might be stereotyped as a "bag lady" approaches. The father and daughter offer to share the warmth of their fire. Each individual represents a significant segment of the homeless population, with the average age of a child experiencing homelessness about 10.

Steve asked if I had any art experience. I told him I once created a pen and ink line drawing of Lech Walesa, who in the 1980s was an electrician in the Polish shipyards. When a foreman announced layoffs, Walesa scrambled up a chain-link fence and socked him in the nose.

Walesa went on to lead the Solidarity labor movement and became President of Poland. Years later, he again became a dock worker. My drawing had hung in the 1199c Health Care Workers union hall in Philadelphia for ten years. I told Steve that Lech Walesa was a true working-class hero. I added that I had made some peace pipes out of pallets and made jewelry out of coins. He said, "Okay, we can work with that." I was impressed that he didn't laugh. Right then and there, I felt relieved and at ease with this gentle stranger whose age I had underestimated. He was actually 70 and as vibrant and patient as any man I ever met.

So, for the next year, I would come to the studio and learn to sculpt. It started with just becoming familiar with clay, rolling it evenly, and learning its properties. I then shifted to Plastiline, a brand of clay with oil in it. This allows you to sculpt today and return in a week, and immediately start working with the material where you left off. Clay needs to be constantly spritzed with an atomized water mist to keep it pliable.

I learned to make "slip" or liquified clay that acts like magic glue. This would come in quite handy, as Steve would often walk by, pause, slice off a body part he didn't care for, and walk on. I would use slip to attach the new replacement part.

After what seemed to be a very long trial period, I then moved past three lumps of clay mounted at their core with a pliable wire. Eventually, the figures took on arms and hands.

That whole approach did not really agree with my composite personality, which by that time included not only the ever-recovering veteran but the new craftsman feeling the beginnings of pride.

Steve would stop me dead in my tracks with my scalpel raised while he put on a full-length military-style raincoat and pause before an imaginary fire barrel. He would set his shoulders and asked me if I saw it. Sometimes I did. Sometimes I didn't.

Steve always accommodated me. He would set me up at a separate table so I could independently sculpt my figures just outside the circle of other would-be sculptors. They, of course, were collectively working on their own rendition of some nude male or female model who was striking an endless pose before them.

I would often look at the models and then at each of the artist's miniature figures and try hard to understand what they were seeing as they molded Olympic-type buttocks in some far too rigid a pose or one seemingly too flaccid. It was so much easier to see the mistakes in the work of others and even correct them than to see the pitiful thing I had sculpted.

In the end, I had re-sculpted the same three figures, starting from the very beginning each time, five separate times. This was coupled with dozens of changes at each initiation. Each time, I thought I had done a reasonably acceptable job. Then, I would start anew, and this always exposed my previous work to have been completely amateurish.

A Young Girl's Dreams

The last two renditions yielded the swish and energy of the little girl's dress. We spoke of her spirit and the fact that she was a small, energetic young girl in a man's world. We spoke of her desire to invite the old woman not just into their camp but also into her safe place where she constantly retreated for comfort and security, just inside daddy's coat.

An Old Woman

Steve and I talked for hours about the plight of the old woman, who had lost everything, including her family. Her emotional loss left her dejected and depressed. She was simply trudging. She was coming from nowhere and going nowhere. We spent weeks working on the "energy of her shoulders."

146

I sculpted her over and over and over again. She carried two large satchels and four bags. Her purse was slung around her neck, resting on her back. She was beat down and situationally or chemically depressed, or both. It made little difference. She embodied decay and that part of our society that had once allowed hard-working people to embrace the tenets of the "American Dream." It was our nation's Protestant work ethic. It holds the belief that if you're willing to work long and hard, you can survive; even thrive if you are willing to sacrifice.

Now, this truth is no longer true. Immigrant men, women, and children came to Ellis Island seeking freedom and new beginnings. The Irish, the Hungarians, Scottish, Chinese, etc., all helped build this country. They had their backs strengthened and even broken in the Industrial Age. Their lungs were first filled with the songs of freedom then seared in the coal mines of Pennsylvania while working endlessly only to "owe their souls to the company store." Others had been burned to death in our garment districts, dying for pennies while the Blacks, who had been wrenched from their homeland, enslaved, and brought here against their free will, fought for their freedom in a war that divided the country into two parts over the economics of that slavery. They were now all finding that the economics of hope and prosperity have been perverted into the economics of greed and further repression by the money changers, who freed them and turned them out into a workplace of economic slavery.

These economics have failed them and are now consuming them. The "American Dream" no longer holds a viable promise. Whatever happened to the promise of "a fair wage for a fair day's work?" The working poor have been startled awake in the middle of the night. Today, you can work 40 hours in a week at a full-time job and with a check in your pocket and still end up living on the streets of that American Dream. These are the very same streets that they had loved so dearly and cherished so much and had held the lore of being paved with gold. Now, in a nightmare of endless depression, the old Black woman trudges. She comes from nowhere, and she is headed nowhere. She has indeed lost everything, including the most treasured of all…hope.

The Veteran

The veteran was the most difficult of the three figures to sculpt. He is really young, but the war has made him old. At first, I thought he was in the Vietnam war. A thankless war, ill-defined and purposeless. When the United States fled in disgrace from Saigon in fear for their very lives, other soldiers of the two "real" wars, I and II, ostracized them. They would not let them into their clubs of Veterans of Foreign Wars. Even though these brotherhood institutions were closing right and left due to the lack of new members to sustain their existence, they kept the door closed to warriors of two "illegitimate wars"; Korea and Vietnam. At the same time, they continued to have this great need to bolster their ranks; they told Vietnam veterans to "get a real war."

Real or imagined snarling whispers of "baby killer" snaked out from nondescript crowds leaving a deep wound that you cannot heal and a slice that will leave thick, raised keloid scars on the neck of Vietnam Veterans forever. But as I tried to capture our veteran's youthful yet old age persona and his knurled, crusty hands seeking heat from the fire, other soldiers, Marines, warriors morphed into him. Young men and women from Desert Storm, Desert Shield, survivors of the Iraq War, Afghanistan are all him. Even though he's no longer an object of the ire of the American people, he was still discarded to the streets of America after we had our way with him. All were used, abused, and finally discarded. My veteran wears a camouflaged Marine jungle hat from Vietnam but displays an "Army" patch on his backpack that now holds all his and his daughter's belongings. A composite of all our armed forces, for 50 years, the Veteran has made up one-third (1/3) of the males of all 3.5 million people experiencing homelessness at the time of this writing and this sculpting. Now female Veterans are increasingly finding themselves on the streets of America.

A Chance Encounter

It was winter and also cold. The veteran and his daughter have been doing what so many other people do all day long. They chase opportunities. This may mean looking for jobs or seeking social service giveaways, which might be food on a plate, or food in a bag. Whether it is dental or medical treatment or a stipend from a church or a clothing voucher from Goodwill, or lodging for the night, it always seems to be located somewhere else. This requires movement that either demands elusive, precious bus passes or walking...lots of walking. Every day is full of endless walking in search of sustenance for the stomach, heart, or head, with little to show for it. One cold day the veteran and his daughter come across a fire barrel only recently left unattended. They approach it and move in close. He unslings the old military backpack from his shoulder with one swift movement, lands it on the tip of his left great toe where he can keep awareness and a vigilant eye on it. He opens his full-length coat, and his daughter moves to stand at her safe place under its protection and warmth. Here she has found comfort endless times before. He kisses the top of her head and strokes it gently, saying, "I love you, baby." She turns her face up to look at him. "I love you too, daddy." The mesmerizing glow of the fire soon combines with the weariness, and he slips into a daze, thinking of tomorrow's tasks.

As always, he says, "Tomorrow will be a better day, honey." As always, Colleen replies, "I know, Daddy."

Although weary from the day of walking, she is still full of energy and quite alert. She sees, in the distance, a person coming from the edge of the woods. As the person draws closer, the little girl realizes that it is a woman. She has been with daddy, day in and day out, in a world of other men, mostly daddy's age. But now, a woman approaches. The elderly African American woman trudges forward, simply moving one foot in front of the other, laden with her many bags. They hold socks, undergarments, sweaters, a picture of her children, a brooch wrapped tightly in a flowered handkerchief, pressed deeply into the bottom of a satchel. There are two blouses, another hat, a bar of soap, a well-used toothbrush, and lots of plastic bags that come in handy for so many purposes when a person lives outdoors.

The little girl thinks that the woman, who reminds her of her own "Gammy," can share daddy's coat with her. It's decided. She will invite the old woman to visit her in her "safe hiding place." Slowly, Colleen outwardly opens her daddy's coat in a welcoming fashion. With her other hand, she makes a beckoning gesture as if encouraging a puppy to join her. "Come on, come on," she urges.

Despite the developing cataracts in her eyes, the old woman sees the glow and flicker of the fire and what seems to be a fat man standing in front of it. Cocking her head for a better view, she sees movement from the man's waist and realizes it's actually a man with a small child. A little girl who, poking her head out from this fragile shelter, holds the coat open toward her. Uncertain and confused, the woman hesitates.

The father, stirred by the excitement of his daughter, looks down to see what she needs. His gaze, alerted by his daughter's excitement, follows her line of sight, and he sees the old, rumpled woman. She is laden with bags...a "bag lady." She is stooped over and appears to be very cold. The little girl is inviting her to their fire. He pauses; then he too joins his daughter, and he too beckons the stranger into their encampment.

Despite her numb toes and bone-tiredness, the old woman thinks: *White people. I'm not welcome there.* Then she realized it's not just the little girl beckoning her, but the man as well. Can that be? Are her old eyes tricking her? Almost against her own will and barely audible, her voice says, "It would be so good to be warm again."

The man makes another beckoning gesture and calls out, "Come on ahead, old woman. All are welcome here!"

Overwhelmed, she whispers, "It is true...they want me to share," with a sigh of relief. She drops her bags the last inch to the ground. Her right-hand clutches her heart as a quiet prayer escapes her lips, "Thank you Jesus."

In the finished work, the characters are not larger than life, nor are they on a pedestal. These are regular folks walking on shared earth.

The Maquettes

In the world of sculpture, a maquette is basically a three-dimensional preliminary sketch. More like a scale model, really, and once the original creator is satisfied, duplicates can be made, which are very useful. Because of their miniature size, maquettes can be carried to the offices or homes of anyone who might be interested in paying for the actual, life-size statue to be cast in bronze. Or to TV shows where the publicity might attract patrons.

After months of effort, Steve and I went through numerous progressive steps and about five complete maquette renditions before we decided it was time to make the molds. The next morning, I walked into a totally rearranged art studio. Supply drawers were pushed to all corners of the warehouse. Four matching large work tables were placed center stage. Four 5-gallon buckets were placed beneath the table. Two other buckets with various chemicals were also there. On a fifth matching table was a case-hardened spatula, two fresh one-sided razor blades, a rolling pin, a large box of plastiline, a scalpel, a case-hardened spatula, A and B rubber compounds, and a dozen Styrofoam cups. With a fine greeting, Steve told me to use the scalpel to cut off the hands of the veteran. Slightly taken aback, our eyes met. He said, "We'll need to deal with them separately. We'll create two air bubble feeder tubes without which the statues would be destroyed." Then at Steve's direction, I used the rolling pin to roll out a large sheet of plastiline. And the process of making a three-dimensional maquette had begun. This part of the process took us an entire day—laden with stress.

Finally, we poured liquified resin into the molds and created *one* miniature statue consisting of all three characters. The next day, I painted our characters with a bronze patina laden with actual gold flakes. I thought they looked pretty darned good for the work of an amateur.

Terrance Flowers

Like a proud papa with his new baby, I headed to the homeless shelter, ARCH, with the maquettes. I officed Legal Aid for the Homeless and helped get the guy's disability benefits at the shelter. Through that connection, I met and learned the first names or handles of about 3,000 guys over the years. I set up a table outside on the sidewalk, set up the maquettes, and began to tell the story of John, his daughter, Colleen, and Ms. Anateen. With each story, more of the folks who hung out on that sidewalk every day came to see what was going on. As expected, the response was mixed from "Richard, is you out of your mind?" to "That looks just like Mother Love," who had posed for the Ms. Anateen character, to "That's Richard, he got our back."

Terrance Flowers

About 45 minutes into the retelling, I saw Terrance Flowers halfway up the sidewalk. That was easy to do as he stands 6'1", weighs in at about 290 pounds, and has a gleaming smile. I actually heard his booming laugh that had silenced the surrounding area while folks re-established their focus on whatever they had been doing. I love Terrance; he represents everything I believe America to be. A high school graduate in Chicago, he was out of work in 1982 and read that the unemployment rate in Austin was only 3.8%. So, he bought a bus ticket and came to get his fair share of work. When he got to Austin, he soon realized that it was a high-tech boom. That was not exactly what he had in mind. He got discouraged and distracted and started using crack. In reflection, he told me that was the longest 20 years of his life. He says he was blessed when he got arrested and forced to detox in jail. Vowing never to go through any of that again, and sure that Jesus had taken him under His wing, he tried his father's life job, janitor at the local homeless shelter.

I had launched the Universal Living Wage campaign in 1997. Helen Varty, the Executive Director of the ARCH, recognized that "paying a living wage might just be the thing," so she almost doubled their version of the minimum wage from $5.15 to $10.00 per hour, and Terrance was at the right place at the right time.

When he was arrested, he had also gotten a No Camping ticket. Weeks before, I had stood on a chair at the ARCH and talked to the guys about doing something about the No Camping tickets for which no one could pay the $200 fine. From my vantage point, I saw this mountain of a man and appealed to him directly. Without any hesitation, he shook himself into this deep belly laugh and in a slow booming voice, "Yes, sir, It ain't right. I'll sign up." And just like that, Terrance Flowers became the second plaintiff along with mild-spoken Christopher Standage, who had long wavy orangish-red hair down to his waist. The four of us, Terrance, Chris, our attorney Cecilia Wood, and I went to the court over and over again for the next five years. We had 12 pretrial hearings. But in the end, we won"! The ordinance was ruled unconstitutional, too broad!! Two weeks later, the City Council honed the focus, and the City of Austin had a new ordinance. On that day that I had brought the maquettes to the ARCH, I drew Terrace over to the table and told the backstory of the statues again. When I talked about Ms. Anateen, who was also African American, his eyes lit up, he got a very serious look on his face, and then it came, that slow, rumbling deep belly laugh as he all but shouted out, "Yes, sir, that's it. I'm in! That's a great statue!" silencing half the sidewalk again.

Today, ARCH is still operating and still paying Terrance a Universal Living Wage, $17.90 an hour, for his awesome work as a janitor while he "reaches back" and takes care of the people just as his dad had done.

Quest for Support

I wrapped the maquettes in bubble wrap and loaded them into an oversized backpack which I secured with bungee-cords to a luggage bag stroller. I set out to meet with each of the seven city council members: Mike Martinez, Laura Morrison, Sheryl Cole, Bill Spelman, Chris Riley, Kathi Tovo, and Mayor Lee Leffingwell. They had all seen me advocate for our people. I had also butted heads with most of them at one point or another. However, overall, I felt confident that I could have a reasonable conversation (within the allotted 15 minutes) with each of them. I would show them the maquettes, share our dream and hopefully get their blessings.

With only limited time, I began my greetings even before I walked into the inner office of Mike Martinez. As I spoke, I slipped the maquettes from the bags and placed them on the table between us. I felt like a proud papa. I told him my aim and the pertinent statistics. I related the moment of tender encounter that the maquettes depicted.

Mike smiled and said, "I'm in. I'm with you; what do I need to do?" He immediately answered his own question: "I'll help you raise money."

"You should talk to Megan Crigger with the city arts program." We shook hands, and I was out the door. I had learned long ago, when the answer is "yes," stop talking.

Next was Laura Morrison, who had also sat on the Health and Human Services Committee, which hosted our quest for compassionate compromise under the No Sit/No Lie ordinance. I had taken a chance by using her husband, Philip, and his diabetes to illustrate a major flaw in the law. Laura gave tacit approval along the way and, in the end, full approval, which is what I would expect from a highly intelligent, even-handed, and compassionate public servant. The issue was that fatigue or dizziness are not visibly identifiable, though they are as real as a broken leg. A cast is good proof, but an investigating officer would have to take a person's word for the symptoms of an illness that doesn't "show."

Laura liked the statue project but cautioned me that City Council had set up a process and certified it the previous year, and I would need to go through it. Of course, I had already read the procedures and knew that the last and overriding stage entailed securing City Council approval. That's why I set up these individual meetings with the people who made up the power base, the council members, to get a sense of any obstacles or opposition first.

So I set up a meet with Megan Crigger and Maggie Stenz of Art in Public Places. Before getting into it, just a reminder: the unofficial city motto is "Keep Austin Weird." But on that day, it was easy to believe that in the minds of the people who ran the place, the goal was to "Keep Austin Totally Controlled." With these two, I hit the high points—the early discussions with Colleen and the basic story of the projected sculpture. I reminded them of our previous work on behalf of the city's most friendless population, like the annual Homeless Memorial reading of the names of the ones lost the previous year.

Megan Crigger informed me that the process of "gifting" art to the city had changed. Works of art (known to them as pre-created art or concepts) were, in fact, no longer accepted. A person was supposed to bring a subject or a theme to the committee who, if they approved, would arrange for the art to be created. I think I was expected to slink away, be defeated, but no such luck.

I thanked her for the information, which changed nothing. Our concept had been developing for more than 20 years. I had spent over a year learning to sculpt. Despite the new policy, we would press forward. Their smiles stiffened, and the atmosphere of the room changed, but we understood each other.

Council Member Sheryl Cole, a sharp attorney with a beaming smile, the mother of three boys and an African American, asked what response I had gotten from each of the other Council members and whether I realized that there was a codified process in place for such donations. Yes, I had met with Megan Crigger and been assigned to work with Maggie Stenz with Art in Public Places. Sheryl Cole's response was noncommittal: "Well, go through the process." Her demeanor was as inscrutable on this occasion as it had been the time she took me to lunch in order to pick my brain about low-income housing. My response was that businesses need to pay living wages so folks could afford their own housing. In spite of her vacant stare, I refused to feel discouraged. Randi Shade had been replaced on the Council by Kathi Tovo, whom I came to know as a deeply caring person. At the time, her response was pleasant, polite, and noncommittal.

Remaining on my list were three White male Council members. Chris Riley was an up-to-date kind of guy, short-haired, wiry in build, a bicycle enthusiast, and a supporter of the then-new Uber taxi concept. I saw him as an environmentalist and, perhaps more importantly, as a reader of my first two books, who had extended compliments on the accomplishments described there. It is always good to know that someone is paying attention, and even better to feel appreciated. I didn't do political or social events, but we ran into each other now and then at work sessions on real political concerns. With just a bit of pressing, Chris said he liked the concept and then canceled it out by adding, "Let's see how the process shakes out." Grrr, "...the process." I knew the process was stacked against the project because it certainly wasn't the first time. That's what happens when you have a project that is outside the parameters of the process.

My next council member was University of Texas professor Bill Spelman, who taught in the school of government and public policy, and who was married to a well-known and respected advocate in the field of international cultural affairs. He had been on City Council previously, then stepped down voluntarily, and finally returned because he earnestly feels he can make a difference, and therefore feels it's his duty to try.

I made my pitch, and he seemed unimpressed. "There is a process; let's see how it goes." Those words were beginning to sound all too familiar. The last in this series of meetings was with our no-nonsense Mayor, Lee Leffingwell, a retired commercial airline pilot; he looked the part well enough to be picked out of a lineup. On top of that, he could have landed that plane for Sullenberger. Just after he was elected Mayor for the first time, his beloved wife died. Those who knew his personal story of sorrow and loss admired him for soldiering on. Remember, he was still a Council member when House the Homeless proposed downtown benches, and we kind of had a standoff. When he held the office of Mayor, he took an opportunity to recommend that the city explore the concept of benches in a most gracious and very public way. Of course, that is not the only reason I say he is a good official who has steered his ship well.

I could tell he liked the statutes. However, I could also tell that he would only be supportive so long as it was representing a memorial to the men, women, and children who had lost their lives on our streets. The unstated message was that he would have no part of a monument that celebrated homelessness. His response was ,"Process," and, "Let's see what happens." Translation: Don't bring this to the Council for a vote *if you have not gone all the way through the process.*

Austin, at that moment, was preparing to vote on whether to retain a 7 member, at-large city council or shift to a 10-1 District (local rule) council. If that passed, I would be facing mostly all new, unknown faces with unknown agendas. Among other consequences, that would mean enduring another series of orientation meetings to introduce those newcomers to the project. Only next time, there would be more of them.

My friend, Andrea Ball is an investigative journalist with the *Austin American Statesman*. For a reporter of this caliber, it goes without saying that curiosity is a major character trait. For example, preparing to write

154

an article on proposed gun control measure, she went to the firing range and learned to handle a firearm. As both a feature writer and a columnist specializing in social services, she was familiar with all aspects of the human spirit. A born cynic, she has somehow balanced that with the "insufferable" compulsion to be compassionate. Afflicted with bipolar disorder, she holds a place in her heart for people coping with disabilities.

If a writer takes a stand or even addresses a controversial topic like homelessness, Austin's news consumers will definitely let their feelings be known, and it can get rough.

So, I was pleased when Andrea Ball told me she was not only going to write about *The Home Coming* but also about the people behind the three characters depicted by the statue. The article made the front page of the Metro Section, above the fold comments like "Great idea! Let's build a monument to the homeless so we can bow down to them," offered a supporter of humankind, illustrating why Mayor Leffingwell was careful to make a distinction between that and a memorial.

Another critic voiced a common sentiment: "You should run anyone out of the state that won't pay taxes!" That doesn't stand up because, as citizens of Texas should know, Texas is a sales tax state and anybody who buys anything, even a coke, pays tax. It created so much buzz that the folks in another department of the very same paper, the *Statesman*, felt compelled to re-interview me. They wrote another article and placed it on the front page of the entire paper, above the fold again. But it included a serious error. I had done the preliminary work to determine the cost of the finished statue, which a local foundry figured would be about $250,000. The paper somehow quoted it as $500,000, which is still half a million dollars even on a good day. To many Austin residents, it sounded like too much. That kind of money could buy the homeless a lot of peanut butter sandwiches. (On basic white bread, of course. Folks might be generous, but they're not crazy.) Andrea calls them "the haters," and their favorite venue is "loudmouth radio," the local talk shows, where a troll does not even need to take the trouble to write a letter to the editor. Nope, just make a phone connection and start pontificating about the End of Days. And by the way, Richard R. Troxell should go straight to Hell, preferably right now, which would still not be soon enough.

Cecilia Blanford, Co-Founder of House the Homeless, Inc. and the most God-fearing and God-loving person I have ever met, took the haters head-on. After two and a half days of hearing an endless string of vile comments, the sweetest of little old church ladies got on the radio and challenged all the talk show hosts and all the listeners; "Don't you think that Jesus would want us to care for this little girl?" She demanded, "Why should anyone not support this veteran who had sacrificed so much for his country?" She pressed on with, "Don't we owe a little respect to this poor old Black woman whose ancestors we uprooted and brought over to this country as slaves? Did we not force them to toil in our fields picking cotton so we could grow wealthy as a nation? What do you think Jesus would say?" I was so pleased as she realized the power of the statue and stated it so beautifully.

In the meantime, I was attempting to compare the cost of running a business and what is necessary to invest in advertisement (the Memorial itself), saying, "It takes money to make money," referring to the need to find a way to raise proceeds to house our homeless people.

I even calculated the cost of detoxifying and treating a person's addiction and just getting them ready to be placed into housing compared to this statue, this beacon, this neon sign that will bring new people into the arena of givers to champion the cause to help up-end and prevent homelessness.

I got a phone call from Seth Orion Schwaiger, a world-renowned Scottish bronze sculptor and great talent who has produced many glorious statutes. He was responding to Andrea Ball's article. He said that he was willing to make The Home Coming his next project and asked if I would be interested in sculpting the statute with him. I was floored! I immediately went online and saw his beautiful work. I was deeply impressed and flattered. He said, "All I want for my efforts is a living wage." Unbelievable, it was sweet music to my ears! My head was buzzing. I was having trouble breathing, let alone thinking. How unbelievably exciting!

The next day, I got a call from Tony Frey in Ontario, Canada. He and his business partner Timothy P. Schmalz had both seen the article in the Statesman. Timothy was also a bronze sculptor and wanted to speak with me about my project. Awesome! I said, "Put him on," but Tony said that although Timothy was equally eager to talk, he had just left for Italy. He said, "I don't want to offend your sculptor, but the work was a bit challenged." I calmly explained that I was the sculptor and that it was my first attempt at sculpting, ever, and it would come around before I was done. (Actually, I felt it would take a bit of a miracle to improve much past where I had taken it.)

Before Timothy got back from Europe, I took the opportunity to Google him.

He was indeed a sculptor with a bit of a religious bent, but his work also has a non-sectarian aspect, making a great balance. He has been called "the Michelangelo of our day," and his works reside in major cities all over the world.

I was prepared to be intimidated by this earth-god among mortals. However, Timothy turned out to be an RP...a regular person, a basic, down-to-earth family man who happens to have a calling to sculpt great pieces of work for humanity and God. I can live with that. Timothy was born in Canada and has lived most of his life in the province of Ontario, where his home and studio are located. Coincidentally, I had spent the best two years of my life in Camp Borden, also in Ontario. My father was a Lieutenant Commander in the United States Navy Dental Corps at the time and served as the U. S. Dental exchange Ambassador to Canada.

For two years, we lived in Ontario in a modest suburban house. At the first snow, someone in each household would take on the role of hoser. I was all in from the start. Each hoser would go to the farthest edge of their back yard, turn the hose on mist, and start spraying down the yard with a sweeping motion while moving back toward the house. That laid down the first of many thin ice layers. We would repeat the process over and over again, and eventually, we had real ice, a cumulative quarter-mile of uninterrupted, connected ice. Each night we kids would gear up in thermal under layers, winter coats, hats, gloves, and ice skates. At dusk all the back porch lights went on, and each house of kids, strapped on their skates, mounted the ice and skated on and on. Cold or wet or both, we simply knocked on any door. It would open to display warm, glowing, smiling faces, mothers and fathers who welcomed us in and helped us out of our outer layers of clothing. The snow-encrusted clothes were tossed into the dryer while we sat around a typically brand new, yellow and orange formica covered kitchen table, feasting on steaming hot chocolate with miniature marshmallows and freshly-baked oatmeal or chocolate chip cookies. We felt like young royalty. Then, with freshly warmed socks, we would hit the ice again. We never felt unsafe. All of life happened within a huge extended family. During the day, walking down the street with your ice skates swinging from your hockey stick slung over your shoulder, you couldn't get far before some driver would stop and call out, "Hop in, eh? "How's it going, eh?"

Ice hockey, street hockey, snow tunnels, curling, tobogganing, flying down a curving hill at about a million miles an hour—Timothy and I shared the same memories in slightly different geographic locations. People of all ages were encouraged to engage in all sports all the time. Ninety-year-old women and men were hoisting and "throwing" 40-pound curling rocks down the ice lane. With their bound straw witch brooms, they would madly sweep so fast, and furiously it melted the ice, all to change the course of the rock, as the captain shouted directions...Left! Sweep left! Faster! Faster!!

Excitement was everywhere, every day! We were challenged by the elements and engaged. We were all sharing the experience. In a way, the statue is like the Canada of my youth, unspoiled, alive, sharing, open, compassionate, and demanding to be touched.

In many respects, Canada is a kinder, gentler place than the United States. Having lived in both countries and traveled as an adult to

Canada several times, I understood that the phenomenon of American homelessness involves many socio-economic distinctions.

Given Timothy's limited experience of the stark realities, it seemed possible that he might not have really grasped what life was like for many Americans. For three months, by phone and email, Timothy and I spoke endlessly of the three people in the statue. By the end of that, I was confident that he "got it," or was close to understanding American Homelessness and we were fairly clear on the characters' back stories.

I was up to my neck in both local and national anti-homelessness campaigns and could not simply take a year off to go off and make a statue. Strange as this may sound, we planned to sculpt it together over the phone.

On the day we were to speak and come to terms on verbally signing the contract, Timothy was nowhere to be found. I was dismayed. Had I gotten it all wrong? No, it was just that he had been summoned back to Italy, to Vatican City, for an audience with *TIME* magazine cover portrait and Man of the Year, Pope Francis.

In a singular ceremony, the Pope was blessing Timothy's homeless statue, which is quite impressive in its simplicity. On a full-size city park bench, two-thirds of the seat is taken up by a small person lying on his/her side. The person is cloaked in a blanket that is pulled up over the head like a hood. A visitor who shares the remaining space on the bench may be repelled by the bare feet. But then a second glance confirms, those are very deep gashes in the feet. This bench sleeper's feet have open, bleeding wounds, such as would be sustained if the person were nailed to a cross. Feelings of shock, compassion, and shame flood the participant in that order. The work is called Homeless Jesus or Jesus the Homeless or Jesus on the bench as the guys on the street call it

I was starting to get this very strong and strange feeling that the Divine hand of God was somehow at work in my life for the first time. I could see "purpose" in the death of Diane Breisch Malloy, whose death had led to the creation of the Homeless Memorial itself.

The Deal Is Cut

> *"I closed my eyes, I held my breath, I took a drink. I didn't know if it was day or night..." Jerry Leiber and Mike Stoller*

Like the famous song said, I closed my eyes and held my breath... Not being an overly religious person, I tucked my head down, and continued. Tony, Timothy, and I came to terms, and it was agreed that over the phone, Timothy and I would collaborate on the sculpting of a 3-foot preliminary plaster version of The Home Coming for $10,000 and a life-size statue to be cast and bronzed for $87,000. For another $10,000, he would produce

200 resin maquettes to be used for fund-raising to finance the eventual creation of the life-size statue.

So, for over 4 years, Timothy and I shared the painfully slow experience of sculpting *The Home Coming* over the phone and through the computer. I took umbrage with every clay stroke that he made while he, on the other hand, displayed infinite patience. I bit my lip and my tongue constantly. I would tell and retell the story of each character over and over again in endless detail. I would describe what their life events had been. I spoke about their emotional responses to each of those events. I spoke about their pain, their hunger, sickness, anxieties, feelings of neglect and inferiority, failure, love, compassion, humanity, and renewed faith.

The whole process was and continues to be a "life lesson" for me...about patience...some master plan. This is what strangles me. It is an albatross flung around my neck. It alienates me from others. I feel anguish that I am failing to be articulate. Just like my brothers and sisters who all but scream and sometimes do scream when they talk about their condition. I, too, feel I am screaming to get people's attention. HEY, Look over there! There are people living on our streets! They are even eating out of garbage cans! There are children living without whole families. There are runaway youths trying to escape abuse. There are people who hire them to work and pay them so little that they can't even get a run-down room to live in. There are people living under our bridges and our overpasses! There are some very sick people struggling for their next breath. And so many are people of color! And we are so privileged! I must hurry, but I must find a balance, or no one will listen...I know this, but it's like a coal-fed locomotive flying down the track with the brakes full-on screeching at an ear-piercing volume. I must tell Timothy with such clarity that his hands hear the words and feel the urgency.

Rolling Up Our Sleeves

Our immediate goal was to raise $10,000 for the initial single set of plaster figures that would be between 2 and 3 feet high. With another $10,000, we could purchase and ship to Austin the 200 maquettes. Then, we would then ask people to help us bring the work of the world's premier bronze sculptor, Timothy P. Schmalz, to Austin. Anyone making a gift of $500.00 or more would receive one of a signed and numbered limited edition of a miniature version of *The Home Coming*.

We needed a point person who could help crystallize and carry forward our ideas for the initial fundraising and help hold a series of informal coffee klatch events, with one culminating event at a local art museum.

A short time prior, House the Homeless sent a hard copy of my white paper, *Preventing Economic Homelessness*, to every member of the U.S.

House of Representatives, every senator, every governor, Bill and Hillary Clinton, and the Obamas. That effort had drained us both physically and financially.

HtH is, after all, an all-volunteer organization, and the annual budget only ranges from $40,000 to $50,000, all small-dollar donations from the people. Our "Year in Review" letter keeps contributors apprised of what we are working on and contains our sole yearly plea for funds. Designated funds go to our Thermal Underwear Drive, devised to take care of folks left out in the cold during the winter. Undesignated funds go to the other projects.

We interviewed a few folks with the offer of gas money and glory. A couple of people came, started up, and fell by the wayside before we finally came across an organization called Leap to Success. This program is based on the awesome concept of keeping unemployed professionals employed in specific, short-term volunteer projects. They keep their skills honed and maintain a presence in the public eye with the hope of returning to full-time employment. How cool is that?

Founder and head of Leap to Success is Shannon Mantrom, a charismatic, dynamic, robust individual with neon bright red lipstick, flashy red jewelry, and red hair cast against her very white skin. In short, a dynamo whose enthusiasm is palpable. Leap to Success helped House the Homeless with the promotional "push-card" for the statue project and revamped our Universal Living Wage website.

When a couple of good prospects for the statue project fell through, Shannon offered to step into the role of Project Head, much to our relief. House the Homeless has a working Board of Directors, and we would serve as her support/advisory committee. We were thinking of hosting maybe 100 people at in-home events.

Shannon immediately went into high gear! We were thrilled to have the new blood and new energy. However, before long, we realized that Shannon was talking in terms of at least 5 events, including a social event at the Departure Lounge, a swanky travel agency/bar, and a grand event at the Umlauf Sculpture Garden involving 200 people. HtH co-founder Cecilia and I became a bit concerned.

Because my energies were directed elsewhere, we were excited and relieved that Shannon had taken charge. What concerned us was that she took such a tight grip on the reins. This problem became evident when she would not send out the postcard announcing the initiation for some reason known only to her. She didn't even show us the visual. In response to pressure, it was finally sent out, but, it failed to display our website, which contained all the information about House the Homeless and about the statue initiative generally. We thought we were dealing with Shannon as an individual, but the information also displayed the name of her business, with which we had not signed a contract. (We had done so twice before and believed this was just an initiative that only involved Shannon.) The power of her personality seemed to be overshadowing the initiative. Nothing felt right.

Foreshadowing

The parents of one of my awesome wife's grateful students offered Sylvia liquor products from their new local distillery, Bone Spirits.

Unfortunately, when the postcard came out, it stated "Open Bar." This was a lot different from "Limited Open Bar," which is what it was supposed to say. Cecilia and I had insisted that there would not be a full complement of free drinks. Because we envisioned the events as lasting an hour and a half at most, we figured two drinks per person would be a good number.

Worst of all, the postcard didn't even tell its recipients what the fundraiser was for! When Shannon explained that there wasn't enough room on the card, I thought my head would explode! And that wasn't all. Despite repeated requests for an itemized budget, it was not forthcoming. What did come was an endless stream of phone messages and emails detailing concerns I didn't feel I needed to know about. My requests for distinctive subject headings for each email fell on deaf ears, which meant I had to open and look at every single email to grasp its topic and meaning.

I intended to make the Umlauf Sculpture Garden and Museum the principal focus of the fund drive. Having been told that I was only available in the morning hours, Shannon scheduled this vital meeting for the afternoon and went alone to meet with the president and executive director of that institution. Afterward, she held onto their contact information like a personal stash.

So, we got the Team together. With Sylvia, Cecilia, and HtH board members Blythe Plunkett and Kevyn Meagher, I went to check out the facilities at the Umlauf Sculpture Garden and Museum. The lovely venue has both inside and outside areas. In the 40'x80' covered pavilion, we could set up the bandstand at one end, and use the center for the silent auction tables and display the model of The Home Coming if it arrived from Canada in time. Around the perimeter was space for dining tables, and 75 feet away, a separate, fully enclosed round room where we could set up food tables. The full screen monitor was perfect to continuously show our videos of Timothy sculpting the statue and the characters' back stories. Outside the building, the grounds open up into a massive, rolling expanse that displays twenty-five of Mr. Umlauf's handsome bronze sculptures. They are spaced far enough apart so each piece can be singularly appreciated. The lawn dips down and drops away to a lower uncovered round pavilion perfect for the dance troupe that Shannon had independently commissioned to perform for free. As we moved from area to area, we spoke of contingencies.

What if it rains? We'd gather umbrellas and move things under the closed pavilion and into the round room. Our MC was Byron Weber, a former local weatherman who would move the event along with a great announcer's voice. The Team was feeling elated. This was going to be amazing.

Trouble Right Here in River City

Shannon was also part of the group assembled that day. It was, in fact, intended to be something of a "come to Jesus" meeting. I had thought ahead of time about parameters. Of course, I would start with giving due praise for the three events Shannon had set up—the Departure Lounge, the gathering at the home of the Legal Aid office manager, and one that we were here about today. The positive vibes did not last long. Shannon asked, not for the first time if I was going to sign off on a $54.00 expenditure. I repeated that, to me, the invoice appeared to say $450.00. When she had first turned in the invoice from Premier Productions, I balked because this had not been authorized or budgeted for. I was sure we would have access to plenty of tables. Shannon insisted that the rental cost was only $54.00, and I should sign off on their contract so as not to lose the opportunity.

As we discussed this, Umlauf staff member Jonathan Greiner led us through the mini-kitchen to heat our food. He assured us that there were plenty of tables for our event. This came as a surprise because I had previously reminded Shannon to check with him about that very question, but apparently, they had not consulted him. Unpleasant feelings began to bubble up inside me, and I chose that moment to again ask Shannon for the Umlauf Director's and President's contact information. The importance of that faded momentarily into the background, as we also learned that Shannon had made the unilateral decision to raise the number of available tickets to 300—and to price them at just $10.00 apiece! The feeling that my head might explode was becoming all too familiar.

Cecilia Blanford, in her early sixties and just over five feet tall, is a born-again, church-going Baptist who gently praises the name of Jesus in about every third sentence she speaks. She survived an abusive marriage, bore a son, and lived through the suffering deaths of several family members and friends along the way. Perhaps the most telling testament to her sterling character is that she puts up with me and my strident vision. However, at this moment, Cecilia's patience with Shannon was growing mighty short to the point where it seemed she might hyperventilate.

As she stammered out a protest, I firmly enunciated what Cecilia and I were both thinking. "This is a world-class sculptor. This will be a world-class sculpture in a world-class venue. You are setting this up so that every penniless Jack and Jill in Austin who is looking for some terrific entertainment and free booze will storm our walls."

Cecilia added the point that should have been glaringly obvious all along. "This is supposed to be for our friends who already know and care about us and homelessness."

When we left the meeting that day, I stressed to Shannon the importance of coming up with a rain contingency plan; and passing along to Cecilia the contact information for the Umlauf leaders; and not tarnishing Timothy's reputation in the larger world beyond Austin. Most importantly, we needed her to create an outreach plan to bring people to all three events.

As it turned out, Cecilia was just as upset as I had imagined. She felt that Shannon was out of control, and it had begun with the liquor donation when the concept of small wine klatches fell by the wayside. I decided that the first step toward getting back on course would be to wrest physical control of the liquor from anyone else's hands. This would mean driving to Smithville, a small-town east of Austin that, surprisingly, has its own distillery. It was a 90-mile round trip event

Jeff Peace, founder of Bone Spirits Distillery, is a very nice, clean-cut, easy-going guy who has an MBA from Syracuse and attended Vanderbilt University Law School. He cut his teeth in the alcohol industry doing marketing for Bacardi. He and his wife Carrie not only wanted to get the word out about their venture but to reward Sylvia's teaching skills on behalf of their son. Jeff assured me that if our first two events left us low on alcohol, we could return to restock our bar. One problem: solved. Cecilia and I discussed the idea of issuing two drink tickets to each guest as they entered the venue. When we told Shannon, she was livid and refused to go along with any plan other than an open bar with no restrictions. Still saved in the telephone archives is her irate message saying she wasn't going to do it and that we could fire her if we wanted. Cecilia's reaction was a short email: "Fire her."

I called an emergency meeting of the Board of Directors, who agreed that we would control the booze by putting "limited" Open Bar on all notices. We immediately stopped all $10.00 ticket sales. They would now be $25.00 for a single person and $45.00 for a couple. I decided to personally send invitations to 500 House the Homeless supporters, offering them free tickets as our honored guests. We would get them in the door first and then work the magic. Obviously, this was a risky move, but I was confident it would bring people who were already familiar with our cause to the event. The Board okayed this move, and I rolled the dice. House the Homeless Board of Directors sent Shannon an email outlining the new plans. (We didn't discuss the drink-limiting tickets and just planned to go ahead with the two-drink maximum.) Shannon agreed to comply. Clearly, she was not happy, but at that point, who was?

The Departure Lounge

The first event was in the Departure Lounge, a very swank, first-rate, innovative travel agency with couches and a kind of nightclub atmosphere. The decor featured an entire wall of wine bottles inserted in cubbyholes to stunning effect. On each wall of two rooms were LCD color screens. We would show all our videos about the statue and Timothy there. It was an amazing venue. Shannon managed to get nightclub singer Hedda Lane and her ensemble to perform for free. It was a Thursday night, supposedly auspicious for a fundraising event.

The event was catered for free by Mid-Town Catering. We only paid for the sound man. What an awesome event! Shannon had set up a truly amazing gig. This was all her show.

Our team had been briefed in Square Reader use that would allow us to capture credit card donations on the spot using iPads. Shannon's husband Chip, introduced as a tech guy *extraordinaire*, was on hand to be sure that money-gathering came off without a hitch.

The opening numbers were sung, and the starting time came and went with almost no attendees. So, Shannon madly sent out personal e-blasts to her pool of friends who were supposed to fill the rooms that night. Having no other choice, I made my "ask" speech to the dozen or so people who were present. They included the Team, Shannon, Chip, the three entertainers, the two owners, the bartender, a couple of unassociated potential travelers, and a couple of Social Service folks who came through "outreach."

From the Team's point of view, my speech hit every chord. I relayed the back stories of the individual characters in the statue—the veteran, the little girl, and the elderly African American woman. I related all the facts presented to the reader earlier in this chapter and emphasized that this woman also represents the unraveling of the financial stability of the working poor in our country due to a failed Federal Minimum Wage standard. I covered all the reasons why the statue needed to exist at all. It embodies almost every facet of the abject poverty and suffering of our sisters, brothers, and children experiencing homelessness.

I explained how the statue would help people stay connected to the Community First! Village, designed to house disabled folks currently living on our streets. Finally, I explained how, once the statue was completed and installed in its permanent home location, anyone emotionally "moved" by it could use their iPhones and move to action. They would only need to click on a QR code to see the videos and hear the backstory. They would be able to instantly send a financial contribution to help sustain the Community First! Village. It felt good…not too long, yet long enough and passionate enough to stir compassion. The applause was enthusiastic, even if it sounded like one hand clapping.

The Square Reader's intention to easily accept credit card contributions was a bust. It only succeeded in irritating the two potential givers and the volunteers who struggled with it.

We were given a very generous 10% of the bar ($97.00) but still only pulled down about $700.00 total. Measured against the amount of work that had gone into the event, this was pitiful. It was clear to all that the lack of success was due to inadequate communication, despite my emphasis, at the Umlauf meeting, on the prime importance of comprehensive advance outreach.

At the Home of D'Ann Johnson

Obviously, we now had a lot to think about before embarking on the next planned event, which would be at the home of D'Ann Johnson, the managing attorney at Legal Aid, where I ran Legal Aid for the Homeless. She lives in East Austin, a section of town that, due to its rapid rate of white gentrification, was the focus of my book Striking a Balance. Ever since its purchase in the 1990s, the multi-story home has been under constant restoration.

D'Ann, an activist since the Seventies, has rubbed elbows with Cesar Chavez, Susan Warren, Ann Richards, and Molly Ivins, among many others. She knows people, and political events are held at her home all the time. If she is into you and your issue, she just might tap into her own network of folks. In fact, it was through D'Ann and preparing for the event at her home that I met and later became close friends with Bishop John McCarthy.

When D'Ann confided that she found Shannon and her approach to be off-putting, I could feel myself turning pale. I admitted that I was as surprised as anyone to learn that this was Shannon's first solo fundraising effort despite her professional and capable facade. I may have heard a cock crow three times as I disavowed her and assured D'Ann that another of our team members would work with her instead.

Shannon had scheduled this event for a Wednesday. There was an open but limited bar, a violin quartet, and for a change of pace, local singer Deann Rene and her ex-husband whose name escapes me, blew the roof off the place. Attendance was fair, and we actually had in-and-out traffic. The difference between this and the previous event was that those who came and went left checks. Again, the Square Reader app did not work properly, but all in all, we raised about $2,500. I framed it in a positive light as good practice for the Umlauf Gardens event.

There was tension on another front, too. Where was the two-foot model statue that Timothy and I had extensively discussed via long-distance phone? About a month out from the Departure Lounge event, he returned from his foundry in Asia to his studio in Canada to find that his "mold man" had just up and quit.

With as much gentle finesse as possible, I explained, then stressed to him, with an urgency that became more like pressure, how important that item was to our entire campaign in terms of raising the first $10,000. The first event and then the second event had come and gone with no model on-site, in front of the folks. Why, I insisted, could he not just hire someone new? He busted out with, "The actual model shouldn't matter that much, and anyway, I'll just return your money and be done with it." Scientifically possible or not, I might have stopped breathing for about three days. In my mind, I replayed the conversation over and over. I spoke with several folks, and finally, I prayed. On Monday, I knew what I had to do. I called Timothy and simply told him that I needed his help. He simply said, "Okay." I exhaled.

Hard Decisions

As the Umlauf event grew closer, the weather took a turn. A cold snap was predicted, possibly the coldest night of the year. It's one thing if people have a chance to acclimate to cold, but the sudden onset of frigid weather has a different psychological effect altogether. And our event was scheduled for an outdoor venue. I decided to bite the bullet and rent four outside furnaces for $100.00. Even now, this is hard to write, as I'm part Scottish, and spending $100.00 that I haven't even earned yet on a little cold weather was unacceptable to my DNA. However, upon reflection, I decided that having guests with hands too cold to write checks would be even worse.

Alcohol

Earlier in the year, Austin had suffered a flash flood, and a woman who was foolish enough to drive around a water barrier was swept away into the raging waters. A young City of Rollingwood police officer, Tim Johnson, tried to rescue her and consequently spent weeks in the hospital. Since he would soon return to active duty, House the Homeless wanted to be part of the support team that would help him get back on his feet. We wanted to hire him to ensure alcohol safety as guests came and went.

Police Chief Pryor liked the idea and approved it. Now, all we needed was a person or group to be the financial patron of this idea and pay for the   officer's time.

I thought that it would be great to involve Mothers Against Drunk Drivers in a proactive, alcohol preventative program. I had reached out to this group years before, seeking sponsors for my innovative alcohol bill, which dealt with the fiscally-based treatment of alcohol users. Then, I was told that MADD was not interested, as they only wanted to punish those involved with problems of alcohol use. Now, their website promoted proactive prevention. Perfect!

I left several unanswered messages and finally resorted to leaving a comprehensive message explaining Officer Johnson's story. Also, at our event, we would limit folks to two drinks per person by issuing bar tickets because our goal was to promote responsible drinking. We wanted to hire Officer Johnson to escort folks across the park road immediately outside the Umlauf facility. We recognized our role in ensuring that everybody got home safely. From our perspective, we were offering MADD a quarter-of-a-million-dollar public relations package in return for writing the officer a $300 paycheck. There was no response. Not one single phone call or email was ever returned. Apparently, not every branch of MADD had gotten the memo about a non-punitive response to the alcohol problem.

I'm sure that if I had lost a family member to a drunk driver, I too would not be feeling very charitable. They just weren't ready for our concept of preventative action.

In the end, Alan Graham, my friend and Executive Director of Mobile Loaves and Fishes, stepped up to cover the cost. Thank you! Under the guidance of Police Chief Pryor, the City of Rollingwood police department picked up the cost of the police car (with flashing lights), helping to ensure the safety of pedestrians and drivers alike.

Ashes to Ashes

Two days before the event, I got a call from the curator of the Umlauf Sculpture Garden & Museum, saying that three boxes had arrived. I immediately dropped everything and rushed over to the scene for my first meeting with curator Kate Edwards, who is intelligent, pleasant, attractive and sharp. She directed me to the three boxes posted from Ontario, Canada. I almost breathed a sigh of relief but instead quickly started opening the boxes. The plaster models at the core of each box were bubble wrapped, and surrounded by Styrofoam peanuts, the bane of the 21st Century! I started by painstakingly transferring fists full of these nuggets to another bag while making a terrific mess of the museum floor. Ever gracious, Kate told me not to worry. "The carpet is easily vacuumed."

I didn't really want to see the individual pieces but to view them as a composite scene, as they would be displayed. I was seeking the total effect, but due diligence was the order of the day. I first pulled the fire barrel. It was surprisingly heavy and intact. Next, I pulled the veteran and his daughter, scanning their surfaces for damage. On the backside of the veteran/daughter base was a gouge about the size of a quarter and about as deep. "Odd," I thought. Now I could feel my body temperature rise as blood rushed into my head. As Kate watched intently, I continued to move quickly but steadily. It felt like my emergency brake was on. I removed the old woman from her bubble wrap to find a gash on the top of her head. The floppy ends of the bandana that tied up her hair were smashed, exposing the white powder casting. I steeled myself. "Focus," I told myself. "What do I have here? What is the extent of the damage?" I could hear Kate draw breath, ever so slightly. "Well, this isn't good," I said in a as calm a voice as I could muster. Her voice held a note of anxiety. "What will you do?" "I'm not sure, but it could have been worse. It could have been her face." Kate commented that I was responding remarkably well under the circumstances. What choice did I have? The event was two days away, and I was bringing the show.

I had intended to leave all three figures at the museum, but now I wrapped up the old woman and loaded her into my truck. I called my sculpture professor and got him on the first ring. "Houston, I have a problem," I said. Immediately, I could hear the stress in his voice, "Now?!" he pleaded over the phone. It was absolutely the worst, busiest time of his entire year, with a major city art tour running through his studio in just a couple of days. I told him not to worry; I'd deal with it. No problem. I hung up, watching the digital numbers disappear from my screen.

Due to the nature of the material, I decided that I would carve away the ends of the bandana with a drywall knife. It would look as if the bandana had been knotted, perhaps oddly knotted, but who would question the knotting technique of an elderly homeless woman? I shot over to Michael's craft store and called my daughter Colleen on the way. As I stood before the sea of paint tubes, she guided me through my options. I returned to the house, finished my model-doctoring. Next morning, I placed the individual statue sections on the museum shelf where they would remain until the setup for the fundraising event.

The Main Event—Umlauf

The night of the event was frigid—as promised, the coldest of the year so far. Without any further discussion with Shannon, Cecilia positioned herself at the front entrance table with my friend Patricia Hawkeye who worked with the Texas Civil Rights Project. Every guest received two blue tickets, redeemable for two free alcoholic drinks. Cecilia had researched this issue on the internet and found our concern was fully in line with current non-profit event practices regarding alcohol. In the end, we had no drunken incidents, arguments, fights, injuries, fatalities, or complaints... not even from Shannon.

As people entered the covered pavilion, they were treated to an awesome array of silent auction choices, including trips, gifts, and vacations. Joanna Fernandez, a volunteer, brought in by Shannon, had done an amazing job!

Cecilia had recruited local celebrity weatherman Byron Webber to be Master of Ceremonies. Throughout the evening, he kept up an endless stream of banter to mask the sound of chattering teeth. The already bone-chilling air was intensified by a slight breeze. It wasn't long before the four heaters began to sputter, and three of them surrendered. Some people huddled in the food roundhouse or at the bar, while others circulated around the silent auction.

Fred Butler, our friend and Keynote Speaker was only partially listened to as he deftly lampooned me. I had once received the Fred Butler Community Leadership Award, so I was certainly okay with some good-hearted ribbing from him. At one point, he said it was better to have my camel nose all the way inside the tent of deciders rather than outside lobbing grenades under the tent flap.

Aware that the scheduled dancers might freeze solid in their tutus, I told Shannon they would be totally forgiven for not performing. Real troupers, they chose to dance and freeze. Very few attendees were as brave. Only a handful of onlookers encircled their heater.

When the time came my "ask", toes were simply numb. People were too cold to engage in anything other than mindless chatter to keep their lips moving, except perhaps around the rim of a glass of high-octane moonshine, which is what we were serving. I was sure I would be just one more voice talking in a din of voices.

Perhaps that is how it started, me just talking in my own head. I harked back to when my daughter, Colleen, was just five when she pointed to a house under construction and said, "Look, Daddy, when they finish, the homeless can live there." It had been my Jimmy Stewart, and It's a Wonderful Life moment. Remember that part when ZuZu hears a bell ring? She says, "Look, Daddy, Teacher says every time a bell rings, an angel gets his wings." Ah, the clear vision of the young.

I spoke of my national formula to finally fix the Federal Minimum Wage and my failed efforts to reach people with my book, Looking Up at the Bottom Line because I couldn't get people to stop texting long enough to read a full-length book. Besides, who would want to read an entire book about homelessness? I spoke of the decision, after decades in the field, and literally thousands of conversations with people experiencing homelessness and hundreds of people struggling to end it, to create a life-size bronze statue.

I explained how this statue was being sculpted by the "Michelangelo of our day" and how it would inspire emotion and move the onlookers to action. I also explained how the QR tile embedded in the statue would bring people to understand Community First! Village, being created by Mobile Loaves and Fishes for homeless people with disabilities, and how this statue's very existence would not allow us to forget these downtrodden people and the lives they have been forced to live on our streets. The statue would not let us forget the endless scores of women, children, and men who had lived and died on our streets and how each of us could make those lives and those deaths count for something. I spoke for what seemed to be a very, very long time.

Then suddenly, I was back. All those faces were staring at me. I found a tear in my eye. Or, as the Grinch would say, I was leaking. It was so quiet. I thanked them and signaled, and our beautiful Blythe Plunkett, who sits on our HtH Board of Directors and was the Community Coordinator for Mobile Loaves and Fishes, slid the drape from the statue. All could see Timothy's fine work and my concept of a chance encounter at the edge of woods when people who have nothing to share but the warmth of their fire gladly share it with another human being, who also have nothing. What more could I say than, "It is called *The Home Coming*," Almost frozen solid, the people applauded enthusiastically.

With the help of the lovely Sara Hickman, 2010 Texas State Artist Musician of the year, we celebrated the statue and the moment. We enjoyed her music, and people gave money, and I thanked them profusely. We raised $8,500 from that event. No one seemed to notice or perhaps care that the bandana on the old woman's head was oddly knotted. I reminded the guests that the 22nd Annual Homeless Memorial would be in 3 days and invited everyone to join us.

The 22nd Annual Homeless Memorial

This is House the Homeless service when regular Austinites gather on Auditorium Shores and read the names of the folks we've lost during the past year. In spite of restrictive land construction projects all around the memorial that year, it was one of our best-attended services to date, with well over 100 people in attendance. The songs by Ms. Robyn Ludwick were haunting. Military-style "dog (people) tags" bearing the names of our lost friends were lovingly attached to the Tree of Remembrance as each name was read aloud.

When the service was over, we socialized, hugged and kissed one another, told stories, and warmly remembered old friends. Dee Sera, a new supporter who had attended the Umlauf event, introduced me to her husband, Jeff. "We've been trying to speak with you. A slow-moving feeling of warmth yet chilled on the edges, told me that I was about to get the flu as the feeling swept through my head and across my face. "We want to help." Simple words, but I felt light-headed.

"We want to give you a $50,000 matching grant." Caught off guard, I simply said, "Thank you." Then brazenly, I said, "At this moment, I need $2,500 to reach the $10,000 goal of the Umlauf event. This will enable us to get the maquettes and begin the fund-raising process in earnest." Jeff looked at Dee and back at me, saying, "We can do that too." A prayer of heavenly thanks escaped my lips. Just like that, we were on our way.

It would be several months before I would understand the feeling of dread and premonition that had enveloped what should have been a joyous moment.

Giving It All Away!

Throughout the effort to raise the first $10,000 needed to secure the stature miniatures, I was also waging a more formidable campaign on a parallel track. I found myself in a pitched battle to give the life-size bronze statue to the City of Austin. Craziness!!!

To review, I had cast my own set of maquettes under guidance, and taken them to each City Council member, and told them of our plan to give *The Home Coming* to the city so it could ultimately be placed at the existing Homeless Memorial on Auditorium Shores.

I was met with support but also with a wait-and-see attitude from other Council members, including the mayor, who wanted me to "go through the process."

Laura Martinez from Mike Martinez's office set up my review before the Parks Department at their Zilker Park offices. I had a good feeling about this. I had crossed paths with Marty Stump, a significant player with the Parks Department who now headed up the major renovation project at Auditorium Shores. Twenty-two years before, I had met Marty and told him about the drowning of Diane Breisch Malloy and how we later learned that 24 other folks who lived homeless on Austin's streets had died in the years prior. We wanted to plant a Tree of Remembrance. Marty's response was sympathetic, and we talked about location. We selected a tree barren site for what would become the City wide House the Homeless-Homeless Memorial. It started with the planting of our live oak tree. Next came our two memorial plaques and the installation of the park bench that House the Homeless bought from the Parks Department. Surely, using Marty Stump's name in our proposal, citing his guidance, collaboration, and ultimate joint site selection, would carry great weight. Unable to guess what questions would be asked at the meeting, I tried to anticipate logical concerns, as Margaret "Call me Maggie" Stenz had suggested. I had been to two foundries, the first outside of Dripping Springs. The owner was a great guy but after two months of planning, the project proved to be just too big for his operation.

Next, I met with Clint C. Howard, also a great guy and the owner-operator of the Deep in the Heart located in Bastrop, Texas. He had grown his foundry from a 5-employee operation to 45 people in only 7 years. He was responsible for more than 2 million dollars in annual sales. He had produced some spectacular, larger-than-life bronze statues, including the Texas Capitol Vietnam Veterans Monument. After months of in-depth planning, we were able to present to the Parks Department the sizes, weights, and cost of the Home Coming statue figures, sculpting costs, and installation costs in between $200,000 and $225,000 for a completed installed project, not including landscaping.

The proposal started with our statue characters on a granite base. We evolved this to textured concrete pads that would help us reduce the amount of impervious ground cover required.

Joining me in the meeting were Cecilia and Kevyn from House the Homeless and Shannon from Leap to Success. Laura Esparza presided. Also represented were both the Parks Department and the Watershed Protection Department. Call me crazy, but while questions were being asked, I sensed that an outcome had already been decided. The gentleman from the Watershed Department referred to past flooding in the area. This set off alarm bells in my head, so I assured him that in twenty-two years, while there has been some minor flooding, our existing memorial had never suffered any damage whatsoever.

That's when it hit me. I needed to locate the engineers who had put in the Stevie Ray Vaughan sculpture that sits just 75 yards west of our existing memorial and our proposed site for The Home Coming. It was a shot in the dark. That statue had been placed almost a quarter of a century in the past on the very same day that my friend Skip Beard and I had dedicated the Homeless Memorial at the base of our fledgling tree. I talked to a lot of old-timers and drank a lot of coffee, but understandably the name of the engineer was elusive. I spoke with my friend, Judge Phil Sanders, who is very well connected, who suggested several possible engineers. After following a trail of stale bread crumbs, I located Gary Jaster of Jaster Quintanilla and Associates. He was the man! Amazingly, I got him on the phone almost immediately. I told him I had planted a tree at our memorial on Auditorium Shores on the very same day they lowered Town Lake (now Lady Bird Lake) by ten feet so he could build the base for the Stevie Ray Vaughan statue. He agreed to meet me at the Vaughan statue. He told me how the city had feared that building the platform might hurt a particular bald cypress nearby. After more than 20 years, the tree looked great. Apparently, it simply grew its roots deep underground where it surrounded the subterranean statue base and adapted just fine.

I told Gary I wanted him to help me. Then almost in the same breath, I confessed that I had no money, just a desire to remember folks who had been dying on our streets. He simply said, "I can help." To be sure there was no misunderstanding, I repeated that House the Homeless had no money and added, "I'll do everything I can to compensate you." His response was calm and clear, "We'll work something out." Just like that, we forged what seemed to me to be the unlikeliest of business partnerships I had ever entered into. With a twinkle in his eye, he said, "They'll say no and we'll push back and they'll say no, again," "And we'll push back," I replied. He nodded, and we shook hands, and I knew right then and there, I really liked the guy.

I realized that I needed to create a statue team of professionals. This would not be a committee. It would be experts coming together when needed. Mike Kelly came to mind, a city/state lobbyist, who had taken me to dinner wanting to pick my brain over the statue concept. I think he was fascinated by the whole concept of poverty and those who fought for the little guy. His world was one of politics and closed-door, big-boss deals that forge the course of destiny. I think he lived in that world for the thrill of the lowered lights, the hushed name-dropping, and deal-forging, cherishing them far beyond the money. My world of poverty was so far outside his realm of understanding that he was intrigued by it. So, he gave me the name of his arborist who had worked for the city. When I contacted the fellow, it turned out that he had moved away from any hands-on activity, so he suggested Don Gardner.

As it turns out, Don doesn't believe in email. He uses a phone drop and picks up messages once a week. I left a message and waited and hoped for, but did not expect, a return call. Online, I found a series of videos where he lectured about the science and his love of trees, their planting, growth, propagation, and care, etc. After a week, Don called back, saying that he had followed my advocacy work for years. He was something of an activist himself. A few years before, one of Austin's great natural attractions, Barton Springs, was in trouble. It's a natural aquifer where crystal clear water was purified by passing through limestone rock beneath the surface, and then bubbles up at a reportedly constant 68°F year-round. On the banks of the pool are hundreds of massively tall, beautifully canopied sycamore and pecan trees.

The City got the idea that hundreds of these trees were dying from a disease so hard to diagnose that they would all have to be sacrificed to make the determination.

Don Gardner and a small dedicated team rushed to the site and managed to painstakingly save hundreds of the trees. They were crisis-averting heroes, and Don was named Arborist of the Year.

He agreed to meet Gary and me at the Homeless Memorial. We hoped that he could perform a similar feat by helping us convince the City Council, the Parks Department, and anyone else that our statue should be allowed to reside at the site of the Homeless Memorial counter to the fact that the area is a declared flood plain. We would need to show that the placement of our statue would in no way damage our own Tree of Remembrance that we had planted in 1993 or be swept away in a flood and cause damage elsewhere.

Lean and sunbaked, Don has a southwest demeanor. He measured the girth of our tree. I was proud to tell him that I had watered it every day for 18 years until its roots reached the river. He measured all the trees in the area. We plotted out the exact proposed location where the substantial counterweight concrete blocks for the statue would be sunk. He identified the sycamores and poplars in the vicinity.

Finally, to my great relief, he said, "You can do it...if you follow my directions to the letter, you can do it."

When Don's in-depth and detailed report arrived in the mail, I vowed to follow it strictly. The counterweights to the statue came in at about 4 tons! Within the community of Austin grew a strong environmental movement that began with saving Barton Springs that gave us crystal clear spring-fed water around which our city was built. When urban sprawl threatened its very existence, the people rose up and literally stormed city hall, and SOS-Save our Springs was born. Our memorial sites on the shore of the Texas Colorado river receive water from the springs.

The Team was growing. We had the top guys in their fields and needed only one more—a landscaper. I had made another major change in the statue blueprints. There would be no platform, neither granite nor textured concrete. These three people, John the veteran, Ms. Anateen, the old woman, and Colleen the little girl, were salt of the earth. They were real people, and they needed to walk on the earth itself. Gary agreed. For 22 years, members of House the Homeless and other Austin citizens have adorned the Homeless Memorial plaque with flowers for the Homeless Memorial service. Through the good work of homebound HtH board member Jo Ann Koepke, flower donations have been made by John Dromgoole, owner of The Natural Gardner TV show and gardening business.

I got it in my head that I wanted John on my team. He is Austin famous. He comes on his Saturday morning TV show in his folksy way and fills our living rooms with sweet, simple advice that makes us all believe that we, too, are gardeners. A radio program complements the TV show. After two weeks of leaving messages without a callback, I went to the Nursery off Old Bee Caves Road. It was a gloriously sunshiny Sunday morning, with so many people arriving, the business had to use *parking attendants* to keep the traffic moving. Like many Austin businesses, it started up in the 1960s, and some aspects remain the same today and operate at the same pace.

At one of the two checkout counters, I asked for John. Faces froze; responses were monosyllabic until I identified myself as Richard R. Troxell with House the Homeless. The frozen faces, bodies, and music all started again. I believe it was the mention of House the Homeless (not my name) that opened the door. Someone said they thought he was "in back with Brandi." Someone placed a call on a landline. I was told to "Just hang." I did. Ten minutes later, a young man came out and said, "He's in back." I waited for more, but he just stared as if I should know where "in back" was. The place was a small maze that seemed to have several "backs."

Then he offered, "Here, I'll show you," and I was led past some beautifully flowered, temporarily potted plants and awesome areas of draping vines that I didn't even know existed, although I had been there many times.

So here is the thing, in many ways, Austin, especially South Austin, is an old secretive, closed club of good old boys and gals who grew up together in the 60s. They have always fought against the establishment and those that would unfeelingly step on its flowers.

After being ushered past a small office, I was led into the connecting room where John Dromgoole was sitting in an equally small office and in a very lively negotiation for a fairly large order of plants on pallets.

Expecting to wait in a standing position for at least an hour while the urgent discussion progressed, I was taken aback when the proprietor stopped mid-sentence and asked, "What may I do for you?" Suddenly, I felt unprepared but forged ahead because directness is always best. "I intend to put in the sculpture of three people experiencing homelessness at the existing Homeless Memorial, and I'd like you to help with the landscaping...and I have no money." It didn't even take him a whole beat to say, "Okay, I'll do it." "What about the cost? I injected." "Don't worry about it. Call Brandi to set up a time." He half-turned away and was instantly right back in the middle of the intense conversation. I pivoted and was out the door. I was in and out in 15 minutes and got Austin's most famous landscaper to agree to join me at no cost. Wow, and all before 9:30 on a Sunday morning.

On Site at the Memorial

The city had started its massive renovation project at Auditorium Shores (that included everything south of the hike and bike trail). This left the trail and a 15-foot swath of land that ran north and perpendicular to the trail unscathed.

As part of the renovations, they temporarily closed down the parking lot that entered Riverside Drive and ran perpendicular to the river and parallel to South 1st Street. As a result, Gary, John, and I met in the Hooters restaurant parking lot. We parked and walked to the Homeless Memorial a few blocks away.

John had some great ideas that included dwarf monkey grass, 6" high, that I suggested should be plugged in 2" by 2" spaces between a patch-work of used, reclaimed brick. We would lay the bricks within an oval vegetation ring 17' in length and approximately 7' in width. John suggested that we incorporate the "used" Austin brick even if we had to purchase it. Gary and I loved the idea. John also suggested that we place lantana at either side of the viewing entrance to entice butterflies. Awesome!

I designed a walkway that would half-encircle the oval. I later re-designed the entrance so that at its point of opening, a wheelchair could easily enter, the statue could be fully viewed, and the chair could be just as easily maneuvered to turn around.

Next, we met with the Parks Department and the Watershed Protection Departments. This was a big deal. I had come prepared. I had my team. This was no longer just my project. It was now the work of world-class sculptor Timothy P. Schmalz in collaboration with me, which made a huge difference and imparted gravitas. I also had blueprints and the backing of engineer Gary Jaster who had installed the Stevie Ray Vaughan statue. I had John Dromgoole, Austin's beloved radio and TV star. Finally, we had the support of Don Gardner, who had maintained the grounds of the Governor's Mansion for 15 years and helped save the magnificent sycamore and pecan trees of Barton Springs. In fact, both Don and Gary were present with me at the table. I also had the names of two dozen prominent people and organizations who supported the project.

With the help of my beloved Sylvia, I had a PowerPoint presentation at the ready. We had excellent photos of the existing Homeless Memorial and drawings that illustrated our landscape vision. We had it all! When I was done, one of the people reviewing the presentation stood up and placed a document on the table that must have been 3 feet by 4 feet and measured 1-inch thick. It was open to a certain page. With a bony index finger, she stabbed at the document, over and over again. She was saying some words, and one of them was "water." Other words were, "...and City Council voted to ratify it. This area has now been designated a 25-year floodplain as of last year." Stone silence prevailed. I shot a deadly glance at Margaret "Call me Maggie," Stenz. "How could she not know?" I blasted out into the room as I glared at her deepening red face.

I looked at Gary. His expression and hand gesture indicated that he hadn't known. Almost sheepishly, he offered, "It wasn't like that when we put in the Stevie Ray Vaughan statue." Then some of the others in the room started talking excitedly about the iconic night photos taken of the Stevie Ray Vaughan statue. The city lights backlit its image reflected upon the floodwater. The river had risen to the top of his thighs.

I asked about an appeal or an exception, or perhaps a variance. The woman with the brutal index finger said there was a process for a variance. "Yes, a variance," I said, stunned, gathering my papers together. Gary tossed out, "It never did any damage to the statue." Cecilia tried to make a soothing comment. Shannon, for the first time ever, said nothing. Kevyn was silent. People were standing and leaving. Gary and I mumbled to each other, "Yes, a variance," and we all left the room.

For weeks, Gary and I spoke about the need for the variance. He said he was in touch with that office. Eventually, the report came: Statue accepted; site denied.

Who Will Stand with Us?

Next stop...The Arts Commission. One of the things that has become abundantly clear: we must have plenty of powerful support.

I set up an email that explained our statue project, showed a photo of Pope Francis' blessing, Timothy's *Homeless Jesus* in the Vatican, and provided recipients with a comprehensive letter of support. I invited people to write their own letter of support or simply sign off on the standard letter that I had prepared. People did both.

The first on the list was City Council Mike Martinez, who by then had announced that he was running for Mayor. I then reached out to Jo Katheryn Quinn, the Executive Director of Caritas, a major local social service organization that works with families, veterans, and immigrants. She is and has been a fairly strong supporter for years except for that little bench issue thing. I then called Irit Umani, the Executive Director of Trinity Center, who asked for two benches and who nurtures women and homeless artists as she hosts "Art from the Street." This program had started the same year that we created the homeless memorial. She inspires homeless folks. She does this by restoring their feelings of self-worth by helping put money in their pockets from selling the art of their own making. She, too, got on board. Alan Graham, founder of Mobile Loaves and Fishes and Community First! Village, enthusiastically endorsed the Homeless Memorial site location for the statue as we continue to work hand in hand. Dan Pruett, Executive Director of Meals on Wheels and More, also endorsed. He always claimed to support our project, but now he actually had. Twenty-one attorneys from private practices, and Texas Rio Grande Legal Aid, Texas Civil Rights Project, including champions like Nelson Mock, Robert Doggett, Fred Fuchs, and Jim Harrington founder of the Texas Civil Rights Project, got on board. Peoples' Community Clinic, Casa Marianella, and Safe Place are represented by giants with Regina Rogoff, Jennifer Long, and Julia Spann, who act to protect and promote women and men, also endorsed the project.

Businesses, musicians, elected officials, veterans' groups, and various religious organizations all wrote letters of support.

Walter Moreau, Executive Director and Founder of Foundation Communities, who has built over 15 affordable housing projects of 100 units or more each, endorsed this project.

Mary Morse, President of the Texas Society, and sculptor Joe Gieselman shared their support. Sculptors Susan Green, Heather Tolleson, and my mentor sculptor Steve Dubois added their names and letters of support.

Many others, too numerous to name here, also endorsed this statue project. How could we possibly not be successful? Between our team that consists of the world's premier sculptor, Timothy P. Schmalz, our project sculptor, Don Gardner, the Barton Springs arborist and our tree advisor, along with John Dromgoole, The Natural Gardener landscaper, and Gary Jester, our engineer and that of the iconic Stevie Ray Vaughan Statue, our list of endorsers and my friend/attorney Nelson Mock who agreed to introduce me to present the prepared summation speech so I could just field questions all in front of the table displaying the small models of the statue, it was destined to be our day!

Additionally, I had done my best to reach out to members of the Arts Commission, *who would have an opportunity to vote on the statue and its location.* I also called several well-connected folks that I know and ask for them to exercise their influence on members of the Arts Commission. My neighbor and friend, Mike Kelly, knows Scott Daigle. Mike said he didn't pull Scott's support but felt he might have neutralized him. Scott by the way is the vice-chair of the Arts Commission.

I contacted my then publisher, Susan Bright with Plainview Press, and learned that Bruce Willenzik is a music man who had been involved with establishing the Armadillo World Headquarters (old Austin legendary stuff) and the founder of the Armadillo Christmas Bazaar. He made sounds like he would endorse the project at the Homeless Memorial.

I had no luck contacting Samuel Tinnon, who had some involvement with a local school district. Nor did I have any luck finding anyone who knew the retired Xerox corporation manager and retired Colonial in the US Army.

Mike Martinez Hits the Campaign Trail

Mike is just a basic, down-to-earth guy with a lot of drive, which is exactly what it takes to be a firefighter and a union leader. Just don't get on his wrong side, or he'll write you off hard and fast. He was sure he was going to be the next mayor, and vocally, he strongly supported the statue project. Austin is a very liberal-minded town, to the point where the rest of the state considers us to be outlanders. In fact, the first time I ever had to testify before the state legislature, the chairman had berated me, attacking my veracity, integrity, and political position. He figured he knew everything about me just from my introduction as President and Founder of House the Homeless in Austin. Every couple of years, the legislature attempts to dismantle *Roe v. Wade* and simultaneously strap a gun on the sides of our 60,000 University of Texas college students by pressing for the passage of ever-broadening gun carry laws.

Austin considers itself "America's third coast", naming itself "The Live Music Capital of the World" and acting like a Hollywood movie-style "wanna-be," which includes snarling already impacted traffic patterns by creating impromptu movie sets on our downtown streets. When they come to our capital from the far reaches of Texas every two years to legislate guns and morality, "real" Texans do not much care for our ways.

Regardless of Austin's left-leaning political bent, I felt Mike was slightly misreading things when he pushed against the anti-immigration advocates and instead campaigned to spend local tax dollars on affordable housing and promising to raise the minimum wage to a living wage while promising to sweep compassionate change into place all with the pull of an election lever. Sure, Austin is "liberal," but at one point, we had 2,700 Dellionaires. These are people who invested in Dell Corporation and became millionaires, including employees who accepted stock options in lieu of a salary in the company's early years. They tend to prefer order, and they like to keep their money in their own pockets.

Mike didn't want a fight over a statue that might be seen as creating a monument to the existence of homelessness, rather than simply a memorial to those folks who have died on our streets. The issue might derail his entire mayoral campaign. So, he wanted to postpone making it one until after his election. After all, we had already had to take a back seat when affordable housing advocates failed to plan or execute any kind of campaign to pass a $500,000 affordable housing bond. On the other hand, after Valerie Louise Godoy was murdered, House the Homeless members went to the Farmers Market for months, telling Valerie's story. We spoke to one person at a time and gathered signatures in support of creating a women's shelter. We secured over 5,000 signatures. And when the hue and cry rose to put a separate bond for this project on the ballot, everyone remembered hearing about the tragic murder. The bond for the woman's shelter easily passed.

However, backers of the affordable housing bond thought they had the automatic support of Austin's liberals. They saw no need to run any kind of awareness or justification campaign for the expenditure of tax dollars. Not only was it the only bond to be defeated, it was soundly defeated. So, when they had to start from the beginning and get the affordable housing bond back on the next ballot, they came to Mike and asked us to put the statue on hold. They thought there might be blowback. Mike graciously agreed to postpone the vote on the statue. In a small city like this of only 800,000 people, he felt he had no choice. I was more concerned about the new individual City Council district configuration that was going to take place. A delay might cause us to slip into 2015 with a set of ten new, unknown elected officials. I was convinced that only one of the old cadres would probably go forward. On the other hand, I knew the present Council intimately, and almost all had taken a turn presiding over the annual Homeless Memorial service.

After much pressure and many discussions with his aide Laura Williams, Mike agreed to schedule the statue issue on the ballot of the very last session of the existing City Council before the changeover. The deal was contingent upon my getting general approval from the Arts Commission. With all the letters of support we had ready, it should be a piece of cake. Friends of *The Home Coming* did some gentle lobbying with Arts Commission members they had met in other contexts. Amy Mok, also on the Arts Commission, is known for her work in the Asian community, and the keynote speaker from the Umlauf event, Fred Baker, knew her. He briefed her on our project and gave his stamp of approval. Attorney Maria "Lulu" Flores is an activist for Latino issues and perspectives. A couple of different people made an effort to bring her up to speed on our project.

The only fly in the ointment was a conversation with John Dromgoole of The Natural Gardner, who had assisted with the landscape design, and six months ago had given his "unconditional support." Just three days before the crucial meeting, he called me in an agitated state. Not long into the conversation, he started to pick apart the quality of the statue. Mostly, he focused on the old woman, whose closed fist seemed to be striking her chest in pain. "She looks like she's having a heart attack. This is depressing! Homeless people don't want to see this." I felt a corresponding sensation in the area of my own heart. But I knew what he meant. Her hand needed to open flat over her heart. I met John's concern with the admission that Timothy and I had discussed this exact subject. Timothy had explained that at this small scale, it was hard to convey certain expressions and emotions. I told John that we were going for an expression of joyous disbelief and that this could easily be rectified, on the life-size version, by

180

an upturned mouth and a faint smile. I explained that I had already fought hard for a whole slew of changes, and Timothy had accommodated me.

John would not yield. He burst out with, "Well, I can't support it!" My head began to swim. Unseen by him, I more or less found the seat of my chair. I assured him that this had been the culmination of my life's work and that I would not create anything that did not properly convey my vision of a compassionate, representative statue drawing empathy from the viewer. He had another point. "It's a winter scene in Texas; it's blazing hot here." (Then why, I thought, did House the Homeless go to so much effort every year to provide thermal underwear?) I reminded John that yes, it is hot, except for when it isn't (we actually have ice storms.) Like in the winter, which is when housed people are more likely to feel compassion toward people stuck out on the street. Addressing his points and earnestly assuring him that I shared his concerns, I was doing my best not to let my heavy emotional investment mess things up. He would not be placated.

This was not going in a helpful direction, so I tried to avert disaster. "I'll take care of it. You don't have to come to the presentation." After a spell of silence, John responded, "Well, it's a public meeting; I can come." There it was. He was going to confront me, the statue and Tim's work, in front of the Arts Commission! Quickly, I said, "Of course you can, but it's unnecessary at this point. I can address your concerns, I promise you." I became conscious that I was holding my breath.

It took me back to 1968, to a time when I stared wide-eyed as a torrent of blurred visions raced past. It was me, Reid Lowell, and Johnny Aerosmith in Bill Hampton's slant-6 Chevy II, three on the column, on the Beltway around Washington DC just after a rain. Top-down, we were flying. There was totally untypical tension in Bill's shoulders as he gripped the wheel. 100 mph, 105. Papers from the car floor swirled around us and flew away. 110 mph, 115. One of us choked out, "Bill, what are you doing?" As usual, his reply was a mumble. "Just wanted to see what would happen...118!" Then he backed off. The wind that had been rushing in our ears was again just blowing in our faces.

It was that kind of moment; I repeated, "John, it's okay, you don't have to come. I'll make the changes, and at the turn of every season, I'll seek your advice for the proper seasonal plantings...I promise...trust me. I've been advocating for these people for over thirty years. You know me." I wasn't sure what was happening in the silence that followed, what wasn't being said or thought. I made my move. "John, I'll keep you posted. Thanks for all your help." I hung up. I honestly can't say I remember ever hanging up on anyone before that instant.

On the day of the Arts Commission presentation, Kevyn and I were at the Parks Department slightly early to set up the statue models. I asked the liaison person where to place the maquettes, and she chose a place at the front of the chamber, where everyone's vision would be naturally drawn to them.

As people arrived, my friend Cecilia and I kissed and hugged, and she whispered in my ear that I'd be great. Both Don Gardner, the arborist, and Gary Jaster, our engineer, were present, loyal, and faithful as if we were lifelong friends. I felt warmly comforted by their presence.

And John Dromgoole, the popular and influential local celebrity and former supporter of this project, where was he? More than once, with great trepidation, I scanned the room, uncertain what to expect. Standing with Nelson Mock, the mild-mannered and soft-spoken attorney who was going to introduce me, I felt compelled to warn him of the possibility of a public confrontation.

The room filled, as did the Commissioner's table. All seven Commissioners were present. Before the meeting, I met with Commissioner Bruce Willenzik, who knew me quite well and remembered when I had presented before the Commission almost two decades before. With long scraggly grey hair, he certainly looked like an aging hippie who had morphed into an entrepreneur and now ran the Armadillo Christmas Bazaar.

Margaret, "Call me Maggie"

Stenz began with other Commission business, which went on for almost an hour and a half. Out of nowhere came one proposed new rule intended to *exclude statues* from any area designated as a flood plain. What? Cecilia, Gary, Don, Nelson, Kevyn, and I, who were spread out all over the room, we exchanged horrified looks. We could almost hear the nails being driven into our collective coffin. Just like that, the Commission unanimously ratified it. Apparently, it was a setup engineered by Stenz, the guide (staff) the city had provided to help us navigate the bureaucracy, who was opposed to our project from day one, and who was now leading the group down a path of her own choosing.

She moved on to our topic and said some less-than-complimentary words about the project's failed initial attempt with the Parks Department to okay me sculpting my own concept. She outlined how the Parks Department had approved the statue on our second attempt, if sculpted by Timothy Schmalz, but not the location. She had a PowerPoint presentation that said, right there in black and white, with a bullet point and a City of Austin seal, that we had been to a hearing before the Watershed Protection Department. They had ruled the site unacceptable because it was in a 25-year flood plain, so what could anyone do? Wait, what? Holy Hannah, she was talking about that woman, who had plopped into our meeting with that huge 3 foot by 4 foot by 1-inch-thick document. That wasn't a hearing! That was an ambush!

I was numb. The Commission had unanimously voted to prevent any statues from ever being placed in that small 200-yard square area that had been officially voted upon by City Council to be a flood plain. Funny how no one seemed to know about that previously, not the members of Art in Public Places, not City staff, and not one of the same City Council members who had allegedly voted for the designation and with whom I had individually met on the subject. I had painstakingly set up meetings, put on a tie, loaded up my three-piece statues on hand carts, and while still recovering from another major neck surgery (front and back, receiving an internal piece of titanium, the size of Vermont) when I had presented my precious cargo. Over and over again, I had physically and verbally enacted the story of my three characters and their heartfelt encounter. And yet, not one of the Council members had pointed out that I proposed placing the artwork in a forbidden place. These Council members were supposedly my friends or at least allies. Okay, at least I had believed them to be honest brokers.

Gary Jaster later told me that when "Call me Maggie" completed her presentation, her stance was defiant, and her facial expression was smug, self-satisfaction. She then deferred to me. I slowly rose from my seat and just then glimpsed the backside of Commissioner Brett Barnes, whose hulking figure was framed by the doorway as he exited the room. To have that individual leave at that particular moment was devastating. At this dramatic juncture, we pause for a digression that illustrates and typifies the never-ending struggle to bring the attention of influencers to our cause. Barnes, you see, was Chairman of the Commission, and in the weeks leading up to this presentation, my decision to contact him was not an easy one. It was, of course, totally legal, but it almost seemed shady somehow, like an effort to arrange ex parte communication with a judge before a trial. Barnes was the fundraiser for Saint Mary Cathedral, so my friend Bishop John McCarthy might know him—but didn't. Lora Ann Gerson, who serves as Community Liaison for Senator Kirk Watson, did know Brett Barnes and declared him to be a great, easy-going guy. She insisted that I reach out to him. Still thinking of how such an overture could backfire, I hesitated. But Ms. Gerson was so insistent and so positive, I took a chance.

I left a voice mail message suggesting that we might meet, at his time of choice, possibly at the Homeless Memorial. The freshly planted flowers were in full bloom, and the Tree of Remembrance displayed the names of the year's deceased friends. The site was right across from the Long Center, which any person with serious musical interests would connect with. But, long story short, I never heard from Arts Commission Chairman Barnes, and now, like Elvis, he had left the building.

This left Bruce Willenzik to run the meeting. I was not sure whether to be relieved or concerned. That thought was soon displaced when, as Nelson Mock introduced me as President of House the Homeless, another person left, trailing behind him an attitude almost as palpable as a smell, an odiferous combination of disgust and disrespect. This was Ernest Auerbach, a retired U.S. Army Colonel and former Corporate Manager for Xerox. Since we had never met, there was no objective reason for such scorn, but in my years of advocating for people experiencing homelessness, I had encountered it before, many times.

In front of the remaining audience, I had exactly ten minutes to blow through the PowerPoint and convey quite a number of ideas. Within those minutes, I would introduce Mr. Timothy P. Schmalz, the world's premier bronze sculptor, and the three iconic figures of *The Home Coming*.

Within those minutes, I would explain why Don Gardner was fully qualified to report that placing the statue at the Homeless Memorial would not harm any trees. I would show how I had created a landscape design that incorporated the concepts of former ally John Dromgoole, hoping all the while that he would not suddenly take the floor and denounce the project. Inside those ten minutes, I would explain that House the Homeless would raise every penny for the statue and we would not need any Taxpayer dollars from this Committee to initiate or complete our project.

Also, in those minutes, I would orient the audience to the small ceramic tile that would ultimately be imbedded in the dedication plaque. It would hold the QR code that visitors could activate with their smartphones to learn about the statue and what it represented and how its very existence would help support Community First! Village, the community that Mobile Loaves and Fishes created to help people who were not only homeless but also disabled. I would explain how a compassionate person could make a financial contribution to that village and how 5% of those gifts would finance the ongoing maintenance of the statue's structural integrity and its surrounding grounds into perpetuity.

And within those ten short minutes, I would talk about the significance of the existing Homeless Memorial and how for the last 23 years, Austin citizens had gathered on Auditorium Shores and adorned our lovingly planted and cared for Tree of Remembrance with the names of men, women, and children who had lived and died on our streets.

"Time!"

Nervous Stirrings

Perhaps, I was thanked for my comments, but if so, I don't remember it. I certainly did not feel that my presence was appreciated. And "Call me Maggie" wasn't done yet. She took the opportunity to repeat that the Watershed Protection Department had said no. But I was ready for her. I switched the PowerPoint back on for the audience to view the new slides I had added for just such an eventuality. In the last several months, the city had allowed extensive landscaping that incorporated stone and concrete construction in that very area of Auditorium Shores. I showed photos of stone block constructions that were 15' by 15' and over 3' high and of a long retaining wall consisting of stacks of 175-pound blocks. In a flood, those blocks would be swept off their moorings long before our statue, with its substantial subterranean counterweights.

I literally pointed across the room to our engineer Gary Jaster and asked him the condition of the Stevie Ray Vaughan statue, which had sat for 23 years just 75 yards west of our proposed location. He said, "It's fine." But "Call me Maggie" was on a mission to obstruct any project not generated by the staff or her bureaucracy. And she had her ace in the hole. "The process...they didn't go through the process."

For a moment, everyone froze. Then Auerbach, who must have returned from his break, led the charge. "They didn't follow the process?" With what Gary perceived as a sneer, "Call me Maggie" explained that we had not even made an effort to advance our project by applying to the Watershed Protection Department for a variance.

It was true. We needed a variance. Gary had gone twice to the Department in an attempt to discover the procedure. The first time, he met with some kind of resistance and was turned back. Before trying again to get the actual instructions, he reached out to a Supervisor of the Department. The Supervisor explained what the Watershed ordinance said and that his department would deny our request for a variance. Then, it would be up to the City Council, which was exactly what we were trying to avoid because several City Council members were running for office, and none could afford to be tagged with "skirting the process."

The department supervisor had told Gary that the result was a foregone conclusion. The Watershed Protection Department was going to say no, and going to each department section would not change that. *So there was no point in getting individual noes from each section.* The next step would be City Council, where nobody wanted to stick their necks out, and so would only refer us back to "the process." It was a classic catch-22. Relentlessly, "Call me Maggie" held on to her truth. "They didn't go through the process," she repeated.

Another Commissioner chimed in to articulate and fine-tune the objection and nailed it. "You didn't go through *each step* of the process." There it was. A vote was quickly called. Two Commissioners, Amy Mok and Maria Flores, tried to approve the statue without the variance approval, but Auerbach and Willenzik were adamant, and our application was denied. Someone turned off the lights, but the room had already gone dark and silent.

Hope Springs Eternal

During the next couple of weeks, I had private and candid conversations with two confidantes about getting the statue into the ground. One was a good ol' Texas boy who does septic excavations with his own front-end loader, likes to work, and is about as crazy as I am. We would get some orange work vests and helmets, and fencing. We could move in on the Homeless Memorial just before dusk and set up some lights. Dig the hole, build some wood framing and pour the subterranean cement counterweights. Unload the statue and get it in place by sunup. We certainly wouldn't hide what we were doing, but I'd get a bunch of the homeless guys to join us and stand guard just in case of anything.

At dawn, I would contact the media with a prepared statement. By mid-morning, the police would be confronting us. With our legal representative standing by, we would declare that we were exercising our rights under the constitution to express free speech. By our way of thinking, it was our land ever since 23 years ago when we openly claimed it under the law of adverse possession, and we had made improvements on it ever since. Perhaps we might negotiate some kind of understanding or not. For the moment, I put the idea on a temporary hold.

A Second Dance in the Park

On January 9, 2015, I received a call from Laura Esparza, who had run the Parks Committee meeting that reviewed our first application and who had been interested enough to attend the Arts Commission Presentation. She had been contacted by two members of the Arts Commission and wanted to assure me that she recognized the importance of our issue. Assuming that we would try again to give our statue to the City, she wanted us to be successful on a third try. Could we use some help in identifying alternative sites? Keeping all options on the table, I told her I was interested. I told her I had two criteria: high visibility and accessibility to foot traffic.

Ms. Esparza wanted to set up an exploratory committee. I asked if the process was open to options outside the park and to House the Homeless suggestions. She confirmed and said that to accommodate that, Art in Public Places would have to be involved, in the person of none other than Margaret "Call me Maggie" Stenz. I grunted.

We framed out a plan to coordinate all the committee participants that would eventually include two Arts Commissioners. I left the rest for her to set up and got ready to look for an alternate location. If we rejected this offer out of hand, we would look unreasonable, and that would be the end of the dance.

Banking on It

"Outside the park" covered a lot of ground, and I started my search by walking up and down Congress Ave. This of course is the main street in Austin and it begins at the State Capitol building. I figured we need a space of about 17 paces by about 6 or 7 paces. I came up with several potential sites. The spot that appealed to me most was 111 South Congress Ave., a beautiful site with good foot traffic in front of the Wells Fargo Bank. What drew me to it was a section of extra-wide sidewalk between two trees. I paced it off. It met our criteria. In fact, it was a beautiful site.

My daughter's father-in-law at the time, Doug Steele, was an executive vice president with Wells Fargo. I sent him a copy of the information packet I had presented to the Arts Commission, along with a request to share with me the name of a local Wells Fargo District Manager at the Congress Branch here in Austin.

Two weeks later, I got a call from Ms. Theresa Alvarez, head of the Community Relations Committee for the Regional Bank President Jeff Ferraris at Wells Fargo. She and I had an exploratory conversation. On learning that we wanted no money from her committee, she was taken aback. All we wanted was a letter of support, endorsing the concept of placing *The Home Coming* in front of the bank. She said, "That's the city's sidewalk. We don't have any control over it." Yes, I got that, but I still felt it was important to cover this base. She seemed to appreciate our overture. I mentioned, too, that House the Homeless, the statue project, and Ms. Alverez, who by then had insisted that I call her Theresa, became very enthusiastic about our mission and said she would submit our request to her committee, along with her recommendation that they should write the letter. Wow! This was awesome. Finally, I dared to hope again. She told me that we would have their answer within two weeks. During that time, I reached out to her two more times. First, I sent an elaborate email detailing what *The Home Coming* represented, emphasizing that it was not a monument to homelessness but rather a memorial for the folks we've lost. I also sent several of the House the Homeless plastic pocket guides—the double-sided, laminated Homeless Resource Information cards, in hopes that she would share them with her committee.

And what happened when the two weeks were up? Ms. Alvarez called to inform me that the committee's decision was not to write a letter of support. They were concerned about public opinion. I called back seeking to clarify whether the bank's non-support would end there or if it planned to actively oppose the placement of the statue on the public property outside its building. My call was not returned.

Yet Another Meeting

It had been several months since I'd heard from Laura Esparza of the Parks and Recreation Department, who had been working to form an exploratory committee. Having looked at the Austin parks system from a broader perspective, the department's landscape architect, Rey Hernandez, would gather a list of potential statue sites.

There were several phone and email exchanges involving Ms. Esparza, "Call me Maggie," and me. They were morphing from a simple working exchange into a full-blown PowerPoint presentation. The meeting would also involve Meghan Wells, the Art in Public Places administrator. Additionally, from the Austin Arts Commission were Maria "Lulu" Flores and Bruce Willenzik. House the Homeless was represented by board member Blythe Plunkett along with co-founder Cecilia Blanford and me.

Ms. Esparza led introductions, recapped *The Home Coming* application thus far, and set out the goals of the meeting. Right from the start, I could feel an ache sweeping across the back of my neck, slowly enveloping my head like a hand-twisted vise. The meeting had just started, but it was already running long, and my tolerance was running short.

According to "Call me Maggie," the PowerPoint included "glowing examples of wonderful homeless memorial projects" from around the country, like the Homeless Remembrance Project in Seattle; and the Andres Serrano photographs of New York residents. Also highlighted were Gordon Huether's "Windows" for the Bridge Homeless Center in Dallas and the Ground Cover Project in Phoenix. There was a passing mention of *Jesus the Homeless* by our sculptor, Timothy P. Schmalz, but none of the other examples really seemed relevant or comparable to our project.

The HtH people were not impressed. The Parks people and the Arts people, on the other hand, liked the nondescript touchy-feely approach so that "people could *imagine for themselves*" what homelessness meant to them. I was sure my head would explode any minute.

Bruce Willenzik, our bearded hippie from the Sixties, who had evolved into an extremely successful business entrepreneur (I assume from knowing what Austinites find appealing), felt *The Home Coming* was exactly what people wanted and needed. He embraced the stark realism of the statue and the greater likelihood that it would cause people to pause and reflect upon the actual condition of homelessness.

Chris Frank was not in favor of the statue and stated, "Veterans with Post Traumatic Stress Disorder would not be helped by viewing it." Well, as a U.S. Marine and Vietnam veteran who suffered PTSD, I can tell you this is exactly what I needed. Also, the Travis County Veterans Services Organization had already indicated its support for the statue.

Chris Frank, stated that "Austin doesn't want bronze art. They can't relate to it." After the meeting, I got his contact information because I wanted to share the names and locations of other bronze sculptures in Austin that people seem to appreciate. There is Angelina Eberly in her nightgown, poised beside a cannon with a lighting stick in her hand, braced for action, preparing to blow the hell out of a building to alert Austin citizens about a raiding party. The intruders wanted to move government archives to Houston and make it the capitol instead of Austin, and they might have succeeded if not for Angelina Eberly.

I would have pointed him to our famed statue of electric and electrifying guitarist, Stevie Ray Vaughan, just 75 yards to the west of the Homeless Memorial on Lady Bird Lake. And the statue of our brilliant, honorable, dynamic, and contemplative legislator Barbara Jordan at the Austin/Bergstrom Airport, where her bronze likeness greets travelers and visitors to Austin from all over the world.

I would have directed his attention to *Philosophers' Rock* at Barton Springs, which depicts J. Frank Dobie, Roy Bedichek, and Walter Prescott Webb, intellectuals who helped make Austin different from the rest of Texas. The *Austin Chronicle* named it the "Best Public Art" in the area. Its sculptor was Glenna Goodacre, who also created the Vietnam Women's Memorial in Washington, DC.

I would have focused his attention on the loving, energetic bronze statue celebrating the youth of Texas, at the state capitol. Had he returned my call, I would have directed him to the Vietnam veterans' memorial on the Texas State Capitol grounds, which shows five of our heroes, also cast in bronze, poised to defend our country.

Finally, when Chris Frank said bronze statues are only for people who have been dead for a long time, I would have focused his attention on the Willie Nelson bronze statue. In the heart of downtown, it represents our world-renowned vibrant music scene and draws scores of visitors every day. And oh yes, as of this writing, Willie Nelson is very much alive. *Know of that which ye speak before ye do* (Scottish proverb).

"Call me Maggie" said she thought the depiction of the African American woman was stereotypical. I told her that her remark was offensive to HtH and me. Bruce chimed in with, "An artist interprets a story." What I wanted to tell her was that she was offensive to anyone with common sense. I did not, however.

Lulu Flores said that she had reviewed the criteria for art gifts, and "nowhere does it say that the Arts Commission can call for a redesign of any project. It can simply accept or reject the project." I again asked for possible sites with high visibility and high foot traffic to be identified for the placement of the statue. Ms. Esparza said that Rey Hernandez should/could do that. We were told that we would all be re-contacted with the site options.

Almost two months later, Ms. Esparza called to say that Rey Hernandez had found a possible site and was now vetting it to other stakeholders, a group to which I apparently did not belong because this was news to me. Just two short nail-biting weeks later, she called again. "Mr. Troxell, I have good news and bad news. The good news is that we have found a location on the trail that is out of the flood plain, and we are all but finished vetting it through the various departments. The bad news is that the Parks Department, City of Austin does not own it. It belongs to a private corporation."

The land was owned by the Hyatt Regency Hotel, and I could contact the landscape architect for any other information. Next stop, Rey Hernandez, who sent me a Google map of the far northwest corner of the Hyatt's Barton Springs property. The site being considered was a 30' by 45' piece of richly green, beautiful land, slightly isolated by a buffer of greenery running along a mini stream. If *The Home Coming* ended up in that location, it would be only about 150 yards from HtH's Homeless Memorial along the same trail.

The choice of that site would allow us to leave the City's bureaucracy out of the vetting process and also avoid pushback from the Trail Foundation, a non-profit that claims authority over the entire trail in every detail. Its members want nothing on either side except grass and the boulders that prevent soil erosion. Another school of thought holds that even Mother Nature's beauty can be complemented by a little art. In any event, I scoured my 300-contact phone database and asked friends and strangers alike whether they know anyone in a decision-making position at the Hyatt.

Another week went by, and I was at City Hall meeting with Ora Houston, the only African American among the new City Council members. That was a good meeting, and after it, Vanessa Sarria, an old friend, seemed happy to run into me. "Got a minute?" she asked? I didn't really, but fortunately, Vanessa speaks quickly and gets to the point. She guided me into an upper-level conference room, saying, "You know I work for the Mayor now, and he wants to end homelessness for veterans. You're a Veteran, right?" she asked, "Marines?" I simply said, "Yes." Cheerfully, she asked, "I thought so. Tell me what you would do to reach out to the vets." I wasn't expecting the question, but it wasn't like I had to think about the answer. I told her I would create a Vet's program helping Vets in a safe place where the guys could go and hang out. "I'd call it USO—Stateside (or something similar). I'd fashion it after VFW clubs; I'd also involve the Vets themselves in deciding what should be there. I'd put in a couple of green felted, sound-cracking pool tables, mind-numbing video games, and rapid-fire foosball tables."

I'd create a "gedunk" for snacks, and I'd let the guy's outfit it with signs, flags, mementos...whatever. I'd get my friends Olie Pope, and George Ruiz involved. They are with Travis County Veterans Services (not the VA) and help vets solve problems.

I'd consult a former student of mine who works in Veterans' outreach. I'd set it up so the guys could watch videos as a group (small movie theatre). I'd let it get rolling for a while until the guys claimed it as their own. Once there was a core group, I'd let them know that someone who can talk about jobs is coming in on Tuesday, and someone else is coming in about job training on Thursday. I'd invite folks to join a group discussion around their needs when the time seemed right. I'd invite someone who can offer outside perspective and who might present some opportunities. I would reach out to local business entrepreneurs and get them to *offer the guys living-wage jobs*. I'd start to house them with City of Austin Housing Authority houses or apartments.

I would tell them about *The Home Coming*. I'd speak of respect and honor and how the Mayor is committed to helping get them off the streets. I suggested that the Mayor could make the statue his centerpiece, a show of commitment and real support for the guys. It would take a couple of years, and this could provide a worthy goal to aim for. The guys could get involved in promoting and even raising funds for the project. This would give them something beyond their own suffering to think about and engage in. Vanessa seemed intrigued. I told her I had to run, but I'd send her an email shaping my concept more fully.

Later, when she had gotten my email and a chance to think about it, she called to let me know that the new Mayor and his new staff were headed toward a retreat to discuss all the issues before them, including the ones we had spoken about. While she was at the retreat, Vanessa and I texted back and forth. She asked me to craft a letter to the Hyatt that would come from the Mayor. Elated, I immediately texted back that I would do it that same night.

After taking a deep breath and quickly gathering my thoughts, I called Sylvia's father, Eugene Stickley, a Harvard Business School graduate, to ask what general approach I should take. Should I release very little information and just seek to set up a meeting, or should I put all the chips on the table?

He said, "Everything, tell them everything...photos and all...just don't get long-winded," he cautioned. So that's what I did. I put it all out there. I sent the Google map of the Hyatt property, a photo of the patch of land, and a photo of the statute. It was a good letter...just not good enough. My thinking was, even if the Hyatt turned us down, if it pleased the Mayor to refer to the statue as the centerpiece of his campaign to end homelessness for Veterans, we would be on our way. To this day, I wait for a response.

Meanwhile, I heard back from Laura Esparza of the Parks Department. She and her boss had decided to go back to the first site they looked at. It was mentioned in a prior conversation, but since it was dropped before I even knew about it, I hadn't pursued the topic. But now it was on the table again, so I'd better pay attention. First, the location? She said it was on the southwest corner of Cesar Chavez, on the grass, behind the barrier. When I pressed her for clarity, she said, "You'll just have to see it. You'll just have to see it." At the repetition, my antennae shot straight up because it sounded like hemming and hawing.

The head of the Parks Department had chosen not to look with more intention at the Hyatt site because of a preference for the first site. Ms. Esparza tried to get off the phone, but I quickly slipped in, "I just have one question." "Yes?" "For what reason did Sara Hensley turn down the site location the first time?" "I don't know; I don't think she could fully envision it. We'll Google map it for her so she can get a better idea."

It was exciting that the Parks Department might possibly recommend an acceptable, visible, accessible site on the trail. Apparently, it was large enough for gathering, something both Laura Esparza and "Call me Maggie" were big on. This was another reason for my antennae to reach skyward like blades of grass after a cool summer shower.

It was the end of the regular workday, so I scooted over to the proposed site. The "barrier," as it turned out, was a heavy-duty industrial urban silver metal fence that allowed light to pass between its vertical spokes. In a large semicircle, the fence with a diameter of about 20' protected a viewing area housing two benches that rested on a cement slab. Like the fence, the whole bench/slab configuration had a cold industrial feel. The north side of the fence ran east and west parallel to the sidewalk along Cesar Chavez Street. On the south side of the semicircle lay a cement sidewalk feeder trail that descended the quickly sloping hillside and connected with the primary hike and bike trail about two hundred yards to the west.

Also, to the west of the half-circle lay a piece of flat ground that measured 25' running east and west and 20' north and south. I assumed this was the spot the Parks Department was suggesting.

That evening I brought Sylvia to the area. I tried not to shape her opinion one way or the other. We both felt that the site being at the corner of Cesar Chavez and Congress seemed ideal in concept. While it was not one of my core criteria, there was indeed room to gather. I asked Sylvia about the noise pollution level. She said, "Honey, this is getting to be a big city. No one hears the traffic but you." The question in my mind was, what is the point of having enough room to gather if you had to raise your voice to be heard? Then we drove to the Hyatt property, which was on the main trail. However, it was at the exact halfway point of the trail, where it seemed that most hikers turned back just before they would see the statue. On the other hand, this property was tranquil and separated from the Hyatt by a wall of greenery.

Statue advocates wanted high visibility and plenty of foot traffic. Within just a few minutes of arriving in the Hyatt space, three people had passed us. In contrast, during two visits to the Caesar Chavez/Congress area, not one single person had passed by on the trail spur. Both sites were adjacent to high-value hotels and exactly the kind of people that we wanted to expose to the statute, but only one site seemed to get foot traffic. But science requires a larger sample, so I decided to revisit each place, sit for a while and count heads. At Caesar Chavez/Congress, I met Elsye, a petite, gregarious, 50-something gal visiting Austin for the first time. Big sunglasses pulled back her thinning sandy-brown hair and exposed the gray roots. A nanny by profession, she was from Savannah, Georgia, doing reconnaissance for a family with two young children. Her 55-year-old husband, who worked for the railroad, was about to retire with excruciatingly painful rheumatoid arthritis.

Elsye was interested in "everything Austin," which was great from my perspective. I was already bored with the lack of traffic on my trail spur.

I pointed out various landmarks. There were the gently flowing Colorado River, the Miller dam to the west, and the Longhorn dam to the east. Our flooding had been in the news, leading me to explain that the dam workers often have to respond to a call in the middle of the night, in the middle of a raging storm, and must rush to *manually* open the flood gates, one of which broke in the closed position. When the river backs up, as it recently did, you get water in downtown Austin and a flooded Lamar Creek and Lamar Avenue.

Immediately in front of us was Congress Avenue, where a giant metal mobile sculpture of a bat is located. Although enormous, it spins in the slightest breeze. We pay homage to the bats because they live under the bridge, tens of thousands of them. Every night, families spread out their picnic blankets on the lawn of the *Austin American Statesman* building adjoining "the Bat Bridge." Folks watch in awe, as wave after sky-obliterating wave of bats roll off the bridge in search of the night's bounty—insects including mosquitoes by the ton. While talking, I infrequently clicked my people-counter and ended up having to explain. It all started with the statue and now rested at the need to choose between the two sites. My hour was up with 19 hikers entered into the database. Elsye wanted to come along to the Hyatt. Along the way, she insisted that we stop at the Homeless Memorial.

The plaque had some dirt on it from the recent flood, but not even enough to obscure the words. I brushed it clean, along with the Dr. Martin Luther King plaque. Elsye exclaimed, "This is the perfect place for the statute," and then repeated herself. Twice, she tells me this...twice. It was a little annoying to have salt rubbed into the emotional wound. "Yes, I know," I said. She would never have to confront the layers of meaning that only I knew hid behind those three words.

We walked 150 yards to the Hyatt site. When the trail opened up, I declared, "Here." She said, "Definitely. People can lay down their blankets and picnic here. You can even plant another tree." One hour later, my "people counter" clicked 680 people. The site preference was a no-brainer. Vanessa Sarria met with Sara Hensley, the head of the Parks Department. In response, I wrote this email. I sent her a shortened version at my wife, Sylvia's insistence. She tells me brevity is not my strong suit...go figure.

Mayor Steve Adler happened to also be an attorney specializing in adverse possession property rights. I contacted his assistant, Sly Magid, in a move to gently press the Mayor to reach out to the owners of the Hyatt Regency Hotel in Florida. I basically wrote the letter to Shelly Schadegg, and the Mayor reviewed it, signed off, and sent it on. I out-and-out asked for this isolated piece of property (about 600 square feet) to be given to our non-profit, House the Homeless, Inc. We also offered to purchase the property or lease it in perpetuity (see the full letter in the Appendix).

Another Bend in the Road

Mike Kelly, City of Austin and Texas state lobbyist, my good friend, neighbor, confidant, and member of the Statue Team of Professionals, learned that he had a terminal health condition and died about a week later. Shock...we all felt it. Everyone loved Mike. He was jocular, quick with the latest political story, and he was the ultimate deal maker. He knew about these stories as he was in the middle of them...advancing the action, finding the way forward, forging a compromise, and sealing the deal. His unexpected demise stunned all of Austin.

The wake was held at Threadgill's indoor/outdoor bar, restaurant, grill, and music venue, in the center downtown area just 300 yards south of the river and 200 yards south of the Homeless Memorial. Everyone was there—musicians, senators, lower-level politicians, city council members,

194

past mayors, advocates, deal brokers, young women, matronly women, friends of Mike from across time going back to his high school days. Efforts to prop Mike on the bar as is customary at a proper wake were deflected perhaps by the fire marshal but most likely by Teresa Kelly, Mike's college sweetheart, and wife. It was pure Austin. There was no room to sit and none would have. Story after story was told with gusto. The building was alive with Mike. He filled every corner of it. Stories circulated about how he had just closed a deal to save Threadgill's from a speculator's wrecking ball. A few people asked about the status of the epic tale of the statue, including the former Mayor's aide, Matt Curtis. "Trouble?" he asked. "No trouble...just bumps in the road. The last part of our initiative has only been a few years," I answered. He studied me for a long minute then pulled out a business card. It simply read: matt@smartcitypolicygroup.com. He offered, above the din of the room, "You do good work." I took the card. Due to the press of the throng, I had to look almost straight up at him as he is a full foot taller than me and said, "The statue belongs on Auditorium Shores at the Homeless Memorial of 24 years; I have no money." This time, without hesitation, he said, "We can do that." He offered me the world's largest hand, and we shook. Moments later, a flood of music enveloped us, and the room virtually floated with loud laughter, back-slapping, and well wishes once again. God bless Mike and Matt...and Mike again for having sent Matt so quickly.

Note—As I looked back over my shoulder, I could almost swear that I saw Mike Kelly on the bar among a throng of revelers, doing a little jig.

Matt and I met at the Homeless memorial. As we walked under the giant live oak tree that I had planted so many years before, I shared stories of the almost two and a half decades of memorials when we had laughed, cried, sung, listened to beautiful music of all kinds, prayed, read the names of our friends who we had lost that year and cried again. We sat on the HtH bench. We read the brass plaque:

> *Homelessness:*
> *It is the Essence of Depression,*
> *It is Immoral,*
> *It is socially Corrupt,*
> *It is an Act of Violence.*

The words had written themselves in under two minutes.

House the Homeless 1993

We admired the beautiful flowers that were always cared for. We read the words on the other plaque crediting Dr. Martin Luther King Jr., who wrote from the Selma, Alabama jail.

I pointed out the newly constructed wall the City allowed to be built in flood plain while forbidding our more secure statue in the same location. If the City and the Colorado River Authority were serious about protecting the citizens of Austin, they would live up to their moral obligation and repair the damaged, outdated flood gates at the Long Horn Dam. Then, there would be no flooding, and the whole issue would be moot. I pointed 125 yards to the west to the Stevie Ray Vaughan statue. It came with a lot of money. The Homeless Memorial came with only the hopes of the poorest of the poor.

We then headed east to the Hyatt Regency property. Matt immediately saw the potential and agreed with each of my observations. Still, there had been no response from the Hyatt people.

We walked to the site that I had named "The 3 Trees" that make an almost perfect triangle and fit the dimensions of the statue. "The 3 Trees" is located at the entrance to the park at 900 West Riverside Drive. This is the park road that leads to the trail past a gazebo designed and built by women. Only 125 yards south of the Homeless Memorial, it is not deemed to be part of the flood plain. Altogether, there are about 15 trees, and a particular grouping of three of them would be a very good site for our statue. Unfortunately, there was some intermittent ambient car noise. However, we could probably live with it, and the surrounding trees would protect the statue from any potential automobile damage to the statues. Matt again saw the potential but advised me to get letters of support for the existing memorial site since it remained our first preference. His other advice was, "Don't piss anybody off." I had to remind him that having that effect on other people is pretty much what I do. All of Austin knows this. As an advocate for the least among us, it seems to be part of the job. I knew what he meant, but often people mistake passion for scary.

On the other side of the entrance road was a fairly large fountain that had not been in operation for several years. When I met with Rey Hernandez, he also saw merit in this possibility but added some caveats. "Check with the Vets. I think they have plans for the site of the old fountain. The 3 Trees location could end up being part of a Parks Department master plan. Even if it's not, everything would be placed on hold while in that review process. Could be three or more years, no telling." He agreed to check on the status of that project.

In the meantime, I reported back to my Board of Directors, and Sylvia and I put together a PowerPoint focusing on *The Home Coming*. We also described in detail all of our projects involving the Plastic Pocket Guide, outreach projects, the Homeless Memorial, our citywide Jobs Program, *Let's Get to Work*, and of course, our Traumatic Brain Injury treatment project involving Veterans. Making a presentation before the Veterans' group, Sylvia and I were well received and applauded. We learned that there had been some talk about putting a veteran statue at the park entrance, but there were no real plans for the fountain area, and they had no objection to our statue, which included a Veteran, being located there. Matt continued to speak quietly to various people about the project while I kept looking for new site options. An interesting one was on Congress Avenue at Cesar Chavez. It was on the edge of the park and up out of the flood-plane. It was a few yards away from the Ann Richards memorial bridge. Oddly enough, building and street configurations had muted the ambient sound of the traffic. Its closest neighbor was the side of a motel across four lanes of traffic. It had great drive-by visibility, but it was only a fast glimpse. I brought Rey Hernandez out to see it, and he acknowledged that it was a possibility. (As far as I was concerned, it could always serve as a "throwaway.")

I continued to press Mayor Steve Adler on the Hyatt Regency property. Finally, his office located an intermediary who could check out the situation from the inside. The report was that the Hyatt had gone "radio silent." This means that no one would speak of the subject. I was officially told that it was now a dead end.

Over a few more months, we learned that the 3 Tree Site was indeed an area undergoing a Master Plan review, and we would have to wait for that process to conclude.

The Statue Is Cast!

A major component of homelessness is the disintegration of the family. Whether it is a major cause or a major result, it is certainly a major piece of the story of every person's homeless experience. And who hasn't heard, "Our dog Sparky is just like a member of the family"?

"Look at that poor dog! Why is it skinny? And that homeless guy can't feed himself, let alone a darned dog." This has been said or thought by every person who has never experienced homelessness. And yet, throughout my life, I have heard that a dog is a man's best friend. He'll protect you and love you unconditionally.

The experience of being homeless causes fear...fear of being arrested, fear of being shaken or kicked awake from a shallow sleep. Fear of being urinated on then tased while sleeping, as happened in Ohio repeatedly. Homelessness equates to fear of being arrested at any time, during the day or night, in any city or town USA for failure to pay a $200-$500 fine. Having lost everything, your job, your home, your family, you are ticketed for illegal sleeping, camping, loitering, being too close to an ATM machine, sitting down, or lying down no matter how bad your health condition has become. Then, when you can't pay the fine, you live in constant fear of being arrested for failure to pay the bench warrant. Then you sit and rot in jail because all these tickets have been elevated to criminal offenses, and there are no free lawyers anywhere in the entire US for offenses like criminal sleeping.

Remarkably, on more than one occasion, I've witnessed a police officer give a "criminal sleeper" a stern rebuke and a warning to "get the hell out of here" rather than be bothered with having to deal with locking up a homeless guy *and* having to then shelter his dog. Yes, love you *and* protect you.

Homelessness is wrapped in hatred. In Colorado, six separate incidents were blamed on gang initiations, where the candidate's acceptance depended on killing a homeless person. In Austin, a marauder terrorized down-and-out homeless sleepers when for weeks, their friend's skulls were crushed with massive stones while they slept. Perhaps when you heard about someone being doused in lighter fluid, then set on fire because he asked for some spare change, you became too apprehensive to ask for help from strangers. Do the basic research on how many homeless men have been set on fire, and it will make your head spin.

A dog has become a very important companion for many folks who are homeless. Dogs are pack animals, happiest when they are with other members of their pack, which includes people. Their love, loyalty, and defensive instincts apply to other members of their pack. I have known scores of homeless folks who have dogs and who hold them as their family. Be it a man or woman; they don't eat or drink until their dog has had a little something first. It's a respect thing and a show of affection. And many a time, I have known or heard of a person walking miles to a free veterinarian clinic to get their dog's nails clipped or for free shots.

I wanted to include a dog in the statue to take care of the little girl and for her to love. Timothy said, "Are you kidding me? This is a serious statue." I said, "Yes, it is...and it needs to be part of their story. I'll prove it to you."

I travel a lot, and wherever I go, I talk to people and listen to their stories. I kept hearing one story over and over again. Because women's shelters were not equipped to take dogs, many battered women faced a hard choice because if they left their dog behind, the abuser would take out his anger and frustration on the animal. I kept hearing, "I'm not leaving my other child with him." I started to share these stories with the shelter directors. In the end, I convinced Timothy to include Joey, a mangy, loving, protective, homeless dog in the statue.

I ran an informal survey around my legal aid office to test a theory that had been percolating in the back of my brain. The majority of people said that when making contributions to social causes, they always gave more, or sometimes double if the cause helped animals. I again shared this with the shelter directors, and lots of discussions got underway. The timing was perfect. In Austin, thanks to House the Homeless, a new women's shelter was being designed. Settled! Dogs could stay with their people.

And so, it was decided. The statue was poured and cast. Timothy and I had decided to create *The Home Coming* in three separate sections. The first was the African American woman, Ms. Anateen. The second was the fire barrel. The third crate would carry the veteran, John, his daughter Colleen, and her dog, Joey.

The statues were shipped on a slow boat from China, literally. It took months, and they went to Tim's warehouse in Wisconsin. This was exciting! Our incredible leap of faith was finally landing. Every step of the way, the project felt like a movie script written at the exact same time as the movie was being projected up on the screen.

In fact, the miniatures for which we had raised the $10,000 were launched just as we fully decided to include Joey and they were also being shipped to the Wisconsin warehouse with Joey in place.

To avoid warehouse storage costs, I had Linda of Timothy, Tony and Linda, send them to the church which houses the National Coalition for the Homeless in DC. When they came 95% of both statues halves were knocked off their bases in shipping.

The bases had been attached with industrial adhesive, but for that to work successfully, both the bases *and* the bottoms of the figures needed to be roughened first to give the adhesive something to grip. But only the bases had been scored, not the bottoms of the figures. The first application of adhesive would have to be scraped off, and the bonding process started anew. I was sure it would take me weeks or even months to rectify the problem for all 200 maquette, one figurine at a time. I negotiated a reduction in per-item cost and storage fees. House the Homeless has spent several months of weekends repairing the problem that continues to this day and begins each repair event driving to Washington to pick up another couple dozen miniatures and restart the repair process.

In the meantime, I continued to carry out certain tasks and gather various documents so Matt could position the statue project for another run at getting approval. House the Homeless had been at that site for almost 26 years and had one or more city-wide annual memorial events each year, and showing continuous care and numerous improvements such as two memorial plaques, the addition of our bench, and the planting of flowers throughout every year and caring for our glorious Homeless Memorial Tree. This project should be "grandfathered" in, as if the request had occurred and been accepted back in the beginning and before any of the excluding rules, regulations or laws, had taken place. Awesome!! He was going to pull it off! Matt sent me a series of emails titled "Going loud in a week." The whole homeless community was holding its breath.

Father and Daughter

Woman

Woman's Face

Father's face

The memo was dated October 7, 2018. Then nothing. Absolutely nothing happened. No announcements came. No more emails were sent, and no phone calls came, and no phone calls were returned.

Then one day, a month later, I saw Matt Curtis across Congress Ave. Our gazes locked just for the briefest instant. He pretended not to see me and turned away. I knew then that he had been shut down. Was it the head of the Parks Department or the head of the business community? Perhaps an unknown. It didn't matter. The force was overpowering, and it was done. We didn't need to invest more years in chasing that rabbit. We might never know who had wielded that that much power. But we did know that Matt Curtis would not ride into Austin on a white horse and save the day. He was never going to be that guy, the guy who can solve any problem. No one would speak of it, but everyone would know. His political trajectory was no longer arching up. He had run into a buzz saw, and he hadn't been able to overcome it or be man enough to tell me to my face. I have always hated the no-response response.

On November 18, 2018, I was standing in the Fannie Davis Town Lake Gazebo just next to the Homeless Memorial on Lady Bird Lake. It was our 26th annual ceremony to remember our fallen friends. After the solemn part came social time, with a lot of hopeful people talking about how we would tackle homelessness in the coming year. Next to me was Alan Graham, founder of Community First! Village. He asked how things were going with the statue placement. I said, "You know." After a beat, he said, "We'd love to have it. We'd put it in the ground." I appreciated the offer but expressed my doubt. At that site, we would just be preaching to the choir.

Then Alan did what a friend does; he went the extra mile. He offered a patch of Village ground as a showcase for *The Home Coming*. I could ship everything over there, uncrate the figures, set them up on their would-be subterranean platforms. The people, including those who ran all the councils and commissions and departments, could see how it looked in real life, up close and personal. Maybe they would change their minds.

Timothy's office was frequently asking about when the storage payment would arrive, and there may have been other factors that caused the HtH Board of Directors to see some benefit in erecting the statues at Community First! Village. So that's what we did. There was no formal fanfare, but there was a greeting party of sorts. A couple of formerly homeless guys now living at the Village stopped to exchange greetings. "Richard, how the hell are you? I'm living in paradise. Man, you saved my life," Tom said as he pumped my hand. I could feel the smile on my face pulling back across my teeth.

From Wildman Willie came, "Hey Richard, welcome to our home! Man, you did it. You got me my disability check, and everything fell into place. What have you got there? Is that the homeless statue? Man, I heard about it. That's awesome!" For the rest of the day, people came up in twos and threes and introduced me to their dogs and extended invitations. "Come see my home. It's a tiny house!" "Come over; I want you to see my trailer. It's really cool." The pride of ownership, the pride of accomplishment, was downright palpable. And they were so thankful, "Man, you got me here. I love you, man." They were always generous with their thanks. I would praise Alan, and they would always envelop me in their thanks. I thought about what had been accomplished at the Village, all the battles, the overcoming of NIMBYism (Not in My Back Yard). The place was full of projects and opportunities like the art center, where the artists keep all the proceeds of their sales. The complex included a hair salon, an auto shop, a community garden, a community chapel, and a blacksmith shop, and so much more.

And there were the intangibles, the health and growth opportunities offered by the sanctuary, friendship, help, comfort, peace of mind, and so very much more for all the lost souls...My friends, and then it happened again. I felt a glow of awareness surround me. It felt like my brain expanded throughout my body and my eyes filled with tears, and a single tear found its way down my face just as it had for Ms. Anateen. And just like Ms. Anateen, I felt a small prayer pass from my lips, "Thank you, Jesus." And in that moment of overwhelming joy, it was decided to plant the statue here at Community First! Village. Then, for one split second I that I would do it all over again. After we placed this statue at the Village, there would be another statue. I would take it to Washington, DC, and like the angel Moroni who pointed to Salt Lake City for the Mormons, our statue would point back to Community First! Village, and we would show the nation's mayors and the people of America and the world how to treat all our brothers and sisters with love and respect. We would invite them to come and experience the Village. We would show them how to love the disabled and the abled, and we would preach family and kindness to one another, and we would show everyone how to help others who have less, and how they can help their brothers and sisters live with dignity and fairness. But I wasn't sure. The hill had been so tall, so many battles, so much opposition from supposed helpers. I just wasn't sure. So much hate.

I returned to Community First! Village and introduced myself to Larry Crawford, the Director of Maintenance and Repair, a gray-haired, goateed white man in his mid-50s with a great smile. He is a known solver of problems that involve mechanical things. So, when I shared with him Gary Jaster's blueprint for the subterranean mumbo jumble re-bar, he studied it for about a third of the time that I did and said, "Sure, I can do it." I told him I wanted to be involved. I would pull my weight, and I wasn't interested in investing any more money in this part of the project. He simply adjusted his response to "Sure, we can do it."

In the past, both Larry and his wife worked at jobs where they brought in six figures. After he retired, they lived in a trailer park in Houston, where he was pulling down $90,000 doing odd jobs as a certified RV repair guy. One day, he was on the internet watching 4-wheeler dirt bikes ripping through a mountainside. The video ended, and he clicked on the one next to it. This old guy in a ball cap was walking through the woods looking at a set of plans...to build a village...for homeless folks. What?! He and his wife looked up Mobile Loaves and Fishes and read all sorts of "cool" stuff about this Village that this guy Alan, and some other folks, wanted to build. The information source included a "help wanted" ad for an RV repair guy. Larry's wife sent in a resume for him. He jumped in his truck and started driving to Austin. While on the way, he got a call-back for an interview on Tuesday. It was Monday. Larry said he thought he could do that. He was hired on the spot. His wife quit her job. Larry told me he felt it was a "God thing."

He wasn't interested in the money part. (He was already making $13 an hour, which of course, at the time was the minimum wage according to my website calculator for the Universal Living Wage standard for Austin, Texas.) Inspired by Larry's story, with typical urgency, I said, "Great, when can we start?" His equally-excited comeback was "Now. Let's pace it off." It was 17' from the back of the veteran's heel to the back of the old woman's heel. We drew the foundation pads in the dirt. They landed exactly on the edge of the garden. This would need to be cleared with Heidi Sloan, Director of Genesis Gardens for the Village.

I returned at 9:00 the next morning to meet with Ms. Sloan. She said, "Step on nothing, touch nothing." She drew a line two feet north of where Larry and I had marked the anticipated pad area. Something about her manner communicated to me that this was the new position of the statue. Clearly, I could live with that.

The statues finally arrived, and Larry and I placed them still, fully crated, standing upright on their ground positions. Using a front-end-loader, we positioned them as best we could. It all seemed okay. So, we uncrated them and laid them down. We set their proper orientation to one another, noting that they were not squarely orientated on their own subterranean bases. Both were off by approximately 10-15% each if their eyes and gaze were to align. It was a bit of a challenge and some heavy work, but we got them lined up pretty well.

I had to go and coordinate the arrival of more miniature statues. Using Gary Jaster's blueprints, Larry coordinated the subterranean tidily-wink, rebar construction. Finally, the concrete was poured over the iron configuration for the pads. On the third day, after the pads were poured, we did a good bit more work involving diamond drill bits, an air hose, and quick-setting industrial epoxy and only had to re-drill four holes.

We sweated out copious amounts of last night's beer and used most of our energy drilling the holes and getting through the anxiety of shooting the epoxy into the holes, hoisting each statue with the front end of the tongs on the Fork Lift, crawling under the forks and the statue sections hanging over our heads and guiding the rods into the epoxied holes. We took a 15-minute breather, giving Larry an opportunity to share his observation that people like to collect things and "tend to simply expand their space relative to their new needs or wants." He's right. No matter what we are talking about, 99% of Americans seem to ultimately want *more* of whatever they already have, if they like it: more money, more food, more drinks, more things, more children, more time off, etc. People experiencing homelessness seem, once again, to be no different.

The next day, gravel was delivered, and we raked it around the base of the statues but not covering their feet. In this way, my vision of having these regular folks walking on the surface of earth, not on a pedestal, is accomplished.

Cook-Walden/Capital Parks Funeral Home has been generous to Austin's homeless community for decades. When I called, they were delighted to hear of our project. They checked their warehouse and donated two beautiful, one-foot cube granite blocks to which they added a slant cut to receive the two acknowledgments plaques that I was having prepared. "Major contributors include Jeff Serra, Eric Anderson, Dan Vogler, Cielo Property Group, Gary Jaster, Cook-Walden Funeral Home, and all the Regular Folks who care so deeply." We cannot thank all of you enough.

The Unveiling!

We handed out invitations to "the guys" for a month and a half. House the Homeless went through years of contact and activity lists, official surveys, and support letters. I went through my personal phone contacts, and we all gathered names for invitees to the statue unveiling for May 18, 2019. But Alan tapped the brakes. Because the second half of the CF!V acreage was under construction, front-end loaders, bulldozers, and dump trucks were everywhere. He felt we should limit this viewing to dignitaries. While I totally understood, I was a bit disappointed. After all, the statue is intended for the guys and to tell their story.

As it turned out, I shouldn't have worried. The night before the event, we were informed that a serious storm was coming. The weatherman predicted lots of rain (our parking was on dirt fields, soon to be deep mud) and hail the size of golf balls! Even I did not want to take my truck out in that! I called Larry and asked him to set up "beanbag" barriers to divert water away from the statue gravel yet hold it in place. He said he would. In the morning, I loaded up the truck with my share of stuff for the event. I stopped in the darkness when the earth stands still and hasn't started spinning yet. I asked Jesus to bless us and our event. Then, I caught myself. I guess I even smiled a bit. I'm still very new to this Jesus thing. But then it occurred to me that it was not my event or even our event. Without really letting it crystallize in my thoughts...I am just along for the ride. *"And whether or not it is clear to you, no doubt the universe is unfolding as it should."*—Desiderata

The people came. The sun shone. The gracious Amber Fogerty, MLF Chief Goodness Officer, warmed us with her smile and her words. Donald Whitehead, then President of the National Coalition for the Homeless and my decades-long friend, spoke about our beloved Dr. Martin Luther King Jr. and the struggle for peace and kindness among all people. Reflecting on the statue, he spoke eloquently about Langston Hughes and his question, "What happens to a dream deferred?" And Donald answered, "Nothing...it just waits for its time," alluding to the statue and with spreading arms, all of Community First! Village. Alan, my brother-by-a-different-mother, referred to my advocacy as the "Tip of the Spear" fighting for our people and recalled my original vision for the Austin homeless village 20 years before, my civil rights battles on behalf of Austin's and the nation's homeless folks over the past 30 years. I grew quiet inside.

Then Will Hyatt, another brother and HtH Board of Directors member, unfurled the tarps covering the statues. You knew that gathered people were clearly moved. Then Congressman Lloyd Doggett came to the podium and called for Mayor Steve Adler, City Council Member Jimmy

Flannigan, Alan Graham, and me to come forward to hold the American flag. He told us it had flown over the United States Congress on the day he read a proclamation honoring Alan and me and then presented it to the two of us. It felt like a very powerful moment to me, and blood pounded on the inside of my skull.

House the Homeless had given Congressman Doggett and his wife Libby a set of the maquettes to honor their years of service and dedication to the homeless community. He seemed a bit taken aback to see the actual statues. He kept looking back and forth from John the veteran and his daughter Colleen, and her dog Joey, to Ms. Anateen. He said, "When I look at these statues, I'm reminded of the great naturalist, John Muir, who said, 'Everybody needs beauty as much as they need for bread, places to play in and pray in, where nature may heal and give strength to the body and soul.'" Pausing, he went on to add, "That is what these statues represent to Austin."

When I spoke, I briefly told the story of the people represented in the statue. There is John the veteran, who represents 1/3 of all people experiencing homelessness in America at that time. With him is his daughter, Colleen, representing a million homeless children. The average age at that time, (circa 2013) was nine years of age. They have stopped at a fire barrel that has been recently been abandoned. Coming from out of the woods is Ms. Anateen, an African American woman. Her husband, in his late 50s, was laid off in the downturn. Unable to find work, and too ashamed to return home, he simply gave up and was swallowed up by the streets. With no one to pay the rent, the two surviving daughters headed out into the world. Ms. Anateen, broken-hearted and penniless, gathered what she could carry of her belongings and walked out the door. When people see her on the street, they refer to her as a "bag lady."

Standing at the fire barrel on a cold Texas night, John, quickly becomes lost in his own reverie as he stares into the fire. His dreams of "America the Beautiful" have been betrayed. He sacrificed his youth and in thanks, only gained the aching hollowness left behind by the loss of his brothers. He will go on because he has true grit. But he is shopworn. Yes, he is angry, but he swallows his anger for his daughter. His anger has been supplanted with the drive to bring his daughter into a better world if he can only find it. His gaze is lost staring into the fire, as happens to people late at night at the end of a very, very long day...or after years of searching for "the promised land."

The interaction is between the old woman and the child. The child sees her first, because, in spite of everything, her spirit remains alive and vital. The old woman is defeated. She may well have partial cataracts following decades of lacking a good diet or medical care. She has lost everything. She raised three children. One is now dead, and two are blowing in the wind. Her husband, having been laid-off, just left one day and never returned. She is in the absolute darkness. Suffering chronic depression, she trudges. She is coming from nowhere and is going nowhere. When she first sees the flicker of the firelight in her upper vision, she is not sure of the shadowy figures behind it.

The little girl sees the old woman as a possible companion, who may know the secrets that the future holds for her. They are reflections of one another's past and future. The girl is desperate to strike a spark only found between two gals...the little girl coaxes the old woman as if calling a puppy, to the camp. "Come on, come on," she coaxes. To herself, the woman is barely audible, "I'm so cold. I'm so tired."

The old woman, drawn closer to the camp, is still hard-pressed to see and understand the intentions of the man and the child. John feels the stirring of his little girl, and is roused from his daze. Looking at the little girl and then following her gaze, he sees the old woman and realizes his daughter's desire to welcome the old woman into their camp. He pauses, then immediately follows suit and beckons the old woman to the warmth of their fire, "Come on ahead, old woman. All are welcome here." Haltingly, the old woman closes the gap between them, and then she freezes. The essence of the moment envelops her. She is being welcomed into their camp...their home. She is being beckoned...welcomed home...no questions. She is emotionally and physically overwhelmed. Her satchels... her burdens, drop the last inch to the ground. There is a look of awe, wonderment, relief, joy. Her hand goes over her heart. A tear rolls down her cheek. The energy release can be seen in her shoulders...her entire being. A prayer escapes her lips, "Thank you, Jesus."

The statue is called *The Home Coming*. I tell our people that it is the true story of homelessness that gets told by their actions every day when folks living on the street offer acts of kindness to one another. It is when people who have nothing share, what little they have...the warmth of their fire, and their humanity.

Suddenly, a gust of breeze blew across the crowd. As if on cue, the band started playing. The children ran through the dignitaries laughing and squealing as they scooted past the formerly homeless people, the groups of old friends reuniting. People lovingly stroked the statue figures; John the veteran, Ms. Anateen, Colleen, and of course, Joey, who got her face kissed a lot. Elected officials had their pictures taken with an arm around John. Colleen and Ms. Anateen got hugged a lot as well. Everyone had come alive. People were eating hot dogs with yellow mustard and relish and telling stories. We all felt the camaraderie. We knew at that moment, that everything good is possible in the world, and we stood as one, united. And it was then that it was fully decided that there would be as second statute. After all, I was on a long journey and I had learned that in my life Jesus is the decider.

P.S. Having then raised the funds for a second statue, getting it cast, shipped to a warehouse in Washington DC, surviving the Covid-19 Pandemic, I received a forwarded email on May 10, 2021 that was sent to Monsignor Enzler, the head of Catholic Charities in Washington, DC. It came from Monsignor Rossi who is in charge of the Basilica of the National Shrine of the Immaculate Conception. The missive announced that the request has *gone through the process*. My application to place the *Home Coming* statue on the grounds of the Catholic University just outside of the entrance of the Basilica has been accepted by the Plant and Facilities and Iconography Committees. On July 1, 2021, Sylvia and I again traveled to Washington and met with Monsignor Rossi. I am to make a presentation before the U.S. Conference of Catholic Bishops for final acceptance of the Home Coming statue. If successful, a QR code placed in the plaque will virtually transports the viewer to Community First! Village in Austin, Texas so they and all the Mayors across America are invited to visit and see *national best practices* of how we as a nation should take care of our homeless/disabled brothers and sisters.

14 Community First! Village

Housing Our Nation's Homeless Folks Who Are Struggling with Disabilities

At the close of the unveiling ceremony, I pause and tell the folks that the vision is not complete. I tell them that with their help, I will create another statue, a national statue, and I will travel to Washington, DC, and find a home for it in a prominent place. I tell them that with their help, we will place a QR code at the base of the plaque. I tell them that when people see it, they will use the app on their smartphone and click on it. They will learn the backstory of our homeless family, and Alan will invite our nation's mayors to Community First! Village.

Then, they will see Alan Graham standing in front of the first, identical statute on their screen, telling them all about Community First! Village. It is a dream of mine that began at Bergstrom Air Base that devolved. Then, the dream resurfaced and evolved when fighting some of the same forces; Alan Graham, my brother in peace, picked up the torch and battled city government and wave after wave of NIMBYism until the people united by the power of love for justice, homeless folks, and Jesus came together to create Community First! Village. Men, women, and children have forged 52 acres into a community of goodness that empowers the dream that embraces dignity and fairness for our fellow human beings who have lost everything.

As you watch the video displayed by the QR code you will hear Alan invite all of our nation's mayors to come to Austin and Community First! Village, stay in a tiny house, eat from the community garden, observe the blacksmith shop in action, visit the hair salon, the automotive service-shop, go to the outdoor movie theater, stay at the Community Inn Bed and Breakfast, visit the community mental health facility, visit the grocery store where art made by the residents is sold, and all proceeds go to those very same residents. Stop and participate in House the Homeless adopt-a-tree facility design program. Visit Unity Hall, the Central Village Community Center. Stop at the mini-chapel and offer a prayer of thanks for all you see. Speak with the resident members of the Village Council. See the shared eating facilities throughout the village. Learn about Community Works, the micro-enterprise program that offers job opportunities. You will meet missionaries who have come to live in the village and share their life experiences and skills. Alan says that Community First! Village is a *blank slate,* and the people can draw on it. I know this to be true because he encourages each of us to continue to draw on it, and we do so all the time. It is truly a collective effort. In the words of Reverend Jesse Jackson, "If my mind can conceive it; my heart can believe it; I know I can achieve it."

Community First! Village Micro Homes

Sylvia and Me

As for Sylvia and me, we have both semi-retired to complete our portion of this vision by placing the second statue and writing this book. I still sit on the Board of Directors of the National Coalition for the Homeless. I am now the National Education Director for House the Homeless, and I travel back and forth between Austin, Texas, North Carolina (where we have moved Sylvia's parents), and Washington DC. Sylvia and I made COVID-19 protective masks and supplied them to folks.

Funds for the second statue have been raised. It is all paid for and has been delivered to a warehouse in the Washington, DC, area. We are in discussions with the proper people to help us secure that prominent place that it deserves. COVID-19 has slowed the process, but we expect to have things sorted out by the end of 2021. Plan to be with us for the Washington, DC, unveiling of the 2nd version of *The Home Coming*, when it points to Austin, Texas, and the National Best Practice: Community First! Village.

The END of the beginning.

15 Veterans in Action

Traumatic Brain Injury

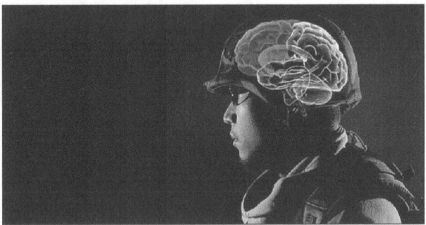

TBI Soldier's Brain

It is proposed to collaboratively engage appropriate participants to administer an initiative to serve homeless veterans in significant recovery from traumatic brain injury, TBI.

For 18 years, House the Homeless has collaborated with Austin's homeless population to learn what affects them and what they need to end and prevent their homelessness. Based on my direct daily field interaction with people experiencing homelessness, I created a different survey each year. The 2010 HtH Health Survey told us that 47% (or about half) of people experiencing homelessness are so disabled that they cannot work.

A Client's Case Had Me Stumped! In 2013, a man in his mid-40s came to my office expressing the inability to work anymore. He was seeking disability benefits which is one of the services that I have provided for the past three decades plus. He was affable, and on the surface, he seemed quite fit. Recently, he had been relatively successful as a master plumber. His articulation failed him in expressing the problem, but through repeated discussion, I realized that he had trouble thinking clearly. He had what's called working memory failure, which is when the short-term memory, attention span, and the ability to manipulate information can't all get together and cooperate.

As far as he could remember, his history did not include any significant injury. No car accident, no exposure to poison, no alcohol or drug abuse, or glue huffing. No near-death drowning, no inexplicable periods of blacking out, no major electrical shock, never zapped by a taser, never tapped out while wrestling. But clearly, something was wrong. Eventually, I learned that he had played football in high school. He had never been carried off the field on a stretcher or sidelined by a doctor, or taken away in an ambulance. Still, I sensed that this was the key. His good-natured attitude, willingness to please others, size, and ability to stop an opponent as a competent high school linebacker led me to further research the issue. While there was no single event that Bubba could recall, he had gotten his "bell rung" so hard, and so many times, without proper recovery between events, that now, 20 years later, he was quite possibly displaying signs of the little-known condition of chronic traumatic encephalopathy, known as CTE.

Chronic Traumatic Encephalopathy, CTE

When the brain is struck significantly without rest, followed by other minor traumas, it cannot fully recover. In fact, without the simple rest that one might provide for a sprained ankle, events can occur that set the law of entropy in motion. There is no readily available test to prove this in a living patient because CTE can only be diagnosed after death by slicing and dyeing the brain. The research, the preponderance of evidence, and the existence of multiple symptoms enabled me to win my argument. On the day when the NFL settled their historic Traumatic Brain Injury contract with their players, we won disability benefits for our man even though he had a "significant" work history after the date of injury.

Hypothesis—TBI Is Linked to Homelessness

Over the years, I had noticed similar situations among other folks. On January 1, 2016, House the Homeless, Inc. once again geared the annual survey toward health and specifically targeted the subject of Traumatic Brain Injury (TBI). The results were amazing. Of the homeless folks who took the survey, 47% said they were too disabled to work. We had listed 26 different symptoms typical of TBI, and 80% of those folks had at least one of those symptoms, if not several. It was at this point that I formed the hypothesis that perhaps the majority of disabled people experiencing homelessness had gotten to that point in their lives due to a traumatic brain injury. I reached out to John Lozier, a friend and past fellow board member of the National Coalition for the Homeless. He had gone on to serve as Executive Director of the National Health Care for the Homeless,

212

which coordinates the homeless healthcare clinics around the nation. That organization joined with HtH to disseminate nationally a joint press release describing the survey's findings.

Dr Mark Gordon's Medical Protocol

As a result, I learned of the Millennium Health Centers, Inc. in Encino, CA, and specifically of Dr Mark Gordon, who had conducted decades of research on TBI. He discovered that when the brain is traumatized and neural pathways are disrupted, the body responds with an upsurge of site-directed hormones. Using this information, he designed a protocol that he has been using to treat our veterans from the Vietnam, Iraq, and Afghanistan Wars. He collaborated with Green Beret Andrew Marr, an Iraq War veteran, who a short time before had been on 13 high-powered medications, drinking heavily, and in extreme danger of losing his marriage. After treatment with the Gordon Protocol, Andrew is off all medications, no longer drinking, and at peace in his life and his marriage. He heads the Warrior Angels Foundation, created in collaboration with Dr Gordon, which treats and helps veterans.

After a series of emails and lengthy conference calls, we formed a team that shares my hypothesis that quite possibly, a significant percentage of people experiencing homelessness got there because of TBI. Furthermore, they have never before been asked about that possibility. No one has ever suggested to them that the symptoms they suffer from—anger, alcoholism, Parkinson's Disease, bipolar disorder, bad decision-making, etc.—may be directly related to a head injury.

When researching Dr Mark Gordon's studies, reports, background, and web interviews, I learned this about the success rate attributed to his approach: "In 98% of the cases, we see from 50% to 100% reduction in the symptoms."

Given their severity, *the reversal of **even one** of these symptoms can greatly improve the lives of our constituents.*

In addition to his numerous publications, Dr. Gordon created a certification program to train and accredit medical clinicians in his protocols, which reduce inflammatory chemicals, replenish deficient brain hormones, and re-establish a healthy neuro-permissive environment conducive to allowing the brain to heal. To achieve the highest degree of healing, he emphasizes the need to improve not only the patient's brain but the external environment in which they are being treated.

Proposal: Treat Ten Homeless Vets for TBI at CF!V

I have shared with Dr. Gordon and Mr. Marr information about Community First! Village and its founder, Alan Graham. I have since reached out to Alan, whom I have collaborated with for over a decade by sending him financially and medically eligible recipients. He has been able to house them using just the small check that I have been able to get the government (SSI stipend) to provide.

One of HtH's previous surveys showed that, of the people experiencing homelessness in the Austin area, 28% are Veterans. Pursuant to our lengthy discussions and having visited the Village, Dr. Gordon and Mr. Marr have agreed to expand their treatment to include *homeless* Veterans.

Alan has now also agreed to the creation of a program to be operated under the name Homeless Veterans in Action as part of Community First! Village. CF!V, House the Homeless, Mobile Loaves and Fishes, Millennium Health Centers, the Warrior Angels Foundation, and local medical doctors will come together to create a first-of-a-kind, ongoing program for ten homeless veterans to specifically treat their TBI.

All we need now is start-up funding.

Community First! Village Contact Information
9301 Hog Eye Road, Suite 950
Austin, TX 78724
512-328-7299
Hours: 8 am - 5 pm
Website: http://mlf.org/community-first

16 Solving Alcohol Addiction Treatment Costs

"One More for the Road"

I'm not sure that anyone has escaped having their life affected by alcohol use or abuse in some way or another. It seems like all of us have known someone whose life has been touched by the velvet/leathery glove of alcohol. If by some miracle, you scooted by without being brushed, you're welcome to skip this chapter. I don't expect to lose many readers this way having been scraped up pretty badly myself.

I've been told that my father, Richard Regnier Troxell, reached the rank of captain in the U.S. Navy before most others his age. In the early 1960s, he was also a U.S. Naval Ambassador to the Royal Canadian Dental Corp, and as such, he was tapped as President John F. Kennedy's dentist. He ran the dental facility in Bethesda, Maryland Naval Hospital. He later became an integral part of the U.S. Naval Defense Medical Materiel Board. I remember clearly when he came home to describe to my mother how a gentleman had brought him a tiny shining light protruding from a bendable wire. This would seem to have broken a major law of physics. The gentleman wanted to know if the U.S. Navy might have any use for what he called "fiber-optics."

Otherwise, I know little about my father. I did know that among his favorite casual reading was a series of books about Captain Horatio Hornblower, a U.S. Navy war captain on the high seas, and I learned through my mother that my father's greatest dream was to become an admiral. Most communications about and from my father came through my mother. Note. Remarkably, it was not until the writing of this book that I learned that the desire to be an Admiral was an effort to find praise in his mother's eyes.

Charged with a Task

I only remember one actual conversation with my father. On my 12th birthday in 1963, I was told to "report" to his home office, the inner workings of which I had only glimpsed on rare occasions. White-glove inspections to detect dust were routinely and rigidly scheduled there on Saturday mornings, after cleaning detail, as my two sisters and I well knew. Still, he might try to spring one of those on me—but I was prepared.

He closed the door behind me and took a seat behind his desk, and I stood in front of it. He handed me a box, about 12" long and 4" wide and 1 ½" deep. It was covered in red leather. On the lid, embossed lettering spelled out the initials RRT. I was instructed to open the box and found a folded sheet of *parchment* paper.

Dear *Son...*

The first of the two paragraphs was much longer than the second. The first contained the name of Adolf Hitler and the statement that he had attempted to rule the world. The letter explained that Hitler had started his political career with stump speeches. Around him, he had bracketed himself with a couple of young men; they were boys really, who armed themselves with old pistols and rifles. The speeches were loud and directed angrily at a government that would allow there to be no jobs for them while others prospered. The speeches were described as loud, hostile, and galvanizing. Government officials soon took Hitler's weapons from him. In their place, he gave his "men" knives such as the one I found beneath the parchment that seemed to be gaining weight at that very moment.

Nazi Youth Knife

Visually, the knife is stunning, powerful. It has a gleaming stainless-steel shaft that 4" later, seamlessly melded into a finger stop. When I was told to "pick it up," it fit my hand perfectly and rested against the top edge of my right index finger. Incredulously, I felt a surge of energy emanating from it. In retrospect, I'm sure it was a feeling of dread. What was happening here?

Making up the "grip" was a 2 and 5/8" long black resin plate, etched by a tightly-knit, crisscrossing, slide-resistant raised pattern. It is held in place by two rivets that extend to and through a similar backplate. Inset into the front plate is the outline of a parallelogram. At each end of the ¾" parallelogram are two diamond-shaped insets that reflect red. At the side of the diamond shapes are two smaller, squat, flat, diamond facings. The focus of the design, set in the very center of the grip, is a jet-black swastika set in a small brown square. My vision began to telescope in and out. I could not focus. Quietly, I was instructed to "Remove the scabbard." A snap on the dried leather attachment held the steel scabbard.

I tugged, and it released. I removed the knife. Deeply etched into the blade in cursive script were three words, which I immediately knew were German. "Blut und Ehre!" came my father's German-accented words, piercing my absolute concentration. "Blood and Honor!" They were the most powerful words I'd ever heard. Dick Troxell intoned those words like an army that had cut a swath across Europe in a ruthless desire to control all of mankind. My ears rang. Almost inaudibly, he said, "Finish the letter." "On this your 12th birthday, it is now your charge and duty to prevent such madness from ever rising again."

Almost compassionately, my father asked, "Do you understand?" "Yes," was all I could answer. I had only the vaguest idea as to what that meant, or how the moment would shape my life. Then, as an afterthought, he offered, "Good. Happy birthday." I really can't remember, but I guess I was dismissed.

A Glimpse of Poverty—The Awakening

With that conversation came the closing of the door to my youth, and something changed deep inside of me. I suddenly wanted to know about the world and developed an intense focus. I got my mother to stop paying me in marbles for work done; I saved every penny and bought a used Schwinn bicycle. I rode it into Washington, DC, every chance I got. and saw all the monuments and some of the slums and looked hard at both. These were some damn poor people. I tried to make sense of it and remembered the "White Only" and the "Colored" water fountains of Wappoo, South Carolina of my still younger days, and it all flooded my brain and everything that I saw after that, was through a different lens. Something horrible had happened to these people. What was it?

As a high-ranking US Naval officer serving as U.S. Ambassador to the Royal Canadian Dental Corps, my father was bound to observe certain protocols and fulfill certain expectations. My mother was expected to be a dutiful military wife, raise several children, socialize like a proper officer's wife, and follow all the rules, both explicit and implicit.

In whatever housing we were assigned, she would work in the yard and grew flowers with the accompanying hand of God. For her children and others, she designed and made clothes. Her position demanded frugality, but that virtue was already in her Scots-Irish blood. In 1919 in Gary, Indiana, Janette McHattan was born on the dirt floor of her mother, Ethel McHattan's root cellar, an indicator of the spartan life ahead of her. My mother survived a car wreck that took her father and left her, her mother, and two sisters to face the echoes of the Great Depression alone. Although the subject was ancient history for most, I heard about it in infinite detail throughout my life.

My grandfather's death must have produced some family income as Janette struck out to put her mark on the world. She attended the Vogue School of Design, where she learned to sew and make clothes, and even secured a U.S. patent for a maternity dress properly with pleats that could be easily released one at a time as needed. As the expectant mother gained in size, the dress would continue to fit her and look good at the same time. My mother was quite clever.

As a student, she was 4'11" with short hair, her mind was as sharp as a newly honed knife, a twinkle in her eye, a ready laugh; and later admitted to being "cute as a button" with "shapely gams." One day, then-Lieutenant JG Dick Troxell entered her life, and only five minutes after my mother and my father met, he was "smitten with the likes of her."

They were drawn to each other like magnets. They became young military swingers. They partied and laughed and enjoyed the hell out of each other and social drinking. However, when the lieutenant found out that she had another serious suitor, he approached his commanding officer and asked for leave "to marry her or forget her." It was a military wedding, and the party continued. He got stationed in Guam in the South Pacific, where my older sister, Lynn, was born. I came next, and then my baby sister, Gail, joined the household, and the party continued.

However, while having children was required in order to rise within military ranks, my father perceived them to be "tiny adults." He saw them as under-developed and not yet grown to the point where they had anything of value to add to any conversation. My father had been an only child, and so he had no siblings to learn social graces with. He was from the school that believed that "children should be seen, but not heard." When my father would arrive at the end of the day in the early evening, my mother, Jan, would greet him with a couple of fingers of whiskey. The kids would scoot off to do homework or watch the Ed Sullivan show.

When we were younger still, our father built an addition to the house, referred to as the "bunkhouse" that was not quite attached to the main house except through a single door. As kids, we would sleep there so we would not be disturbed by the grownups or, more accurately, not disturb them. We didn't realize that living in a separate house from our parents was out of the ordinary. My two sisters and I lived in the "bunkhouse." About 20' by 12', it seemed large enough to us. There was a triple-layer bunk bed, like on a military ship. Lynn, the oldest, was on top, and I was in the middle. On the bottom shelf slept Gail, or "baby bird," as I came to call her. Even as an adult, she was only 4' 10" tall and forever fragile like a newly hatched baby bird.

Richard with Captain Troxell

We each had our own double-paned window at our bunk beds. So, while we could see outside, the view and the sense that we were separate and apart from what we were seeing (the world) was omnipresent.

The bunkhouse had no other windows, and these bed windows were quite difficult to see out of as they were only about 6" by 10". Each window had a separation of about 2" between the panes, with the space containing a cloth bag full of chemicals meant to absorb moisture and prevent the glass from fogging. We were cautioned that the granules inside the bags were poison. Because it was the era of James Bond, "duck and cover," and the Cold War generally, I was always afraid that the inner window might shatter, and I would be gassed to death by the packet of granules. My sisters and I lived in isolation, literally right on top of one another, and yet we didn't discuss these fears. I found it rather odd that we didn't talk about things. The truth is that I think we, the children, were traumatized by our relationship with our father. A constant pensiveness was only buffered on sporadic occasions when our mother would seemingly step over an invisible line and enter our world but not in the presence of our father. The two built-in ladders rose straight up. Lynn would climb right past me to get into or out of her bunk. She "lived" right above me but never stopped to chat. Nor did the three of us speak from bunk to bunk. We just knew instinctively that such discussion would be frowned upon, perhaps not by our mother, but certainly by our father, who undoubtedly would chastise us, not with harsh words or any words at all, but with a mere look. The second ladder led up to our custom-designed clothes loft, about 8' off the ground, a narrow platform that did not allow any room for sharing the space or passing. This made it a little awkward when scrambling to get ready for school. It was strongly constructed, "Like the Rock of Gibraltar!" I'll never forget how we'd be startled when a deep male voice would burst out with, "Like the Rock of Gibraltar!" It was our father, who would declare this to the air with no further context or comment.

The two women, with rigid posture and dressed for outdoors, clutched their coats to themselves as they scurried out the door. With pursed lips, they shook their heads slightly, apparently aghast at what they had seen. In a low, distinct tone, a male's voice kept repeating, "Utterly unsafe, utterly unsafe." One of the women focused on her own issue. In a disbelieving, shaky voice, she came out with, "Oh, the isolation!" I remember wondering at the time if she thought that was good or bad. However, it did not seem good to my ears.

It was not until years later that we three children learned that the three people were inspectors from a *Better Homes and Gardens* magazine contest, one man and two women were there one day as Lynn, and I returned from school. I was in first grade, and Lynn was in third.

My sisters and I had no plumbing in the bunkhouse, so that meant we had to be sure we had drained our bladders thoroughly prior to bedtime because once it was "lights out," we couldn't return to their house..."unless it was a matter of *life or death.*" What is a life-or-death matter? I would hear that phrase in my head a thousand times.

What Is a Life-or-Death Matter?

Richard and sisters eating in a tub

Because there was no plumbing in the bunkhouse, the three of us used the bathroom and tub in the big house. After a meal, the shower would serve as the perfect kid cleaner. Our mother had lived through the Depression, which meant we would constantly live vicariously in that grim era. Everything seemed to be framed by it. We, the children, did chores, and our allowance was paid in marbles because kids liked marbles. I sure did. My sisters, not so much. Money simply never left the closed system of the "family pot." We always thought it strange that it was always referred to as the "family pot," and yet, we the children never got any money. We were frugal with water, too. After bath time, the tub would be emptied with buckets and used to water the yard and vegetables. In our family, the Depression produced efficiency, conservation, and sturdiness.

One day, while in my bunk, I was playing imaginary soldiers in my head when I saw a couple of young boys skipping down the sidewalk in front of our house. I used my right hand in a closed fist to insistently tap on the window, loudly chastising them, "You're out of uniform, Mister!" I remember saying this repeatedly as I continued to knock on the glass with my voice rising. Then it happened. I shattered the glass. I knew instantly the poison gas was flooding my space, and soon the entire bunkhouse would fill with deadly gas from the packet of granules. I looked down as blood gushed from my knuckle where a significant shard of glass was lodged, making my hand unusable. I was bleeding all over the sheets. I rushed to the door that divided their house from our house. With my left hand hanging above my head, ready to knock, I suddenly stopped. What should I do? I didn't know. Timmy and his dog, Lassie, from TV, would know, but I didn't. Was this a "life or death" thing?

Lynn was yelling something, and I told her I just didn't know for sure. Lynn saw the blood gushing and started crying. She remembered the other admonishment, "...only if you are bleeding arterially!" I started crying. Chaos ensued. More shouting, then from me, "I just don't know!" Lynn finally pushed past me and pounded on the door. It opened. Adult chaos ensued. Apparently, it was enough of a glass shard that I wear the scar to this day. No, the children's bunkhouse (built like the Rock of Gibraltar!), in competition for the cover of Better Homes and Gardens, never did have its photo opportunity or receive a prize for the Best Children's House Ever Built. Go figure.

There was always something. There was either alcohol consumption or alcohol residual thinking. The adult parties were awash with alcohol by the case and mirrored by the youth parties in the park. I planned my military career while drinking in the basement watching war movies. My parents thought it was good parenting to build separate living quarters for the kiddos. In fact, both my parents were very handy with tools, having built their own workshops. Each project was measured in the number of beers or number of cases of beer required to finish a job (e.g., the bunkhouse was a ten-cases-of-beer project).

My father, as tired as he was from working, and the obligatory interactions with fellow and senior officers at the Officers' Club, would proceed to tell very lively stories with flair. With a glass of whiskey in one hand, he would gesture with the other and regale his wife with tales of his day. At one point, he became president of a Toastmasters International club. He shared amazing stories that everyone loved and toasted with great zeal.

"The Road Goes on Forever, and the Party Never Ends!"
—Robert Earl Keene

As my father received one promotion after another, we moved into a quiet home in Bethesda, Maryland, on the outskirts of Washington DC. As time passed, the 495 Beltway was built, and the family home literally became "inside the beltway," which is supposed to be a pretty big deal. Clark Clifford, the Secretary of Defense, lived just down the street. Bigwig highway contractor Mr. Marinelli lived across the street. It was the "Days of Wine and Roses." We were always having parties, not small. There might be 200 guests. When I say "we," I mean the adults. We kids were now teenagers, bunched together in age. We had one thing in common. We were all Dr. Spock babies. All our parents prescribed to the teachings of Dr Spock. One of his recommendations was that if a baby cried, one shouldn't pick them up and cuddle them until they stopped crying…"Enlightened parents" were to just let them cry it out. How did that work out? Well like any good salad bar, people select some things and pass over others. Vegetables or ideas that seemed less desirable or failed to fall into the basic common-sense category should not have been put on their plates. To me it seemed clear that even at that time, both of these beautiful, very smart girls, my sisters Lynn and Gail, were not getting the kind of love and reassurances that they needed. None of us were really. Sadly, the alcohol fog seemed to override common sense. In hindsight, now decades later, I can't help but reflect on comments of my mother whose friends had questioned her selection of the tough love approach. Today, both Lynn and Gail face serious mental health challenges. Perhaps because of the isolation and never being responded to when crying out for human relief we were all damaged.

Well, as the adults rocked the house, we would go down to the park formed by the greenbelt around the beltway, just below our house, and have our own parties. We would simply help ourselves to a case of beer from the stack and a bottle or two from the other stack and walk away.

No one ever seemed to notice or care. We were young, and it was the '60s. We talked about sex, drugs, and rock and roll…everything. We tried pot. We listened to Bob Dylan, Donovan, Vanilla Fudge, Joni Mitchell, Simon and Garfunkel, the Mamas and the Papas, and Jimi Hendrix.

The day following an adult party, the kids were expected to help with the cleanup tasks. On more than one occasion, I would come across shots of booze, half-drunk beers, and "party puzzles," as my mother would call them. When guests first arrived, they would reach into a large bowl and retrieve a 2" by 3" piece of a puzzle that my mother had carefully cut out of a sheet of Masonite. An attached brightly-colored ribbon allowed the new owner to dangle it from his or her neck. They would attempt to find their match throughout the night by trying to insert their half into the other matching half found around the neck of another searcher. As far as I know, my mother was always into a boy-girl theme. The whole idea was a great icebreaker and maybe a little more. After all, it was the '60s. The alcohol flowed like tap water, and there were always party horns and party hats. Imagine two hundred of Washington DC's most powerful people gathered in our house, all letting their hair down, so to speak. I'm sure that careers were made and dashed at those events. I had a young person's first question about why, among such massive crowds, there were *no* Black people in our house. I had just lived in South Carolina but I somehow thought the military was supposed to be above that.

My older sister, Lynn, had curly blonde hair, an impish persona, and a brilliant mind reminiscent of Shirley Temple (White America's picture-perfect child in the 1930s) before she rebelled against everything. In some ways, Lynn reminded me of Patty Hearst, who in the early '70s was first kidnapped, then absorbed into the Symbionese Liberation Army mind meld. Lynn took up smoking, dyed her hair black, donned leathers, and became a motorcycle momma. Literally—she got pregnant. The non-verbalized undercurrent seemed to carry the idea that she did it to destroy my father and his career. After all, she was the first child. With a genius IQ, she somehow believed that she had been robbed of her due amount of parental love when a year and 3/4s after she came into the world, I was born. Then, a year later, my baby sister, Gail, joined the small family. Being left alone to cry for a hug was bad enough but having to share was one bridge too far. Lynn did not like to share.

News of Lynn's motorcycle antics and her pregnancy reached Gail and me in that order. In those days, girls were sent away to hide their conditions and await their delivery, quickly followed by adoption. Lynn disappeared, and our mother had to sneak us out of the house and drive us "somewhere" to see Lynn. But even then, only our mother saw her, while Gail and I had to wait in the car. We often stayed in the car for over an hour, not knowing what the hell was going on. These things may have knocked Dick Troxell off his elevated military path. His alcohol consumption increased a bit, but it seemed on the surface to just make him go to bed earlier. He still got up just as early every single day and headed off to work, all shaved and fresh-pressed in his naval officer's uniform. Or, it may have been one of those parties. You never knew whose half a puzzle piece a guest might randomly draw or how a spouse might later react.

As it turned out, without discussing it (or almost anything else) with me, my father was shocked to learn that I would not be accepting an appointment to the U.S. Naval Academy (that had not been offered and that he had not pursued.) Somehow, he thought that because my mother was assigned to take me to the Naval Academy in Annapolis for church on Sundays, she would take care of my application and remind him to call the appropriate senator. Perhaps it was all those youth parties in the park or too many   years in our finished basement drinking draft beer from my parents' refrigerator keg every night while watching Vic Morrow fight Germans on the TV show, "Combat," that set me on my path as a Marine. Just as alcohol may have had some effect on the course of my father's military career, it might have also affected mine. A vision of myself in an officer's uniform kept flickering in my brain like the clicking of a torn reel-to-reel movie theater tape when you just sat there in the dark thinking crazy thoughts. Nothing made sense. I sure didn't want a repeat of my 2nd, 3rd, and 4th-grade military school experience of getting beat up every day. It provided no enticement to compete with my father as a naval officer. Also, at the time, my father and his pristine dress whites, immaculate fingernails, and eloquent diction seemed a bit prissy to me. I was bound and determined to be a man's man and a leader of men, like Vic Morrow.

It was 1968, and the Vietnam "conflict" was raging. Bobby Kennedy had just joined his brother Jack in the hereafter. The world had come undone. All my buddies were avoiding the military draft. Fred got help from his father to lay tracks down his arm with a saline solution to look like a junkie. Bob, the real ladies' man among us decided to put on frilly pink panties. Tom, a good Catholic boy with 12 siblings joined the U.S. Coast Guard Reserve, as perfect a compromise to the real military as he could find. Rick, 2 years older and one of my role models was just too drug fried to pass the entry exam. He was stamped *Reject, Unfit for Service*.

Sure that I would be drafted eventually, I grew up and joined the U.S. Marines. My super-intellectual rationale was that if I was going to be shot at, I had better get the best training possible. Initially, the Marine Corps didn't draft, but because so many of them were getting killed, they opened up to the draft, and Black guys flooded in. They needed the money, and the military needed the bodies. Mine became just one more.

Vietnam introduced me to the war and, accordingly, to Chu Lai Bombers (marijuana cigarettes laced with opium) and, of course, more alcohol. By 1970, President Nixon started pulling us out of Vietnam and parked us in Iwakuni, Japan, all the while hoping to convince Congress to send us all back at some point in the future. My choice of escape was Akadama wine, reported to have killed a half a dozen Marines up to that time, or that year, or who knew which, and who cared? It was a semisweet, red wine concoction that caused nightly vision loss, and that was all I really needed.

Finally, they scooped me up and sent me back to the states for my remaining third year of military service. Most guys got discharged upon returning to "the world." Not me. I had been suspected of organizing a revolt against the United States military. They seemed to feel that having left Nam, and after being jammed onto a tiny military base on a tiny island, with enough gear and men to fill the entire state of Maryland, I may have become upset. We literally crawled over massive military crates to get from point A to point B and then got thrown into the brig for being late because we literally couldn't move—after putting our lives on the line for that same government. They found it unreasonable that it would upset me to the point where I would attempt to shut down their little base and open their brig so my brothers could escape the insanity. No dots on such a fairytale were ever connected, and no insurgency was ever proven. I was shipped back to the "the world," otherwise known as Camp Lejeune, N.C.

There, I was put in charge of funeral details, but apparently, my combination of sadness and inebriation wasn't a good fit, and I was quickly shifted to a stint of guarding the mess hall, which consisted of standing at attention from dusk 'til dawn. Apparently, that task interfered with my inebriation to an unacceptable level.

Digressing back to the mess hall for a moment, at the end of every meal, each Marine was required to scrape uneaten food into one barrel, toss paper products into another, and place the cups, plates, and silverware into a third. Not unlike me, short-timers didn't give a rat's ass about anything, so you just slammed everything into the first barrel. The service upheld the fiction that the ceramic and metal items were "inadvertently" discarded. (Lots of guys simply emptied their entire trays into the of food waste. These barrels were then transported to the military's own hog farm, the site of my next posting, where it was my responsibility to recover all the government property from the hog pen. I got to live my dream of bending over all day, reaching into the slop up to my elbows, retrieve dishes and stainless-steel utensils from the muck, and then throwing up, over and over again. Fortunately, there was more to the job, which also provided the hog-slopping experience I had always longed for. The reinforced cast aluminum barrels weighed a ton and had to be picked up and spilled into the hog pen. No matter how many times I practiced my art, the slop covered my boots every time. Almost every night after exploits at any number of town bars, I would return to base, find a bunk to fall on for about an hour and a half (otherwise, I bunked off base), get up still quite drunk, and head off to flip eggs on a 3' by 6' blistering sheet of steel called a grill. There, I would profusely season everyone's eggs with pretty much pure alcohol in the form of fresh sweat. In other words, that's how I received the honor of guarding the mess hall on a nightly basis.

The military apparently took a final dislike of me when, after I was discharged, I burned my uniform and headed off in my skivvies to the local bus station. In my absence, they passed a regulation that would make such a farewell gesture punishable by arrest and a free return trip to the base brig.

Back in the World…Taking Care of Business

I came back to my parents' home. Everything was different. All my friends were gone. They had all gone to college or just off to life. Finding out that I no longer had the emotional support of my friends nor the

U.S. government for the 4 years of college that my "friend" Harry, the asshole recruiter, had guaranteed me, I borrowed a car from a guy I knew. He was too mentally compromised from excessive amounts of LSD and booze to be drafted. Like so many others who stayed behind, he could do little more than sweep the floor of a gas station while watching the world in living color. The world seemed to have lost its collective mind. Or maybe it was just me.

I drove to Rockville, Maryland, where I had first grown up in the "bunkhouse." I didn't go there. I didn't even want to look. Instead, I drove down the street, parked across from Checkie Chevlovski's house, and turned off the ignition. Checkie had tied me up with a clothesline and whipped me with it. No reason, except that he could. I was littler than him. He was the world's biggest asshole, and he had even set his own parents' house on fire.

I had come for him. I thought about it for all those years. Every time I drank (which was pretty much every single day and night that I could), I'd think about Checkie Chevlovski. Sometimes, it was the only thing that kept me going. Now, I am reminded of *Man's Search for Meaning* by Viktor Frankl.

There was, of course, alcohol involved here, along with rage like I had never felt before. My ears filled with blood. I could no longer hear anything. I knew that I was about to stroke out. I was sure of it. My hand was on the car door latch when I saw him, Checkie, the source of so many sleepless nights. He came out to get something from the bed of his pickup truck. He was a fat slob, and he still lived at his parents' home, like I'd been sure he would. But he was nothing. He was so big, but he was nothing. He was a slug.

I'd thought about revenge so many times. Then my ears popped, and every pore in my body opened up. Suddenly, tears were streaming down my face but at first, I hadn't noticed. I was breathing so hard, and then suddenly, I snapped back to the here and now as they say. After all those years, my eyes cleared and I realized that I was staring at the corner of his house. Through a thin layer of paint, I could still see scorch marks on the edge of the wood siding from the fire he'd set to burn his parents' house down. I realized what I was seeing was really as good as I could hope for. He was already in a hell of his own making. I'd come to that house and imagined that moment so many times. Somehow, for some reason, I just stopped. It was done. It was over. I turned the key in the ignition, put the car in gear, and drove away. All I could think of was a prayer that slipped my lips—"Thank you, sweet Jesus, for your hand upon my shoulder."

The Phone Call

After the discharge, I entered Montgomery County Community College and attempted to engage in the pursuit of a college degree. I finally got into a rhythm but felt like I was holding my breath and trying to catch my breath at the same time. I got a room in a shared house in Silver Spring, Maryland. I had built a separate room by simply walling off the kitchen. It was like a mouse hole, but I didn't care; I had my own space. I hung in there for almost two semesters. I was focused on getting into the Massachusetts Institute of Technology to learn printing technology and offset lithography. I got lost in the work. My activities included photography, graphic design, operating several types of presses, the works. I pretty much liked it. However, I was concerned about the noise of the press room. Because of the war, I was no longer good with noise.

Then I got the call, the one that told me I needed to come home. There had been an accident. My father was hurt.

It really wasn't much of an accident, but more of an event. My father, USN Captain Richard R. Troxell, at the age of 50, was dead. He had always been the smartest guy in the room. He had been "that guy." I guess that's how he knew he would die. He apparently had the foresight to tell my mother every day for a year in advance that he would die. Maybe it was my sister's rebellion and her pregnancy. He had organized a shotgun wedding, giving the baby a father, and then according to what I was told, worked diligently to cause the first annulment in the state of Maryland to be granted after a baby was born. I suspect that he left it to my mother to find "a proper home" for that baby to be adopted into.

Or maybe what did him in was my rebellion, the choice to not be a naval officer but a Marine. Or was it President Nixon's meltdown and ultimate self-destruction? My father had spent days, nights, and weeks at the officers' club going over the details of the situation with his fellow officers. Working late in the night, every night, looking for solutions. He felt it was the "courtiers" around Nixon who had failed the President and caused his disgrace, Watergate, the break-in, the missing 18 minutes of tape and his new place in history.

Perhaps it was the kidney and liver problems that began to surface after almost 20 years of drinking a nightly half quart of Guckenheimer whiskey, a taste he had acquired in Canada. Perhaps it had something to do with the James Bond era parties, held in his very own home, designed to help clear his path to admiralship in hopes of finally stop hearing his mother's relentless urgings to succeed.

Perhaps he just couldn't see a path forward anymore. But in any event, he had prepared my mother, so she must have suspected he was sick enough to die. He had pulled out his service pistol and dutifully cleaned it regularly. My father, who could describe the intricacies of a small nuclear detonating device with words so precise you could envision it, had left a multi-faceted, multi-page document that detailed everything, where every penny was stashed, where every life insurance policy was stored, when the fuses in the basement were to be changed...everything. How could she not know? He did everything to prepare her.

But there was one thing she was not prepared for. She did not know that all her "friends," all the officers' wives and all the officers, would immediately distance themselves from her and what was left of her family. Then, and I think even now, that kind of death was considered unacceptable. It was like the third rail beneath a subway train. You just don't go there. You just don't touch it. It implies failure of the system. The implication is that somehow, a career in military life did not provide every single thing that any human being would ever need or should ever want. In fact, a coroner's report of such a death on a military death certificate meant that there would be no widow's benefits paid to the family. Suicide in the military is considered a disgrace to one and all. Everyone knows that, and everyone distances themselves when they are needed the most. This response, believe it or not, is part of the military culture.

He did not prepare her for that Easter holiday that began with Good Friday when he left her bed, put on his full-dress uniform, went into the garage, and closed the door. He had not prepared her as to the best way to remove splattered grey matter from the wall...flesh and blood, brain cells, and dreams that had once been her beloved husband.

A Moment of Clarity

All I knew at that moment was that he was wrong-headed. This brilliant man who had literally only ever spoken less than 500 words directly to me had lost his grip and the logic which he had clenched so tightly. It was now clear to me that his brain was pickled from alcohol. It was then that I fully realized that alcohol had tainted every plan, every decision, every action from his first college drink to building the bunkhouse to his last dying day. Hell, he had raised his children like they were show dogs...but at bay. I wanted to hold on to this epiphany. I was not sure what I was to do with it, but I knew I should hold tightly to that moment of clarity, so when the right moment came, I would be able to pull it up. I would hold it up to the light. I would examine it quietly and I would address it properly and make something positive come out of it.

One for the Road

Shell shock, trauma, post-traumatic stress disorder makes little difference what you call it. Soon I headed out on the road. I didn't stay for the funeral. I walked out of college and out of Maryland. I had no real destination. I pretty much drove across the U.S. for the first of many times.

My father was gone, my friends had moved on, and I hadn't yet begun to recover from the war. I was mad...I was so damned mad and in pain, and I hit the road. I drove and I drank. At night, I would go to some local bar and drink Johnny Walker Red. At some point, I'd jump up, yell "Hoorah!" and hit the biggest damned son-of-a-bitch I could find. I would smash him with my right fist. I'd smash him as hard as I could, then I would be smashed. Beer and whiskey would go flying. Other boys, infuriated with the jostling and loss of their drinks, would join in. That was the thing of it. That's what I wanted. Chaos. It was always the same. I'd wake up hung over, with a rubber-mallet head and a busted lip and split knuckles. I was always bloody and caked in dried blood. Vomit often plastered my hair to the side of my face. I'd crawl to a sitting position, wrap my more serious gashes with one of my bandanas, drive to a gas station. I'd hang out in the washroom for half an hour to rinse off the blood, try to drink water from the sink, and screw my head back on straight. After changing into shorts and running shoes, I'd stash the VW somewhere and run. All-day, every day, I ran and ran and ran. Then I drive some more...do it all over again...and again....

I drove a brand-new red VW bug, a gift. In 1972, I had just gotten back from the war. My father, Captain Richard R. "Dick" Troxell, USN, had ordered it for me. When I say ordered it, I mean just that—from his chair in his special dining room that he had built with his own hands. Every day of his married life, he sat Japanese style on a square pillow, placed on the carpet, and he ate the same evening meal, a cheeseburger with thinly sliced fried potatoes, with a draft beer, in the room he had designed and built so he could close off the world. Just prior to my return, while seated in his chair, he picked up the phone, called the operator, and had her connect him to the Volkswagen dealership. I'm sure he politely introduced himself, gave his address and the name of his banker. I suspect he said, "Would you please deliver to me a red Volkswagen car? I believe you call it a beetle. Thank you."

Today, ordering a car from one's living quarters is not unusual, but in 1975 I'll bet he was among the first to do so. After all, He was the captain of his ship.

When I temporarily moved back into my parents' house, he handed me the key and said, "Welcome home." That was all. Not another word was spoken aside from my apprehensive "Thank you." Not then, nor throughout the remaining three years of his life. I know this sounds unbelievable in retrospect, but my father's policy was that children, "were not to speak unless spoken to." Remember that as children, we were not considered to have much to offer. This continued into adulthood as we were still the children of the household.

Now I was driving that red VW "bug." It was my only possession aside from the Hitler Youth knife, I landed in New Mexico. By this time, I guess I was too sick from drinking and too busted up to fight. I stayed there for a year and just kept running ten miles a day. I traded my cramped

VW for an International Harvester utility truck that I loved and lived in. I swung a Pulaski ax for that full year, restoring trails for the New Mexico Park Service in the Sandia mountains. I was on a crew with ten Mexicans. During lunch, we drank mescal, and the rest of the time, we smoked marijuana. We forged international relations in our own minds and restored 25 miles of trails.

I had all the time in the world on my hands on that trail. I had enough time on my hands and on the steaming asphalt that I kept running and stopped drinking and started to reflect ...on all of it. Over the years I kept coming to the one constant that had pretty much enveloped my life from the very beginning. This included my mother's imbibing while celebrating her pregnancy of me. Alcohol had been the center piece. Then as I began to work with homeless folks; I realized that many of them were also looking for shelter from their stormy lives. Alcohol had become the center piece whether it was my father's consumption, my friend's consumption or mine. I remembered that focused moment that I had examined after my father's death. I had stored it away and vowed to myself that one day when the time was right, I would pull it out again and do something positive with it. That day was coming...

When that job ran out, I got a job humping tables in the Thunderbird Bar (where else?). I guess I hadn't stopped drinking entirely. One day, the bar got torched. The only bar for miles and it got torched! A professional basketball player named Ira Harge failed to pay his note to some impatient dudes, who got tired of his slow-pay practices. As a volunteer firefighter but thoroughly undertrained, I ran around that blazing building assisting various lieutenants until the dawn broke, the smoke cleared, and the Thunderbird bar had burnt to the ground.

Buddy

At this point, I parked my truck in front of an adobe hut that belonged to a friend of mine with a note, "Jose-Enjoy! I'm on the road again. Ricardo." I made my way north, leaving New Mexico in the mirror, hitchhiking with my new dog, Buddy. This gal, Holly, told me he was being held against his will and mistreated by her one-time friend. The dog was clearly out of his mind. Despite being just a springer spaniel, he was the scariest dog I'd ever met. If you got anywhere near him, he'd turn his head sideways with a laser-intensive stare from bulging eyes, and bark at you at the top of his lungs without stopping, while drooling and throwing snot the whole time.

Holly was right; her dog was being abused. His fur was matted, and he stunk to high heaven. I decided to help her out. He was chained to a mesquite tree where he had wound himself around several times, and then pulled on it as if he was trying to choke the damned tree. I could tell it would be awkward to get past the ranch house for one thing, but the dog wouldn't be of any help either. I couldn't figure out how to sneak up on him without getting myself chewed to the bone. So, I took a different approach. I waited until Saturday night when the gal who took the dog from Holly had gone to the Red Rose saloon. I got my truck one last time and simply plowed down the mesquite tree. This threw up a mountain of dust and stunned the dog enough for me to throw a water-soaked blanket over him, chain and all. I got the damned dog to the edge of the truck and dragged him in the truck bed, by the chain. I wrapped him in a dry blanket and stayed with him through the night.

The next day, I cut the blanket free, and Holly, who gotten me into this mess, hosed the dog down while I pumped water from the well. It was a muddy mess. We talked sweetly to him the whole time. I took a day and a half to calm him down. I appreciated that he hadn't eaten me, so I named him Buddy. I guess I thought that the name would suggest something favorable to him, and he might act like a buddy to me. I pulled one end of the chain through an old cedar tree and short-chained it so I could hack-saw it off. That still left about ten links.

For my trouble, Holly had said that Buddy belonged to me. I didn't know what to say. I had not thought about a dog in years. Not since I'd gotten in a drunken, hung-over-state after my father killed himself, and I'd inadvertently left my beautiful stray Irish setter in the red Volkswagen and failed to return for two hours. By then, it was too late. I had killed the most beautiful dog I'd ever seen. I guess simply baked him, and God took him back because perhaps I had unknowingly failed to support my mother when my father so tortured her with his upcoming act of suicide. And because I had failed my father, he killed himself. And, of course, I had somehow lived when so many of my buddies hadn't. But I know for sure, I sinned against God and my dog, Rusty, and will carry that to my judgment day. I was stunned, ashamed, and frozen with the pain. I was numb.

So anyway, I had taken the dog from Holly. Maybe to make amends for Rusty, to start over fresh, if that was possible. He was still crazy, and after all the abuse and the waterboarding and all, he had just sat down. As I say, I talked to him for more than a full day. Time was irrelevant. I explained how we were alike, and I told him more about what had happened on my end, then his, I guess. I told him about all of it, every beating I got in military school, the bunkhouse, the whipping, the isolation, my "charge" to save the world from the fascists, my brothers who never came home from Nam, my other brothers who are still in the woods all over the world, breakout at the brig, losing my father, killing Rusty, smashing faces in as many bars as possible as I ran across country, my years of trying to numb my mind with alcohol, everything, I told him everything and I cried for hours. Soaking wet, I guess I just finally fell over. When I awoke, his head was on my chest. Slowly, I pulled back and sat up. He was still just as crazy and still barked out one side of his mouth and threw spit out at people with his eyes bugged out, but he never ever did that to me again. I got some dog food, put it in my backpack, and together we hitch-hiked across the country, then up north and ended back east over to Philadelphia where I got a pair of bolt cutters and cut off those last links of chain.

I still ran between hitches, but Buddy somehow realized I would be coming back. As time moved on, I too came to ease up on myself and I came to realize that I really wasn't being punished through Rusty but all those alcoholic encased events of my life made me look at every bit of it pretty hard.

Apparently, I was done with the bars, and Buddy had a new life. It turned out he loved to hitch-hike and would hang his head out the window. He still had a crazed look about him, but it was only because the wind blew his beautiful auburn feathers on top of his ears and his ears themselves, back, and it pulled the skin around his eyes back, so they again bugged out. But replacing the crazed fear of abandonment, he had a look of excitement and joy. When a big rig would stop, he'd instantly jump up in the cab, take his place on my lap, and stick his head out the window, always looking forward. Buddy Trucker, as he got named, and I shared a life together until he was a very old dog. He would go camping with me and Eric, who would become my other traveling buddy.

Richard and Buddy

The three of us hiked through western Pennsylvania to beautiful areas like the Pennsylvania Grand Canyon and Pine Creek Gorge. It was glorious. It was full of vistas of endless mountain ranges crossing us in the distance. I have a picture of Buddy on the top of a wooded mountain surrounded by beautiful blooming mountain laurel, sitting there looking out across several of those mountain ranges with a breeze blowing back his feathers, his sniffer in the air.

He never lost his ferocity and was always on the alert for invaders. Many a time, he had scared off marauding bears or returned to camp with a snout-full of porcupine quills. He was fearless. But it always hurt me to remove those quills because they were barbed, and they bloodied his nose. But, he trusted me and always let me do it. Eric loved him, too. In the end, he had cataracts in both eyes, and his teeth were worn down to the gum. He died in my arms, and I buried him in the woods. He was the best dog friend I ever had. We came through a lot together.

He was God's gift to me, and I guess I was God's gift to him.

Having a Conversation with the Devil in the Room

As I say, buddy and I landed in Philadelphia. There Garland Dempsey found me and Buddy squatting in one of his houses but instead of having me arrested, gave me housing and a job as an automotive apprentice. Buddy became a junk yard dog and loved running with the other dogs. Thanks to Garland's connections, I soon enough got hired straight from the streets to become an ad-hoc paralegal and Buddy and I found a home of our own. You can read all about that and many other adventures in *Looking Up at the Bottom Line*. But it was years before I fully found my bearings and decided to pull out of my pocket, that little jewel, that epiphany that I had had about alcohol, and chose to examine it more fully. Here is what I found...

Cheers! Prost! Compi! Salud! Down the hatch! A toast! I'll drink to that! One more for the road! (scary). To your health! Mazel tov! L'chaim! These are just some of the words that, like the wine, scotch, vodka, beer, margaritas, etc. that we drink to enliven, enhance, and celebrate our lives, add flavor and joy to our moments of importance or when we need to express or repress our pain or sorrow.

Alcohol brings us joy, and makes us feel good about ourselves and often engages us in an activity that involves others and brings us together as community.

In contrast, alchy, bum, detox, skid row, crawled into a bottle, wino, boozer, blackouts, drunkard...these are the words that are associated with the negative side of alcohol.

Alcohol—A Product Liability Case

When one prepares to exit the grocery store with goods on the conveyer belt, neither the checker nor the first-time alcohol imbiber knows which of the two categories he/she will fall into. The checker only know that the customer has produced their identification, shown themselves to "be of age," and with money in hand, made the purchase. He knows that the customer has been instructed to "drink responsibly" but little more. Neither of them has any way of knowing if the customer will react with joy or suffer a life-changing addiction that will lead them down a path of misery for them and their family. Simply, alcohol could take over and ruin the rest of their lives. There is no way of knowing...not even within one's own family.

As I looked back to write this chapter, I see alcohol invading every corner of my life. It seemingly began with my parents and their parties with 200 guests, cases of whiskey, and uncounted full kegs and cases of beer. It involved endless teenage park parties with friends, enhanced by stolen fifths of whiskey and packets of drink mixes. It included tapping my parent's refrigerator, always filled with a baby keg of beer, and drinking in quiet solitude while watching the black and white glow of our basement RCA wood-encased TV. I did this throughout my entire junior and senior high school years when I should have been studying. If not for escaping to the basement to drink, I might have had a college plan, avoided Vietnam, and never made the acquaintance of Akadama. These were just the first of many years when I consumed alcohol in such quantities that it literally dripped heavily from my face and the pores in my head.

Or did it begin with my mother's consumption of alcohol while I was in utero. One cannot tell for sure and that's the point or at least one of them.

In order to fight the demons in my head, alcohol was my weapon of choice, and it was alcohol that later dragged me across this country through the front doors of countless bars and saloons, only to crawl out the back door soaked from sloshed beer and bleeding from broken whiskey bottles.

Years and even decades later, astonished to still be able to drink a beer without it ending in a full-blown brawl, I reflected on all of this. I also learned about the financial and human costs of alcohol.

Diggin' in the Weeds...Looking for Real Answers

In 2010, the Centers for Disease Control reported that excess alcohol consumption costs the American economy $249 billion in lost productivity in a single year.

According to Statista.com, total alcohol beverage sales in the United States in 2019 amounted to almost $253 billion. According to the National Institute on Alcohol Abuse and Alcoholism, the cost of alcohol to society can be broken down into three categories.[40] Two teams at different times using two slightly different methodologies created the following statistics compiled by D.P. Rice and his colleagues, and H.J. Harwood and his colleagues.

Cost of treating medical consequences of alcohol use and treating alcohol abuse:

Rice $70.3 billion   1985
Harwood $89 billion   1980

Health-related cost loss in productivity by workers:

Rice $27 billion   1985
Harwood $54 billion   1980

Health-related costs due to premature deaths due to ETOH abuse:

Rice $24 billion   1985[41]
Harwood $14.5 billion   1980[42]

So, the total cost (not including other costs like property damage) to society in 1980, according to J.G. Harwood, would have been $157.5 billion. The cost to society in 1985, according to D.P. Rice, would have been $121.3 billion. The point is this, even taking the low estimation established in 1985 (the most recent statistical study of this nature), the cost to society in terms of medical consequences, lost worker hours, and premature deaths associated with alcohol use was an eye-popping 121.3 billion dollars. What would be the cost if calculated today with the increase in alcohol use factored in?

These are two different pots of money to be considered.

One pot of money is based on alcoholic beverage sales ($223.26 billion) paid to private industry, and the other is the cost of the alcohol sales paid by society ($121.3 billion). Texas, North Carolina, Indiana are among the five states where the alcohol industry contributes *zero dollars* to cover the medical care, including alcohol detoxification, treatment, work production loss, premature death-related costs, or the heartbreak of relatives and friends caused by the disease of alcoholism.

The alcohol industry's only contribution is "Drink responsibly," whatever that means. It isn't even a campaign. It is just a tagline, a slogan, a commercial jingle. It is the industry's attempt to insulate itself from any damage their product may inflict on society. Their line is, "we told them to drink responsibly. These consumers are adults. They know the negative consequences of their actions." Caveat Emptor—Let the buyer beware!

The alcohol industry causes real damage to human lives. Their only defense to not participate in addressing that damage is that, "If they (society,) ask for a penny today, then they'll ask for two pennies tomorrow." I get that. The alcohol industry is afraid of the "slippery slope."

The alcohol industry is afraid that once again, legislators will simply "pick a number out of the air" to address the cost of alcohol treatment and that over the years, that amount will creep up, seeing the $223.2 billion pot as a *deep pocket* with no bottom. I can see that as well.

In fact, as a capitalist (with reservations), I am sympathetic to that perspective. However, as a person who looks at issues from both practical and ethical perspectives, I wish to offer an even-handed, practical proposal based on ethics.

The Proposal

There is no mechanism to identify someone with the alcohol gene as of yet as they pass through that grocery store checkout line with their bottle of wine or 6-pack of beer. Nothing would set off alarm bells, stop the conveyor belt, or the monetary transaction. The seller will sell to any individual of appropriate age a substance that could cause serious medical complications, ruin their relationships, devastate their financial stability, and even result in their premature death or the demise of others. At the same time, the alcohol industry wants to avoid a "slippery slope" of endless increases in financial support to address societal costs. Let's take an unusual approach to the problem.

What if we simply identify alcohol as a product? Any other product that fails or hurts the consumer would be addressed in our court system as a product liability case. If a head gasket on an engine is manufactured improperly, it may leak and probably overheat the engine block, which in turn, could cause a worn push-rod to shoot through the firewall and pierce a driver through the heart. We might hold the manufacturer responsible, right? If the brakes gave out when the vehicle reached 55 miles/hour and was later proven to have locked up, causing a crash, or a bad part caused the car to accelerate uncontrollably, resulting in injury or death, we would hold the manufacturer responsible, right? Yes, in 2010 Toyota recalled 2.3 million cars for a stuck accelerator after four people were killed.

Ice Cream, Anyone?

Several years ago, Blue Bell Creameries discovered that their ice cream was contaminated with listeria, a bacteria-based food poisoning. After weeks of intense public outrage and pressure from local health authorities, Blue Bell finally pulled all of their suspected ice creams off the market and toothbrush-scrubbed every piece of equipment until they felt the consumers were no longer in jeopardy. Then, they covered medical costs for injured parties. Our proposal falls along similar lines, inasmuch as it involves the beneficiary of product sales while also involving them in addressing any adverse consumer consequences caused by their product.

But when Blue Bell did not simply resolve the matter in a responsible fashion; the courts stepped in, and the Associated Press reported that on May 1st, 2020, "A Texas-based ice cream manufacturer pled guilty to charges of distributing contaminated ice cream products and was legally forced to pay $19.35 million in fines, forfeiture, and civil settlement payments, which the Justice Department said is the second-highest amount ever paid to resolve a food safety matter." And so, *my eureka moment,* "Aha!" moment, my moment of clarity, my moment of sobriety arrived, and I knew I could make a difference in the lives of others. And so, for the want of a better phrase, I chose to place this alcohol proposal under the title of *Product Liability.*

No Slippery Slope. Instead…

However, our approach would have no slippery slope. We would address the concern without court system involvement and without blaming the entrepreneur, without unjustified, unanticipated, compensatory costs, and in such a fashion as to not unduly burden any one portion of the alcohol industry or associated business for people suffering an adverse reaction (alcoholism) for consuming a product...*their* product.

The idea is to go to the local health authorities to identify and share the costs they are experiencing necessary to *help people who suffer adverse reactions to the alcohol product.* For purposes of discussion, let's call this Product Reaction Recovery Fund or PRRF. To collect these funds, we will establish a Value Added Tax collection system. Now, we collect the PRRFs.

For the sake of argument, we will use Texas as our impact area. So, when alcohol crosses the Texas border, or if the product is made in state, starting from wherever that point of entry is, some entrepreneur receives that product and then sells it in some form or fashion: (a pallet of wine (56 cases of wine) a case of wine, a glass of wine, or a bottle, can, case, pallet or keg of beer, etc.) For example, Budweiser has a brewery where they manufacture a product, package it, load it onto trucks, and send it out for sale and distribution (even if it is their own distribution point). Each point of distribution and sales point will be charged a pre-established amount that reflects the number of people who sold and profited from the sale in the past year. This is counted as one unit of sale. Those funds or the Value Added Tax go into the Product Reaction Recovery Fund, PRRF.

For example, when 100 cases of beer are sold, they are then distributed to points of sale and distribution (PSD), e.g., bars, convenience stores, liquor, and beer stores, etc. which pay into the PRRF for having profited from the resale for each unit of product.

Then, we take the known annual cost to provide medically supervised detoxification and treatment (RX$) and divide that cost by the number of people who need treatment in the county (the number of county detox and treatment beds available where that treatment is provided.) Note—We realize that currently the number of beds does not yet equal the number of people who *need* treatment, because there aren't enough available treatment beds anywhere in the US, but it is a place to start.

This cost of treatment is then divided by the number of units of sale by individual sellers and then passed on to each distributor.

Note—It is a benefit to society as a whole to help those citizens who have had *an adverse reaction to the product of alcohol.* It is best to remove alcoholics from behind the wheel and provide them with appropriate medical treatment in a first-step response.

By using this approach, there is no "slippery slope" to the alcohol industry. The cost charged to the alcohol seller for medical treatment is just a portion of the cost rendered and *equally proportioned and reflecting those that suffered an adverse reaction* (becoming an alcoholic) *from the use of the product in question.* The alcohol industry will take full advantage of the free market while proudly touting *good corporate responsibility* for providing good medical treatment for all people who have suffered any adverse reaction caused by their product. Clearly, this approach would help to mitigate any corporate liability while the corporate industry becomes a true community partner.

As I said, initially, there may be an adjustment period to the capacity level available to treat *all* consumers with the adverse reaction to the product. At first, a county may only have the capability of treating, say, 20 people. As funds become available, beds and medical staff may expand to, say, 200 beds in a small city. This can be addressed to meet the size of the medical need, given the capacity of the healthcare community involved in that area. Also, over time, the alcohol community and the science community may find new ways to reduce the level or number of people that suffer an adverse reaction to the alcohol product.

Cost Estimation to Alcohol Sellers

Because we are all human, and therefore all different, so is the level of treatment and the duration of treatment required. This is reflected in the cost. The current medical practice for alcohol treatment consists of three components: Detoxification, substance abuse treatment, and sponsorship.

Detoxification ("Detox") is usually a 7- to 10-day program. In Austin, Texas, in 2020, this Detox program costs between $2,500-$7,000 per person. Also, in Austin, the 10-day detox program costs between $4,000-$10,000 per person.

Treatment in Austin, Texas, is either a 30, 60, or 90, day program.In Austin, the 30-day treatment program, costs between $8,000-$20,000 per person. The 60-day treatment program, costs between$10,000-$40,000 and the 90-day treatment program, costs between$15,000-$90,000.

Because various government departments, in addition to health departments, want to encourage reduction in alcohol-related automobile accidents, gun violence, suicides, domestic tragedies, loss of job productivity, etc., various subsidies are offered to reduce alcohol detoxification and treatment costs. However, given the overall annual alcohol sales gross ($120 Billion in Texas alone, according to Statista.com) and the number of points of sale and distribution (PSD). *It is estimated* that the overall cost to the alcohol seller is *less than one cent* per unit sale.

The Benefits: Mitigation for the Following Costs Relating to Year 2000
- 15 million Americans suffer from alcoholism.
- 100,000 Americans die each year in alcohol-related deaths.
- 90% of those afflicted are binge drinkers.
- Alcoholism makes up ¼ of all emergency room costs.
- Alcohol is involved in 1/3 of all suicides.
- Alcohol is involved in 1/3 of all traffic fatalities.
- The cost of American productivity was $185 billion.

The alcohol industry is like the tobacco industry, where their consumers suffer and die from diseases like cirrhosis of the liver and kidney failure, which are akin to emphysema, lung disease, COPD, etc. In 2000, a Florida jury awarded $154 *billion* in a class-action lawsuit in a tobacco case.

This concept foresees a hypothetical case in which an alcohol user who had a negative reaction to the product could qualify for a program of medical screening, detoxification, and treatment. The program would be created, in part, by the local Health Department in conjunction with the alcohol industry. Costs would begin at a known economic rate that never exceeded the cost of treatment for the individual having used that product. This program, approved by the Drug and Alcohol Commission and the alcohol industry, would only apply to those who suffered an adverse reaction to consuming any of their alcohol product. For having participated in such a healthcare program, the liabilities of the alcohol industry would be capped and limit their overall costs to financially maintaining that healthcare program.

Imagine a court's response when a potential alcohol litigant asks to sue the industry if they had not availed themselves of such a program following a relapse. How sympathetic will the courts be if someone's response is that they failed to seek this free healthcare program?

Many have perceived the tobacco industry to be "public enemy #1," and it has been the target of the nation's ire. By using our approach, would the alcohol industry not (while limiting its liability exposure) become the positive poster child of industry and heralded as a community partner in the same fashion that Smith & Wesson was praised? The gun manufacturer was renamed American Outdoor Brands in 2016.

Participating in President Bill Clinton's "comprehensive efforts to reduce gun violence in America," they were praised for promising gun cartridges that would hold only 10 rounds and guns that could only be fired by their owners. On a parallel track, savings to the alcohol industry might be in trillions of dollars, while at the same time, the savings in lives, families, and workplace hours recovered might be of equal or even greater value in our society.

House Bill #611 Will...

I reached out to State Congressional leader Lon Burnam in Texas. After lengthy discussions, House the Homeless, Inc. and Lon Burnam introduced House Bill #611, designed to reflect my concerns and those of House the Homeless in the 76th Texas Legislative Session.

It was a proud moment. There had been so much. So many friends lost, so many fights fought. So many homeless men and women, my street friends, beaten by their fathers and their mothers. My sisters endured suffering; my mother suffered stoically; my father experienced pain and suffering. Checkie Chevloski, Marine drill sergeants, the frigging war itself. Enough! My comfort and sense of pride come from realizing that, at the very front of the protest line was my daughter Colleen, age nine, by my side. It was all going to be just fine.

Colleen Marching with Richard

House the Homeless had painted our demonstration signs, and Colleen had painted her own. We marched through the streets in the downtown Austin entertainment district. "Make Business pay for Addiction!!" They could stop the enhancement. But they didn't (don't) want to stop it. The businesses in the Austin entertainment district wanted to *enhance the public intoxication jail time and increase the fines against people experiencing homelessness*. House the Homeless stopped them this time...but they'll push back...they always do.

Homeless folks are down for the count, and the businesses that sell the addictive alcohol come with their knee...then twist it on the necks of the downtrodden when folks continue to have an adverse reaction to their product. The businesses see to it that when people with no homes and no doors to close, like everyone else, have become publicly intoxicated, they are arrested and fined. The ironic thing is that many of these homeless folks are homeless due to skyrocketing housing costs and *insufficient wages* paid by the businesses themselves.

The House the Homeless Texas House Bill #611 carried by representative Lon Burnam would "enable Texas municipalities to set aside a percentage of all alcohol sales to create substance abuse treatment programs for all Texans based on the number of afflicted as identified by local health departments."

Response to Our Concept and Legislation: The Booze Brothers

Butchie (representing the beer lobby) and Mike (representing the whiskey lobby) were better known as the Booze Brothers. They seemed to be joined at the hip and went everywhere in tandem. A lobbyist and dear friend of mine, Mike Kelly (not a Booze Brother), lived just down the street from me in Austin. He said the Booze Brothers have always been there, and there will always be someone filling those roles of beer lobby rep and whiskey lobby rep. Our alcohol-related bill would have to go through these two fat, white guys. The way Mike Kelly told it, if a member of the Texas Legislature entertained even a fleeting thought about having a fundraising event, he would turn around to find the whiskey Booze Brother holding a case of it. Turning around again, the legislator would have to untangle himself from tripping over Butchie, the beer Booze Brother (and incidentally, labor lawyer) who was extending the first of several cases of beer.

I asked Mike Kelly to please reach out to the brothers and tell them I had a great alcohol bill unlike any other. I said to them that "It avoided the slippery slope and would put the alcohol industry in a favorable light forevermore."

Apparently, the Booze Brothers had 3 principles: 1) do not allow any legislation that would reduce consumption, 2) do not permit any legislation that would interfere with wholesale distribution, 3) do not open the door to the "slippery slope."

It was the slippery slope that held my interest. I learned that the idea of making citizens whole for damage done by their product embodied the fear-yoke that hung from their collective over-fed necks. They believed that if the citizenry asks for and gets 1% of the proceeds today, they'll ask for 2% tomorrow. Their bottom line was then, and is now, to keep all the cookies in the cookie jar.

However, the Booze Brothers were quite focused in their approach to bullet point #3 of their marching orders. Apparently, they saw the subtlety of my argument as a distinction without a difference.

So, I never got a direct response from the alcohol industry, nor could I speak directly with the Booze Brothers. However, I did get one phone call. It came from Lon Burnam; he said, "I will say this once and once only. If you quote me, I'll deny it. I received a phone call from the Booze Brothers. They said that "The bill will never come out of committee. It will never get a hearing. If you ever again attempt to introduce another alcohol bill, your career in the Texas Legislature will abruptly end." Lon told me the caller did not wait for a response. The line had gone dead. Likewise, Lon never waited for my response. In fact, that was the last time I ever spoke or heard from Lon Burnam.

I still think that the concept of product liability as applied to alcohol is a pretty good idea...but then again...it is my idea and one of my short stories in a long journey.

PS—It was just two days later that the House Clerk announced that House Bill # 611 had died in Committee...there had been no hearing.

PPS—I checked. Lon Burnham is no longer a member of the Texas Legislature.

Final Food for Thought

Effects on alcohol consumption by stress in the outside world: in January 2020, the public became aware of coronavirus disease. By March 2020, the illness was renamed COVID-19, and alcohol consumption had risen by 55% throughout the U.S...according to market research firm Nielsen. According to Nielsen, alcohol consumption through online sales was up 243%!!!

Sweet Jesus, please, help us.

Personal note—For the last forty years or so, when Saturday night comes around, I find myself able to put my feet up and drink a couple of Miller Lites with a bowl of chips and feel satisfied. Not every alcohol abuser is so lucky. At this point in time, consumers simply do not know if they were born with the alcoholic gene or if alcohol will destroy their life.

17 How You Can Help to End Homelessness

"What if God was one of us? Just a slob like one of us
Just a stranger on the bus, Tryin' to make his way home?"
     by Eric Bazilian, sung by Joan Osborne and my friend Sara Hickman

1. Practice Your Humanity Skills.

In February 2020, Sylvia and I were on a rare date night, headed to an Arlo Guthrie concert in an old Charlotte, N.C. church converted to a concert hall.

The words of his father, Woody, were running through my head..."This land is your land; this land is my land..." when a filthy man broke into my thoughts. "Can you help with a dollar?" He stood clutching a grease-smeared 4" x 6" piece of cardboard. I said, "Sure," as I gave him one. I offered, "I'm Richard," as I reached to shake his hand. "What's yours." In a low, reserved voice, he replied, "Chris." His grip was almost flaccid and coupled with jutting arthritic, bony fingers. The physical connection seemed to have transformed him into a humble Abe Lincoln. I tensed ever so slightly as my hand pressed his palm and felt an abnormal growth, coarsely leathered, the size of a semi-flattened golf ball. My gaze took him all in. He was a bent 6'1". He wore a denim jacket like mine, except his held together a crumpled, middle-aged man along with what appeared to be a pair of blue jeans now tattered and torn almost beyond recollection. In my mind, the expression "shopworn" surrounded him like a dense fog.

Hesitantly, he took a half step toward me, holding up the stretched-out dollar with two hands, and offered, "For five dollars, I can get a burger, fries, a coke..." So as not to extend his disappointment any longer than necessary, I cut across his words, "Sorry, I don't have change...but if you're here when we come back, I'll help you out."

Two hours later, re-energized by the motorcycle song and a full rendition of *Alice's Restaurant*, Sylvia and I were swept along the sidewalk in the stream of very satisfied and nostalgic Arlo lovers. Three columns of people and a large planter box away, Abe Lincoln stood with his "please help" sign as people diverted their eyes and flowed past him. Sylvia saw him first. I called his name, and as we continued to be swept onward, "Chris...Chris," I yelled again. With a waving arm, I directed him to go up ahead and meet on the protected side of the huge planter.

I handed him the five. He was stunned. He burst out with, "I can't believe you remembered my name." His eyes lit up his whole being, and his appreciation showed all around him. Stunned, I simply said, "We do care...we're trying." What had meant more to him at that moment was not the dollar or the five dollars, but that we had come back and cared enough to remember his name, that we had called out his name across a crowd of people. It was the human connection. Dr. Martin Luther King, Jr. had declared, "I am somebody." Others carried signs, "I am a man." I say to you that you can help by simply reaching out, connecting.

Look folks in the eye. Touch them. Share a personal thought. Share your humanity. "What if God was one of us..."

2. Pay a Fair Living Wage.

Are you thinking about getting some yard work done? Are you going to hire someone to shovel snow or rake leaves? Individual people working at a minimum wage job need to afford the basics in life: food, clothing, phone, shelter, and access to public transportation to get to and from work. If so, know this: between 1997 and 2007, the United States Congress did not raise the Federal Minimum Wage by even a penny. When the FMW was raised, it went from $5.15 per hour to a pitiful $7.25. Since that time, Congress has again failed to do its duty and has not raised the wage to this day...another decade. As a result, even a person working a full-time, 40-hour a week job is unable to afford a roof over their head. This is a slave wage that renders full-time minimum wage workers homeless!

If you think that at the end of the workweek, full-time minimum wage workers should be able to get off the streets and into an efficiency apartment, then as a full-time or part-time employer, you should pay a wage that can make that happen. Even if you only hire someone for two hours or 20 hours of work, you should pay them at that rate. Remember that when they are able to put in 40 units of work each week, they win the jack pot...they get housed!

Become a *common-sense* giver! Pay people who work for you at that rate. Don't wait for someone else's ethics to kick in!

Throughout the life of my daughter, *regardless of her age*, if I felt she could do a job I needed to have done and felt it was safe, I paid her to do that job, and I paid her a fair living a wage—the proper rate for a unit of work. Find your local ULW here—http://www.universallivingwage.org/wagecalculator.html

According to House the Homeless Inc.'s annual surveys, 48% (nearly half) of the folks experiencing homelessness nationwide (3.5 million every year) are so disabled that they cannot work. As a result, even disabled people who do not have a work history are eligible for a Supplemental Security Income stipend (SSI). The federal government continues to operate as if we live in a single-wage economy (nationwide) and provide only a single support amount for every eligible disabled person (regardless

246

of where they live). Long ago, we learned that we are a nation of a thousand or more economies. Heck, don't members of Congress ever travel? Don't they realize that it costs twice what it costs to live in Washington, DC, as it does to living in Harlingen, TX? And it costs much more than that to live in Santa Cruz, CA, etc. Everyone else seems to know and understand this simple truth. Clearly, you will need different size checks that relate to the single most expensive item in the budget of every American: *housing!* But even beyond that, the current SSI checks are so low that twelve states have added more tax dollars into the pot to help tenants. But nowhere in the US is even that enough money to house these folks. Here's the deal. These people have no funds, no support system, possibly no work history, and they all need to be housed and cared for because they are disabled and determined to be so by the US federal government that may have taken as much as 1.5 years to determine that they are disabled. But even then, the government only covers a fraction of what they need to survive. As a result, they then become homeless and living under one of our nation's bridges, like 100,000 of their brethren.

But before disparaging any of these folks for not having work history (remember, they are disabled), consider that half the workers of America are women. At least half of them were married and stay-at-home moms raising entire families—as such their value as paid employees being determined to be over $100,000 per year. But as stay-at-home moms (or dads) with no W-2s...they get no paychecks; there is no work history (pay stubs) for them, so they get a one-size-fits-all $794 per month stipend.

Make a difference: Write your congressperson and your senators. Tell them that anyone getting an SSI stipend because they are disabled needs sufficient funds to cover their housing costs plus food, clothing phone, and public transportation, wherever they live in the United States. Then go into the hospitals and nursing homes, etc., and share copies of your letter. Register folks to vote. Demand positive results from your elected officials. Tell them, if they will not help our disabled folks get a livable income, you will organize and campaign to replace them with someone else who will.

3. Call for the Federal Minimum Wage to be Linked (Indexed) to the Local Cost of Housing.

INDEX IT! INDEX IT! INDEX IT!
Half the people experiencing homelessness, 52%, are capable of working, and an even greater percentage of those responding, 89.7%, have declared their desire to work (see http://www.housethehomeless. org/surveys/).

However, according to several US Conference of Mayors reports, almost nowhere in America can a full-time minimum-wage worker get and keep a one-bedroom apartment at the current Federal Minimum Wage of $7.25 per hour, which is about $14,000/year. Compounding the problem is the fact that the federal government continues its multi-decade-long practice of treating the country as a single economy. The reality is, we are a nation of more than a thousand economies. This means that any response such as raising the wage to $15.00/hour has distinct consequences. At $15/hour, minimum wage continues to fall far short of empowering people to work themselves off of our streets in our larger cities. At the same time, $15/hour will devastate the "mom and pop" businesses so prevalent in rural America. To address this condition that has added so significantly to our nation's homelessness problem, the Universal Living Wage, ULW campaign has set out to fix the Federal Minimum Wage for the entire nation once and for all.

The ULW is a 3-pronged formula using existing government guidelines (see www.UniversalLivingWage.org) that ensures that if a person completes 40 hours of work, be it from one job or more, they will be able to afford basic housing, pay for food, clothing, a phone, and public transportation to get to and from that work.

To advance this solution that fixes the Federal Minimum Wage, Google your congressional leaders in both the House and the Senate. Leave your message of support for the Universal Living Wage that indexes the Federal Minimum Wage to the local cost of housing to ensure that a full-time minimum wage worker can get and keep housing wherever that work is done throughout the entire United States.

4. Get Out Basic Information to Our Homeless Folks.

To adapt Austin's Plastic Pocket Guide concept to your town would be to undertake an ambitious and much-needed project. Once they are produced, how do you get them in the hands of the people who need them? For distribution, secure the help of libraries, churches, youth programs like the Boy Scouts and Girl Scouts, social workers, local college fraternities and sororities, the police, your local downtown business alliance, and any courts that routinely deal with unhoused people.

In Austin, members of House the Homeless, including the directors, keep guides in their vehicles. We fold a dollar into each one and hand them out to people standing on street corners, exchanging first names to affirm their humanity.

As you can imagine, the Plastic Pocket Guide provides crucially valuable information, especially for those who do not have internet access. It also conveys the very personal message that society—your community—cares about the safety and well-being of people experiencing homelessness.

Note—When we give out cards to churches, etc., we invite a donation of $1.00 per card. We print 10,000 at a time. People are very happy to do this as they love the cards. We have covered postage in the past, or the cards are picked up at one of our local churches. In this fashion, the cost is "a wash" while providing an invaluable service to providers and our constituents.

Due to limited card space and failed start-ups, entities on the card should be successfully functioning for two years before they are considered for placement on the cards. Not everyone expresses interest to be on the cards because they often do not have the resources to handle expanded outreach.

As you can imagine, the Plastic Pocket Guides do what the internet cannot; it provides valuable information along with the very personal message that society (the community of Austin, for example) cares about them. Good stuff...and it slips into your pocket. (See Appendix).

5. Give Out Hygiene/Treat Bags.

You can make care packages in sealed baggies. People need:
Fresh fruit that can be put in a pocket (apples, oranges, etc.)
Granola bar, dried fruit, or other individually wrapped snacks
Nuts
Mini boxes (or snack size zip-loc pouch) of raisins to slip into a pocket
Small peanut butter in a plastic container
Mini tissue packets
Hand sanitizer-4 oz. bottles
Small packets of hand wipes
Small note pads and pens
Socks
Gloves
Space blanket
A couple of bucks Sunglasses
Plastic Pocket Guide (list of resources in their area)
Hat (seasonal type)
Safety whistle
Comb
Toothbrush & paste
Travel soap
Washcloth
Mini water bottles
Pet food

6 Give Out Face Masks.

COVID-19 or other air-borne disease prevention masks (nothing says someone cares like a couple of hand-made masks). On April 3, 2020, the Centers for Disease Control announced that face masks could help minimize the spread of COVID-19. Sylvia and I had been making and distributing homemade masks since early March 2020. To us, it just seemed like common sense. After Vietnam, I pulled a tour of duty in Japan. At all times, about one in 20 people wore a mask to stop the spread of the common cold or flu.

I cut the fabric, make the nose bridge wires, and Sylvia sews the cloth. We gave out hundreds to the homeless community, our neighbors, and the healthcare community in Weddington, NC, Austin, Texas, and Washington DC through the National Coalition for the Homeless. This act alone brings people together.

When you give a bag of resources, exchange names with the person you give them to, open up a dialogue. Share personal information about yourself—marriage status, children, and work. (It is not recommended to include address or phone numbers other than those on the Plastic Pocket Guide.)

7. Volunteer Your Time and Skills.

I was rocked back on my heels the day I learned that the City of Round Rock, just outside of Austin, had generated 2,700 "Dellionaires" from stock options. Dell Computer Company established its HQ in Austin in 1984. I was similarly stunned to learn that in Travis County, where Austin is located, one person in five is *illiterate*. Think about the income divide that this suggests. Volunteering to serve dinner on Christmas or Thanksgiving can be awesome, but teaching someone to read is amazingly rewarding...for everyone!

If you really want to make a difference and increase your understanding of people experiencing homelessness, volunteer at a homeless shelter (day and night), at a soup kitchen, on a board of directors of an organization serving the homeless, etc. Organize homeless folks to collaborate with parks and recreation departments for creek and woods *clean-up* where lots of homeless people live. Volunteer for periodic counts of homeless people. This is very important because the distribution of federal dollars is based on need. Need is determined by counting an area's unhoused people during a designated 24-hour period, once or twice a year. This is not for everyone, but it is very helpful and a true learning experience. Almost any service provider can direct you to the "counters."

8. Create Little Libraries.

Take all your used books and magazines to shelters and create little libraries. Get your friends to contribute on a regular basis. Educate your readers to take a book and leave a book. Go to used book stores, make connections, and get them to donate surplus books. Feed your libraries constantly.

9. Create Speakers Bureaus.

Empower people who have experienced homelessness, past or present, to form local speakers' bureaus. Encourage them to tell their stories to groups at places of worship, civic clubs, book clubs, business luncheons, etc. They should talk about who they are, how they became homeless, their families, what their dreams are, and how they expect their homelessness to end or how it did end. Reach out.

Focus on civic organizations, e.g., Masonic Temples, Rotary Clubs, garden clubs, churches, synagogues, colleges, universities, police departments and fire stations, hospital nurse groups, unions, etc. All these groups are looking for speakers. If you are clever, you can ask for donations at the end of presentations and divide these among your speakers. Get the word out and get your folks some cash! The National Coalition for the Homeless uses this as an organizing tool that financially helps our homeless folks and puts a few bucks in the coffers of the organization.

Speakers Bureau Game Plan
- Tell the attendees how they can help.
- You might want to print up a list of suggestions to pass out.
- Hire people experiencing homelessness.
- Pay living wages.
- Donate clothing.
- Create a work tool lending library.
- Pass the hat, etc.
- Reach out to homeless **children.**
- Give the children crayons and coloring books. Watch them light up and go to work.
- Then help the children create their own coloring books. Get the children to tell you the story they have created. Ask them if their characters are happy or sad. Ask each child how the characters in the story might be helped. Collect their answers. Use your instincts to help.
- Get sponsors for the children's after school activities (e.g., band, dance, sports).

- Raise money to upgrade their shoes and clothing so the other kids won't bully them over fashion.
- Contact whatever organization is working with homeless children under McKinney-Vento Act funding in your area, and see what help they say the children need. These folks usually make sure that every student has all of their vaccinations, weekly planners, school supplies, backpacks, etc. Remember that without their immunizations, they will not be permitted to attend school.
- Make sure they have lunch money and a means of transportation, and rain gear. Finally, make sure they have after-school care.
- Become a Big Brother or Big Sister.
- Think. Take Action. Speak out! Get into some "good trouble," as our mentor John Lewis would tell us.

When the Ku Klux Klan came to Austin and spoke their hatred, members of House the Homeless took buckets of soapy water and scrub-brushed the spot at City Hall where they had stood until you could eat off that spot. Of course, when you do something like this, you want to invite the public to help and be sure there is media coverage of the wash brigade in action.

Think—Preamble to the US Constitution...

> *"We the people of the United States, in order to form a more perfect union, establish justice, ensure domestic tranquility, provide for the common defense, promote the general welfare, and secure the blessings of liberty to ourselves and our posterity, do ordain and establish this Constitution for the United States of America."*

Masked Police

In 2020, our nation began wringing its hands and feeling angst and helplessness about the militarization of our country's municipal police forces. I saw a squad of about eight male and female City of Austin police officers traipsing through the alleyway between the homeless shelter and the Salvation Army. They were dressed entirely in black, full-combat, strike force, SWAT gear that included flack-jackets, armed with 50,000-volt tasers and mace. I approached one of the officers asking what they were doing in the alley between two homeless shelters. The one officer replied, with a wink, "sending a message." Another officer, in a booming voice, asked, "Yeah, you got a problem with that?" I responded with, "Yeah, I do," as I peeled off.

Shaken, I got to where I was calm enough to think. Obviously, these fine folks were there in the alley to enforce all the "quality of life" ordinances against the unhoused.

Well, I wanted to know where all the military equipment had come from, now in the hands of our police. In addition to assault rifles, they get *tanks* for carrying out SWAT attacks. You've seen them. We have all seen them. It turns out that these weapons come from our very own federal government, for free. They come from the General Services Administration (the federal government) as "military surplus." I didn't vote for that. Did you? No, you didn't. Who pays for it all? You and I do, with our tax dollars.

10. Make a Proposal.

Simply tell your city council person that you want to place all military equipment donated to the city budget for $1.00 and charge the people because all budget items are subject to discussion. Council members and citizens alike can openly discuss their acquisition. Who will pay for weapon storage? Who will pay for weapon, machinery replacement, and vehicle operational use? Who will pay for training? What happens when these items break down or become obsolete? Do we even want replacements? Under what exact circumstances can the equipment be used? What are the rules of engagement? Do the people of your city actually want to live in a heavily militarized zone?

We, the people, need to regain control of our municipal police forces. We need to engage and decide these issues through a democratic vote. Perhaps, it turns out that we want to have and pay for such additions to our police force. Okay, at least then, we will have decided our own fate, not simply fallen into it. We need to vote on all of our issues.

Go get into "good trouble," as our good friend Senator John Lewis would tell us. Be the change you seek. Don't wait for the other guy to do it. You may not be happy with the outcome. Let's ensure our domestic tranquility. All politics are local.

11. Promote Community First! Village as a National Best Practice.

I urge you and your mayor to come to Community First! Village to see national best practices of how to care for disabled homeless folks. Stay in a mini-house for the weekend. Urge your mayor to return to your community, share their findings and build your own Community First! Village.

Note: As of 2021, the earth is still in a pandemic relating to COVID-19. Google the Village before you decide to go.

Appendix

Homelessness
It is the Essence of Depression
It is Immoral
It is Socially Corrupt
It is an Act of Violence

Words on the HtH Homeless Memorial
on Lady Bird Lake in Austin, Texas 1993

House the Homeless, Inc.
P.O. Box 2312 Austin, TX 78768-2312
512) 796-4366
www.HouseTheHomeless.org
www.UniversalLivingWage.org

Endorsers of the Universal Living Wage Campaign

These businesses, unions, nonprofits, and faith-based organizations beginning in 2001, were presented with a synopsis of the Universal Living Wage and asked to sign and return a letter of endorsement along with 42,000 others. This is the fruit of that labor.

Endorsers can be found on the Universal Living Wage website: http://www.universallivingwage.org/advocates.html
They can also be found in the author's book *Looking Up at the Bottom Line: The Struggle for the Living Wage* on page 262 in the appendix.
This QR code can be scanned to see the endorsers on the website.

International Endorsers

Communications Workers Of America, International
Nonviolence International
Centre for Social Justice- Ontario, Canada
The Big Issue in Scotland- United Kingdom

National Endorsers

American Federation of Teachers AFT
CCW/AFTEF Center for the Child care Workforce/ The AFTE Foundation
Center for Community Change
Center for Economic and Policy Research
Central Conference of American Rabbis
Church Women United
Citizens Policies Institute
Citizens Policy Institute
Coalition on Human Needs
Communication Workers of America, National
Community Family Life Services, Inc.
Community for Creative Non-Violence (CCNV)
Community IT Innovators, Inc.

Co-op America
Friends of the Earth
Gray Panthers
Green Party of the United States
Homeless Children's Playtime Project
Housing Assistance Council
Jobs with Justice
Labor Council for Latin America
NAACP
National Alliance of HUD Tenants
National Association of Social Workers
National Coalition for Asian Pacific American Community Development
National Coalition for the Homeless
National Community Reinvestment Coalition
National Council for Urban Peace and Justice
National Council of Churches/ Economic/Social/Justice Program
National Health Care
National Law Center on Homelessness & Poverty
National Low Income Housing Coalition
National Network for Children
National Network for Youth
National Organization for Women (NOW)
National Priorities Project
National Rural Housing Coalition
Network: A National Catholic Social Justice Lobby
North American Street Newspaper Association
Pax Christi
Physicians for Social Responsibility
Presbyterian Church (USA)
Religious/Labor Coalition
SEIU
Spina Bifida Assoc. of America
The Coalition on Human Needs
The Salvation Army-WDC
Union of American Hebrew Congregations
United Methodist Church Board of Church and Society
Universalist Service Committee
Washington DC Bureau of the Rainbow/PUSH Coalition
Washington Legal Clinic for the Homeless
Women of Reform Judaism

Resolution Implementation

Because many states and cities are passing and enforcing laws targeting poor and homeless people, and the fact that homeless people are targets of senseless assaults, murder and unjust laws due to their condition of homelessness, House The Homeless feels the need for the adoption of this resolution by City, State and the United States governments.

HOMELESS PROTECTED CLASS RESOLUTION

Whereas, the United States Government has adopted and is party to the United Nation's Document referenced as the Universal Declaration of Human Rights, which " confers on every member of society a right to basic economic, social, and cultural entitlements, that every (nation) state should recognize, serve, and protect, of which food, clothing, medical care, and housing are definitive components of the right to a minimum standard of living and dignity," and

Whereas, the United States Government has adopted, and is party to the United Nation's Document; the Habitat Agenda, which calls for certain actions that include but are not limited to: protection against discrimination, legal security of tenure and equal access to land including women and the poor; effective protection from illegal forced evictions, taking human rights into consideration, bearing in mind that homeless people should not be penalized for their status; by adopting policies aimed at making housing habitable, affordable and accessible, including those who are unable to secure adequate housing through their own means, and

Whereas, the United Nations Document: Habitat Agenda, calls for the "Effective monitoring and evaluation of housing conditions, including the extent of homelessness and inadequate housing policies and implementing effective strategies and plans to address those problems," and

Whereas, there is a shortage of affordable housing stock nationwide, and

Whereas, the national minimum wage or the Supplemental Security Income stipend is an insufficient amount of money to secure safe, decent, affordable housing, phone and public transportation even at the most basic financial level, and

Whereas, more than the minimum wage is required in every state to be able to afford a one-bedroom apartment at Fair Market Rent, as set by the U.S. Department of Housing and Urban Development, HUD, and

Whereas, the Supplemental Security Income stipend is an insufficient amount of money to secure safe, decent, affordable housing, food, clothing, phone, and public transportation, and

Whereas, the combined effect of these and other circumstances create a group of people that have no alternatives to living on the streets of our nation, and

Whereas, it is estimated that nationwide, there are at least 760,000 persons living without a permanent, fixed, individual residence on any given night, and

Whereas, at least 28% of our nations' homeless are United States veterans, and

Whereas, approximately 45% of the homeless population suffers from some form of mental illness of which approximately 25% is considered serious, and

Whereas, the fastest growing segment of the population is women with children, and

Whereas, 36.5 million men, women and children of all ages are living in poverty (many of whom are already homeless), and

Whereas, there has been a collective, concerted effort at city and county levels to devise laws and ordinances that find homeless people guilty of having committed a crime for simple acts such as sitting, lying down, sleeping in public, or even in their own cars and

Whereas, there are certain life sustaining acts such as eating, breathing and sleeping that must be conducted by all persons including those that are homeless who must conduct these acts in public, and

Whereas, these laws and ordinances are designed to criminalize and sweep these homeless persons form our nations' streets and imprison them, without regard for their personal safety or care for their personal belongings, for no reason other than they are lacking housing and as a result, are characterized as non-citizens, and are deprived of their human rights, and

Whereas, these impoverished persons are targeted and often made victims of malicious hate crimes and selective enforcement of these laws and ordinances, and

Whereas, camping, sleeping, sitting, lying and other anti-homeless laws including those that restrict the feeding of people who are hungry, are being enforced at a time when emergency housing shelters are consistently full and no housing alternatives remain available, and wages paid are wholly inadequate to afford people the basics of life: food, clothing, phone and public transportation,and and shelter, and

Whereas, the enforcement of such laws under such circumstances constitute cruel and unusual punishment and impinge upon these persons access to travel,

THERFORE, BE IT RESOLVED: That persons without a fixed, permanent, individual place of residence, and those that are earning 100% of Federal Poverty Guidelines or less, are sufficient in number characteristics, and vulnerability to compromise a distinct class of people, and as a result, shall hence forth constitute a **Protected Class** with all rights and protections under such a designation. Herein after, this Protected Class, will be referred to as the Indigent Homeless Population.

AND FURTHER, BE IT RESOLVED, that as a Protected Class they will be protected:

From laws against sleeping, sitting, lying down in public,

From laws that restrict them from being provided food,

From acts or laws interfering with their right to travel,

From wages that are so low that they are denied access to housing,

From laws or practices that disregard their rights of ownership, and protections for their personal belongings,

From being made targets of hate crimes/violence, and

From being characterized and treated as non-citizens.

From being denied employment due to one's homeless or formerly homeless status.

From laws or practices that discriminate against people and deny them any type of housing based on their present or past condition of homelessness.

Richard R. Troxell
Author/Founder 1989
House the Homeless, Inc.
BOD National Coalition for the Homeless, 1997-2022

Signature	Print Name	Email

Complete and return to House the Homeless, Inc.
P.O. Box 2312 Austin, TX 78768

Email with History of the Homeless Memorial and Statue Justification on Lady Bird Lake

Vanessa, Hi,

On behalf of House the Homeless and our Board of Directors. I'd like to convey our heartfelt appreciation for all of your efforts to help us site *The Home Coming* statue. We thank you for your most recent meeting with Sara Hensley of the City of Austin Parks Department.

You have explained that in that meeting, Ms. Hensley restated her support for the Cesar Chavez/Congress Street site. Our Board of Directors believes that while the site is clearly out of the flood plain, it comes with other equally serious *negative* aspects.

Our Board of Directors have visited the site many times and found:

- The site to be subject to very loud traffic noise that is disquieting and distracting,
- The volume of the noise is so loud that at times it becomes very hard to hear one another speak;
- The visibility of the site is and will continue to be compromised at the proposed location;
- The level of foot traffic is quite nominal as access is by a secondary feeder trail that is rarely used. During similar hours of the day, this area received only 19 people as opposed to the existing Homeless Memorial that during the same time period had 282 pedestrians.

Please understand that House the Homeless greatly appreciates the recommendation, however, the site is again rejected as inappropriate for our memorial site.

The Parks Department inventory of land is vast in size and we are open to consider alternative suggestions.

You have stated that you are now prepared to explore the possibility of acquiring access to the Hyatt Hotel property site. We applaud your initiative and look forward to details as they unfold as we feel this would be a reasonable accommodation.

Finally, please allow me to restate that the existing Homeless Memorial is our 1st and foremost preferred site. You conveyed that two significant points were raised in that conversation. The first point is that the shoreline is fragile and needs to be protected and preserved. We are in complete agreement. It is for this reason that House the Homeless has partnered with John Dromgoole, "The Natural Gardner," for landscaping and with John Garner, "The Barton Springs Arborist," both of whom have prepared detailed plans and prepared statements that the placement of the statue will not interfere or have any negative impact on the area if specific directions of the statue placement are followed.

So, you can see, we clearly share the concern and have taken specific steps to protect and enhance this environment. To that point, let it be noted that I personally watered the Tree of Remembrance for 20 years on a weekly schedule until its roots finally reached Lady Bird Lake, and it could drink for itself from the river. Additionally, House the Homeless has removed dead branches from the tree throughout the years. On three separate occasions House the Homeless volunteers have made major soil reparation involving the tree's roots at the surface where we loosened the soil and add bags of mulch and soil to turn and aerate the soil while protecting the roots from foot and dog traffic. Finally, before the area was turned into an off-leash dog park, we nurtured the grass that once completely covered the area and trimmed it around our bench and both the Homeless Memorial plaque and the Dr. Martin Luther King, Jr. plaque, which we are currently in the process of tiling.

The second significant point raised but not discussed in details in the conversation with Ms. Hensley is the flooding issue. Our second application before the Parks Department was turned down because of the flooding issue. When we went through the application process we were denied specifically because our architect, Gary Jaster of Jaster of Quintania who put in the Stevie Ray Vaughan statue was told by that section head that he was signing off for his entire section saying that we would be denied at each point within his section because the area was a flood plain and therefore each response would be denied.

However, all of the Auditorium Shores restoration project including the retaining wall, revamp of the exercise area immediately adjacent to the Homeless Memorial beginning with the water fountain and shower within 10 feet of the trunk of the Tree of Remembrance and all of which share the same Lady Bird Lake shoreline and environmental sensitivities and all the massive *tree planters* made with two hundred pound blocks and the multi-sectioned water fountain with electrical compressors were all upgraded or newly constructed after House the Homeless initiated its application to site *The Home Coming* statue in that very same area.

In addition to all of the massive construction in late September 2015, having renamed Auditorium Shores the Vic Mathias Shores, a 300-pound memorial stone with bronze plaque was placed less than thirty feet from the Tree of Remembrance at the Homeless Memorial site.

The final point conveyed about the discussion with Ms. Hensley and the Parks Department is that placing *The Home Coming* statue at the existing Homeless Memorial would make a lot of people *angry*. The point here is that almost no one has even seen the statue (not even my humble version of it.) I am intimate with it as it is my concept. However, after I had first presented it to the Parks Department and been denied based on my humble efforts, I was approached by the world's most prominent bronze sculptor because of the message of compassion for one's fellow man/woman that it conveys. Timothy P. Schmalz the current sculptor and my partner in this project, has art work in countries all over the world. He sculpted *Homeless Jesus*, which in a singular ceremony was blessed by Pope Francis.

The organization of House the Homeless was founded in 1989 with the stated/ registered mission of *Education* and *Advocacy* around issues of homelessness. Following the drowning of Diane Breisch Malloy in Waller Creek at the mouth of Town Lake (renamed Lady Bird Lake), we created a memorial to the women, men, and children who have died in poverty on the streets of Austin. We did this with the help of Marty Stoop of the Parks Department, who was in charge of the Auditorium (Vic Mathias) Shores renovation. He helped us select the site, locate and plant our Tree of Remembrance calling it, "the perfect place" as there was no tree in that area, which was basically barren at the time. Every year since that time, for 23 years, we have held the City-Wide Homeless Memorial Sunrise Service. We always invite an elected official to demonstrate that there is a very real human cost to not solving the problem of homelessness. The core purpose behind the Memorial is to put a "positive face on homelessness." Anyone who has experienced homelessness will tell you they feel *invisible*. People will not feel angry when they see this statue. They will feel compassion.

House the Homeless has thoroughly discussed all of these factors and is prepared to proffer a compromise recommendation regarding the site.

Clearly, the Parks Department has found the site of the Vic Mathias monument to be an appropriate setting in this flood area. It is worth noting that the sub-ground counterweight of *The Home Coming* statue exceeds those of the current block construction in this area. Additionally, the Stevie Ray Vaughan statue was placed in the ground on the very day that the existing Homeless Memorial was constructed only 75 yards apart. Neither have sustained any flood damage for these past 23 years, and in as much as there is considerable concern for the Lady Bird Lake Shoreline, it is recommended that *The Home Coming* statue be placed away from that shoreline where the Vic Mathias monument is presently located.

Having said all that, please realize that we do greatly appreciate all of your efforts, and we are keeping our minds and options open. Please let us know of any progress on the Vic Mathias suggestion.

Thank you,

Richard R. Troxell

City of Austin Letter to Shelly Schadegg

 City of Austin

Steve Adler, Mayor

301 W. 2nd St., Austin, TX 78701
(512) 978-2100, Fax (512) 978-2120
steve.adler@austintexas.gov

Shelly Schadegg
Corporate Vice President Admin & Development
Edinburgh Management LLC
1500 Sand Lake Rd
Orlando, FL 32809-7081

Dear Shelly Schadegg,

On behalf of Mr. Richard Troxell and his not-for-profit organization, House the Homeless, Inc., I would like to express my support for the placement of an important statue symbolizing the struggles, the humanity, and our community's resolve to end homelessness. Mr. Troxell has identified a site on the property of the Hyatt Regency Hotel in Austin at 208 Barton Springs Road that could serve as an ideal location for this work. The statue, sculpted by Timothy P. Schmaltz, reflects the values of our city and expresses our commitment to both memorializing and ending homelessness while leading the nation in changing the face of homelessness.

The prospective site of the statue placement is near the 25-year old "Homeless Memorial" site, where citizens honor those who never made it out of homelessness. The 'Homeless Memorial' currently resides in a floodplain and therefore cannot accommodate the statue. The location on the Hyatt Regency property is a short distance away from the memorial and represents an ideal alternative. This small piece of property is separated from the rest of the Hyatt Regency property by a wall of foliage, a bend in the Town Lake Hike & Bike Trail, and a two-foot-wide creek. This piece of property is both accessible and in a location that allows for solitude in order to reflect on the statue's meaning.

Mr. Troxell and House the Homeless, Inc., wish to discuss the possibility of the placement of this statue on your property; or the purchase, leasing, or donation of the property. I support this endeavor and would like to see this statue find a home at this location in order to emphasize the importance of this issue and those experiencing homelessness in our city.

Mr. Troxell can provide you more information and photos of the statue.

Thank you for your time and consideration.

Sincerely,

Steve Adler
Mayor

CC: Richard Troxell

The City of Austin is committed to compliance with the Americans with Disabilities Act.

265

House the Homeless Health Survey Results 2010

Check ALL that apply.
Do you have?...
   High blood pressure 204
   Mental Illness 175   What Type? Schizophrenia 16   Bi-Polar 86
   Diabetes 84   Shots 16   Panic Attacks 70
   Arthritis 123   HIV/AIDS 10   Seizures 45
Are you a regular illegal drug user?   Yes—59
Do you believe you are an alcoholic?   Yes—92
Have you ever had a brain injury?   Yes—83
Do you have cancer?   Yes—83
              What type?   Prostrate   6
                           Throat   3
                           Liver   3
                           Testicular   2
                           Cervical   2
                           Bone   2
                           Skin   2
                           Kidney   2
                           Colon   1
                           Lymphoma   1
                           Fibroid   1
                           Pancreatic   1
                           Hodgkin's Disease 1
What other serious disease or condition do you have?
Debilitating Chronic Back Pain   21
Debilitating Chronic Knee Pain   14
COPD   11
Post-Traumatic Stress Disorder (PTSD)   9
Asthma   8
ADHD   6
Generalized Pain   4
Anxiety   4
Fibromyalgia   4
Metal Plates/Ankle   3
Hypoglycemic   3
Stroke   3
Sciatica   3
Emphysema   3
Hip Problems   3
Heart Disease   2
High Cholesterol   2

ADD	2
Intestinal Hernia—Massive	2
GERD	2
Metallic Ankle	2
Neuropathy	2
Paranoid Schizophrenic	2
Hyper Active Deficit Disorder	2
Pancreatic	2
Eye Injury	2
Severe Hearing Loss	2
Chronic Viral Bronchitis	2
Degenerative Joint Disease	2
Carpal Tunnel Syndrome	2
High Cholesterol	2
Glaucoma	2
Degenerative Bone Disease	2
Neurological Disorder	2
Tinnitus	2
Shoulder Plate	2
Scoliosis	2
Circulatory Problems	2

What other serious disease or condition do you have?
They wrote in:

Sleep Apnea	1
Hyperthyroid	1
Graves Disease	1
Pregnant	1
OC Disorders	1
Walking Pneumonia	1
Delusions	1
Cirrhosis	1
Dizziness	1
Bad Feet Due to Circulation	1
Arterial Sclerosis	1
Irritable Bowel Syndrome	1
Muscle Control Loss	1
Kidney Disease	1
Degenerative Rheumatoid Arthritis	1
Degenerative Disc Disease	1
Phlebitis	1
Standing and Mobility Issues	1
Missing Digits	1

Tendonitis	1
Brain Bleeds	1
Hip Replacement	1
Cirrhosis of the Liver	1
Broken Pelvis	1
Hepatitis B	1
Anti-Social Behavior	1
Heart Pacemaker (Endocarditic)	1
Heart Murmur	1
Faucet Disease	1
Totally Blind in One Eye	1
Thyroid	1
Gunshot wound (GSW) to Head	1
Degenerative Nerve Disease	1
Parkinson's Disease	1
Gall Stones	1
Chronic Gastritis	1
Plate in Elbow	1
Chronic Ulcers	1
Osteoporosis	1
Degenerative Heart Disease	1
Acid Reflux	1
Hallucinations	1
Arm Amputated	1

Are any of these conditions keeping you from working?	Yes 241
Do you smoke cigarettes	Yes 381
Do you have severe shortness of breath?	Yes 145
Do you ever need to stop and rest when you are walking, before you can continue?	Yes 330
Finally, have you ever needed to sit down and been unable to locate a bench?	Yes 472

Note: Of those surveyed, 241 said that they have a health condition that keeps them from working (48.1%) This is about half of a very large sampling.
Copies of the disability statistics were distributed to the council members.

House of the Homeless Plastic Pocket Guide

PLASTIC POCKET GUIDE©
Published by House the Homeless, Inc. July 2021
POB 2312, Austin, TX 78768 HousetheHomeless.org

Current Resource Info: Dial 211 (Live, 24-hr, multilingual)
Unitedwayaustin.org/ConnectATX
or go to FINDHELP.ORG or call 833-512-2289 (8a-4:55p, M-F)
CapMetro GO Line: 512-474-1200

SOCIAL SERVICES - MULTIPLE
ECHO: Coordinated Entry Assessments (housing/vulnerability). Call 211 for assessment sites; AustinECHO.org/ca or FindHelp.org
Front Steps/ARCH: 1st Point of Entry to Services System/Serv. Card IDs, library card, case mgmt, clinic, laundry/showers/restrooms 6:30a-5p, M-F, 500 E. 7th@Neches, 512-305-4100, web:bit.ly/3droyOf
Austin Public Libraries: 21 locations, Free public computers, Wi-Fi, Reading, Classes & Events. 512-974-7400, library.austintexas.gov
Caritas of Austin*: Housing, food, educ, employment. Housing programs require referral via Coordinated Entry system. Daily Lunch, 11a. Office: 8a-4:45p M/W/Th, 8a-6:45p T; 8-11:45a Fri. CENTRAL: 611 Neches NORTH: 9027 Northgate Blvd. Caritasofaustin.org
Sunrise Homeless Navigation Center: Hot meal, mail, showers, hygiene, limited clothing, laundry, triage referral/navigation; Service Point ID, Coordinated Assessment, MAP/Food Stamp sign-up; Medical clinic, Integral Care; job resources. 9a-1p, M-F (varies by service type). 4430 Menchaca Rd, 512-522-1097. SunriseAustin.org
The Other Ones Foundation: Workforce First jobs, 512-568-7557 or brian@toofound.org, mobile hygiene/shower trailer toofound.org
Trinity Center: Navigation/service ctr, meals, case mgmt, ID docs, Coordinated Assessment; MAP, SNAP, Food Stamp sign-up, bus passes, ltd. travel asst., clothes/showers-women (M/T); mail, phone, computer access; housing referrals. Open 9a-1p, M-F, 3-4:30p, Sun. Come in person/no appts. 304 E. 7th, TrinityCenterAustin.org.
First Baptist Austin: Case Services/Navigation, M-W-F, 9a-4p; Snack packs & hygiene kits. 901 Trinity St. Appt: 512-476-2625 fbcAustin.org
El Buen Samaritano Episcopal Mission: Comm. Health Worker Training, Adult Educ, Youth Progs, School Readiness, Food Help M-F 9-5, 7000 Woodhue Dr., 512-439-8900 ElBuen.org
Comm. Court/DACC: Walk-in Soc. Srv. 8a-4p/M-F. 512-974-4879

MEALS & MORE
Austin Baptist Chapel/Angel House Soup Kitchen Food Pantry/breakfast/ lunch 9:30-10a,11a-12:30p., 512-643-2327, 908 E. Cesar Chavez, AngelHouse@Austinbaptistchapel.com
Central Presbyterian: Breakfast, coffee, hygiene 8-9a, T/Th; 200 E. 8th, 512-472-2445 cpcaustin.org
First Methodist/Feed My People: Food, hygiene, AA mtgs. T/Th 5:30a-7a; At the Well- (women only), Fri. 9a-noon, showers/rm. laundry, clothing, hygiene, breakfast, fellowship, 1300 Lavaca, 512-453-6570, fumcaustin.org
University United Methodist/Open Door: Food/clothing/hygiene, Sat. 8-9:15a; *Micah6 Women's brunch/support/care Tues 10-noon, 2409 Guadalupe, 512-478-9387 UUMC.org/Open-door
University Ave. Church of Christ: Dinner, fellowship, Bible Study., Wed. 6p. 1903 University Ave., uachurch.org
Micah6Austin.org*- Partial, Services vary: see contact info:
-**University Ave. Christian:** Food pantry: Call 512-477-6104 2007 University Ave., ucc-austin.org
-**University Presbyterian:** 2203 San Antonio St., 512-476-5321, upcaustin.org
-**University Baptist:** 2130 Guadalupe St., 512-478-8559 ubcaustin.org
-**All Saints Episcopal Loaves & Fishes:** 209 W. 27th 512-637-2826, bit.ly/2TQWYW
Mosaic Church: (North) 12675 Research Blvd. 512-537-0027 MosaicChurch.austin.org
Texas Oaks Baptist/Solid Ground Ministry: (South) Food, fellowship, other services. 9910 Billbrook Dr. 512-280-9500. T/Th/Sat: 10a-1p showers/hygiene/laundry; Block Party, 2nd Sat. ea. mo., 10a-1p food, clothing, hygiene/showers/laundry TOBC.org
Mobil Loaves & Fishes Trucks: Food, clothing, shoes, socks, books, hygiene, today's stops, 512-328-7299, mlf.org/truck-schedules/
Violet Keep Safe Storage: 7a-7p daily, 606 E. 12th enter northside alley
Project Help: Homeless students. Austin schools, 512-414-3690

ADVOCACY/LEGAL
Texas Legal Services Ctr: Advice/represent/govt. benefits/+ 512-477-6000
Catholic Charities Central TX: Immigration Legal Srv. 512-651-6125, cctx.org
Texas Fair Defense Project: Contact atty here if receive a ticket (camping, asking someone for assistance, or related to your inability to access housing) or if were arrested for unpaid tickets. Mon. 12-5p; Th. 10a-1p, 512-637-5220, press 0 (lv msg if nec.) or apply at https://bit.ly/2RAcwuM
Texas RioGrande Legal Aid: FMI 512-374-2700 www.TRLA.org

Crisis/Suicide Hotline 800-273-8255
Immediate Emotional Support 512-472-HELP (4357)
Veterans 24-hr Help/Crisis/Suicide Hotline 800-273-8255
National Domestic Violence Help 800-799-7233(SAFE)
Text START to 88788
SafeAustin.org: If experience abuse, call 24hr SAFEline 512-267-SAFE(7233); text 737-888-7233

(vertical text on left:) HELPFUL NUMBERS

Linea De Defensa Communitaria/Deportation Crisis: 512-270-1515
Challenger Street Newspaper: Voice of the people, no barrier jobs.Valerie Romness, 512-560-4735, http://Challengernewspaper.org/
Disability Rights TX: Legal Protection of Rights for persons with Disabilities/Serv. Referrals/COVID vaccine info. 512-454-4816/ 800-252-9108, M-F, 8-5. www.disabilityrights.org. Online 24/7 at Intake.DRTX.org

MEDICAL/DENTAL
Medical Access Prog/MAP Card: Accepted @ Lone Star Circle of Care/ People's Community Clinic/El Buen, 512-978-8130, CentralHealth.net/MAP
Manos de Cristos: Dental/Basic Needs/Educ., 8a-5p, 512-477-7454, 4911 Harmon Ave, manosdecristo.org
CommUnityCare (CUC)-ARCH clinic: Onsite or help to schedule offsite dental and vision, 7:30a-4:30, closed for lunch. 500 E, 7TH 512-978-9920 +27 sites Manor to Rundberg! 512-978-9015. CommUNITYcareTX.org
-**Southeast Health & Wellness Ctr:** Walk-In Clinic-Med/Dental, M-Sat, 7a-8p, appts: M-F, 8a-5p. 2901 Montopolis Dr. 512-978-9901
-**Ben White Dental incl. pediatric dental:** 7:30a-6p M-F, 1221 W Ben White Blvd. #112B, 512-978-9700 gen.#
-**Hancock Hlth:** Walk-In. 7a-8p daily, 1000 E 41st #925, 512-978-9940
ViventHealth.org: HIV Serv/rapid testing/more. 512-458-2437

MENTAL/BEHAVIORAL HEALTH
Integral Care: 512-472-HELP (4357), including PES
-**Urgent Care Walk-In Clinic:** Psychiatric Emergency Service (PES) M-F 8a-10p; Sat/Sun 10a-8p, 1165 Airport Blvd., 2nd Flr.
-**Adult Integrated Care Clinics:** M-F, 8-5, 512-472-4357
East 2nd Clinic / Central Austin, 1631 E. 2nd St.
Stonegate Clinic / South Austin, 2501 William Cannon Dr., Bldg 4
Rundberg Clinic / North Austin, 825 E. Rundberg Ln., F-1
Oak Springs Clinic / East Austin, 3000 Oak Springs Dr.
-**PATH-Programs for Assistance in Transition from Homelessness:** Call 512-804-3700. email: PATHoutreach@IntegralCare.org
-**HOST-Homeless Outreach Street Team:** UT/Central 512-804-3720
Salvation Army Adult Rehab Center: 4216 S. Congress, M-F 7a-3p.
Call first for Appt: 512-447-2272 salvationarmyaustin.org
RecoveryATX: Peer support-recovery/harm reduction (multiple), re-entry. 1816 E. 12th, call for appt Google VM: 512-273-7329 RecoveryATX.org
A New Entry: Substance Use, incl.Vets 512-464-1250 bit.ly/recsupport

VETERANS
VA Homeless Vet Hotline: Screening; local connect to housing options, transitional & permanent (VASH) 1-877-4AID-Vet (877-424-3838)
Austin VA Outpatient Clinic: M-F 7:30a-4p, 7901 Metropolis Dr. 512-823-4000, 800-342-2111
Caritas of Austin & Front Steps: Support for Vet Families (SSVF)
Catholic Charities of Central Texas/ St. Michael's Veteran Services: bit.ly/stmichaelsvr, 512-651-6154
Samaritan Center: Help for veterans, 512-451-7337 opt.4
Travis Co. Veterans Srvs(notVA): Disability benefits/homeless referrals/S help. 5325 Airport Blvd. 512-854-9340 tcrvet.org

YOUTH (Mid-twenties and under)
Lifeworks: Youth Resource Center. Food, hygiene, bus passes, Coordinated Assessments. Emergency Shelter/Rapid ReHousing 512-735-2100, 835 N. Pleasant Valley Rd. Check Hrs - Insta: @lifeworksyrc; Facebook: lifeworks.yrc; call/text 512-473-9125.
Street Youth Ministry: Guidance, food, clothing, toiletries, books, items for young adults. 408 W. 23rd. 24-hr helpline, 512-553-3796 StreetYouthMinistry.org OR http://help.SYMin.org (info@SYMin.org); Online support groups-voice (help.SYMin.org -> groups). Outreach in San Marcos: Fri. 4:30-6:30p. Skate park/library or Southside Comm. Ctr.
Texas Youth Hotline: Runaways, abuse, truancy 800-989-6884, 24/7

SHELTER (211)
Cold Weather Shelter Hotline: 512-305-ICEE(4233)
Salvation Army Center: Emergency shelter, services, men/ women, Office: 8a-4:30p M-F, 501 E. 8th, 512-476-1111, salvationarmyaustin.org
ARCH Men's Shelter: (case mgmt clients) ARCH/Front Steps, 500 E. 7th
Salvation Army Rathgeber Center: (Family shelter) 737-256-6926; &
Austin Shelter for Women/Children: 512-933-0600 both: 4613 Tannehill Ln

PUBLIC RESTROOMS
716-1/2 East 6th Street | 403-1/2 Trinity Street | 507-1/2 Brazos Street |
Library Restrooms | Park Restrooms | Restrooms in other Public Buildings

All info subject to change-Call 211 for updates; contact resources before going Guide not to be copied.

Flood and Water Quality | Safety & Health Tips
FLOOD: Culverts, bridges, roads, ditches and creek beds can flood quickly. Subscribe to https://warncentraltexas.org to receive alerts. Move to higher ground with your belongings.
WATER QUALITY: Avoid creeks for 2-3 days after it rains and avoid water that isn't flowing, is brown, discolored, or has a bad odor. Harmful algae may be present in lakes, creeks, and ponds. Stay safe- do not touch algae and keep dogs away. AustinTexas.gov/algae
HELP KEEP CREEKS CLEAN: Use public restrooms. Put trash, cigarette butts, and pet waste in public trash cans. Call 311 to request "Violet Bags" to collect trash and litter. Call 512-974-2550 to report pollution.

WATERSHED PROTECTION

HOUSE THE HOMELESS

No Sit/No Lie Disability Card in Spanish

A partir del 1 de mayo de 2011, la Ordenanza de No Sentarse / No Mentir se modificará para proteger a las personas con discapacidades físicas y mentales.

Puede tener un descanso de 30 minutos para "recuperar el aliento" si está discapacitado y siente (pero no se limita a):

debilidad,
dificultad para respirar,
problemas del corazón,
mareado,
dolor
migraña, etc.

Entonces, si necesita sentarse o acostarse porque está discapacitado ... **DEBE** decirle al oficial de policía que está discapacitado porque sufre de:

diabetes
insuficiencia cardíaca congestiva
esquizofrenia
trastorno bipolar
depresión
parálisis cerebral
o cualquier otra discapacidad

Si un oficial de policía se le acerca y le pregunta por qué está sentado, dígale que está discapacitado, "Tengo diabetes (etc.) -ver arriba, me siento mareado (o lo que sea-ver arriba). Solo necesito un minuto o dos." El oficial debe preguntarle si necesita atención de emergencia y, si no, debe decirle: "Está bien,

(over)

volveré en unos 30 minutos. (Es posible que se le emita una multa de advertencia en este momento). Si después de los 30 minutos Si todavía está allí y tiene un problema, lo revisarán nuevamente para recibir atención médica de emergencia.

Si no necesita la atención médica de emergencia, se le pedirá que continúe de inmediato. Si no se mueve, recibirá una multa. Si se emite una multa, el caso irá ante un juez.

Tampoco debe obtener un boleto si:

Usted está:

-Visualización de un desfile, manifestación, mitin o similar.

-en un área de parada de autobús esperando para usar el transporte.

-en fila esperando bienes, servicios o evento público.

-en una silla o banco proporcionado por una agencia pública o el dueño de la propiedad privada contigua.

O cuando Austin está experimentando un clima extremo, por ejemplo calor / frío / día de acción del ozono, etc.

Si obtiene un boleto, lléveselo inmediatamente a Richard R. Troxell en el

Endnotes

1. Pollin, Robert, and Stephanie Luce. The Living Wage: Building a Fair Economy. New York: The New Press, 2000. pp. 26-27.

2. Ibid.

3. Ibid., pp. 26-28

4. Ibid.

5. Ibid.

6. Next Century Economy. Rep. San Rafael, CA: ICF Kaiser Economic Strategy Group, 1988.

7. Bernstein, Jared. "America's Well Targeted Raise". Issue brief no. 118. Economic Policy Institute, Sept. 2, 1997. https://www.epi.org/publication/issuebriefs_ib118/.

8. Bernstein, Jared, and John Schmitt. "The Sky Hasn't Fallen", Economic Policy Institute, June 1, 1997. https://www.epi.org/publication/epi_virlib_briefingpapers_1997_skyh/.

9. The History of Tipping: From Sixteenth-Century England to the United States in the 1910s, Ofer H. Azars, https://papers.ssrn.com/sol3/papers.cfm?abstract_id=397900.

10. Pollin, Robert, and Stephanie Luce. The Living Wage: Building a Fair Economy. The New Press, New York, 2000.

11. Ibid.

12. Shulman, Beth. The Betrayal of Work: How Low-wage Jobs Fail 30 Million Americans and their Families. The New Press, New York, London, 2003.

13. "Summary." Fair Market Rents. U.S. Department of Housing and Urban Development. Accessed on web: July 16, 2010. www.huduser.org/periodicals/ushmc/winter98/summary-2.html.

14. Koidin, Michelle, San Antonio Express-News, Sept. 29, 2002.

15. Schlosser, Eric. Fast Food Nation/The Dark Side of the All-American Meal. New York, Harper Collins, Perennial, New York, 2002.

16. Ibid.

17. Ibid.

18. Pollin, Robert, and Stephanie Luce. The Living Wage: Building a Fair Economy. The New Press, New York, 2000.

19. Ibid.

20. "The Sky Hasn't Fallen." Economic Policy Institute in Washington, D.C..

21. Pollin, Robert, and Stephanie Luce. The Living Wage: Building a Fair Economy. The New Press, New York, 2000.

22. Report •David Cooper • February 3, David. "Balancing Paychecks and Public Assistance: How Higher Wages Would Strengthen What Government Can Do." Economic Policy Institute, 3 Feb. 2016. https://www.epi.org/publication/wages-and-transfers/.

23. "The Realities of Poverty in Delaware 2001-2002." Welcome to DHC. N.p., 2002. https://www.cds.udel.edu/wp-content/uploads/2016/03/delAwarewinter2005.pdf.

24. Troxell, Richard R. "2011 Health Sleep Study | House the Homeless."

25. House the Homeless. N.p., 18 Feb. 2011. Web. 03 Mar. 2013.

26. Ibid.

27. Estelle v. Gamble, 429 U.S. 97 (1976).

28. William Wayne Justice, "The Origins of Ruiz v. Estell," Stanford Law Review 43 (1990):1.

29. Mark Collette, "Telemedicine has a global reach," Galveston Daily News, (30 March 2008) https://www.galvnews.com/lifestyle/article_367663b4-d90a-559f-b63b-5db41b48f6f9.html.

30. Texas Department of Criminal Justice, "Statistical Report Fiscal Year 2008," (January 2009): 15, https://www.tdcj.texas.gov/documents/Statistical_Report_FY2008.pdf.

31. Scott Henson, "How about some balance on the Board of Pardons and paroles?" Grits for Breakfast, (7 July 2007) https://gritsforbreakfast.blogspot.com/2007/07/how-about-some-balance-on-board-of.html.

32. Scott Henson, "AIDS drugs, healthcare for elderly inmates driving TDCJ medical costs" Grits for Breakfast, (3 April 2008) https://gritsforbreakfast.blogspot.com/2008/04/aids-drugs-healthcare-for-elderly.html.

33. Marc A. Levin, "Policy Perspective: Mental Illness and the Texas Criminal Justice System," Texas Public Policy Foundation: Center for Effective Justice, (May 2009): https://files.texaspolicy.com/uploads/2018/08/16093244/2009-05-PP15-mentalillness-ml.pdf.

34. Mental Health Association in Texas, "Factsheet," Mental Health Association in Texas. (28 February 2003): http://www.mhatexas.org/mhatexasmain/FACTSHEET1final3_03.pdf.

35. ibid.

36. Levin.

37. Coming Home: An Asset-Based Approach to Transforming Self & Community, A Report on Re-Entry by the Phelps Stokes Fund Co-Production at Work, Volume 1, Submitted to the W. K. Kellogg Foundation, November 2008.

38. No More Throw-Away People The Co-Production Imperative Edgar S. Cahn Creator of Time Dollars and Time Banking Second Edition 2004 Essential Books publisher.

39. C.A. Visher, "Returning Home: Emerging Findings and Policy Lessons about Prisoner Re-Entry," Federal Sentencing Reporter 20, no. 1 (2007): 94.

40. J. Travis, "Reflections on the Re-entry Movement, 20 Fed," Sent. Rep 84 (2007).

41. National Institute on Alcohol Abuse and Alcoholism report No. 11PH293, dated January 1991.

42. Rice, D.P.; Kelma S.; Miller, L.S.; and Dunmsyers, S. The Economic Costs of Alcohol and Drug Abuse and Mental Illness: 1985, Rockville, MD National Institute on Drug Abuse.

43. Harwood, H.J.; Napolitano, D.M.; Kristiansen, P.L.; and Collins, J.J. Economic Costs to Society of Alcohol and Drug Abuse and Mental Illness: 1980.

More Praise for *Short Stories in a Long Journey*

"Richard R. Troxell is a true American Hero. Richard's book *Short Stories in a Long Journey* is a magnificent blend of Richard's personal story written in an inspiring and insightful manner. Richard's book is a catalyst for a long-ignored discussion about income inequality in America. Income inequality and workforce investment has long been ignored in the quest to end homelessness in America. Richard also provides a roadmap to end homelessness in America when he identifies solutions to several of other pieces in the puzzle. Richard is an amazing advocate that I choose to call my friend. People experiencing homeless are very fortunate to have Richard as an ally."
—**Donald H. Whitehead Jr.**, Executive Director
National Coalition for the Homeless

"I remember as a young mental health professional telling my supervisor about an idea I had. She said 'that is a great idea, how are you going to pay for that?' I had identified a problem and a method to address it. The remarkable thing about Richard's remarks are not only his honesty about his personal experiences, and his ability to identify the impact and cost of these issues, but his ability to begin the dialogue of 'how are you going to pay for that?' This book continues that dialogue. It not only proposes realistic "methods of finance" such as a modest surcharge to finance substance treatment but it also addresses the counter arguments. We recognize what the counter arguments are but also that the industries will pass the cost onto consumers. Regardless, Richard continues to press the discussion about the most serious issues facing us today—living wages and access to substance use treatment."
—**Greg Gibson,** MA, MAHS
35 year Activist for health and human services, policies and programs
U.S. Army Veteran Combat Medical Specialist, Advisory Board Member
Chairperson of the Texas Interagency Council for the Homeless

"I was fortunate to have read Richard R. Troxell's new book, *Short Stories in a Long Journey*. I found the book most interesting and informative. Clearly a lot of thought went into developing and writing it, and it seems obvious to me that Richard used his head guided by his heart in writing the book. He seeks to discuss the issues of homelessness honestly, letting the chips fall where they may. If there is a theme to his book, I would say he is saying let's use our hearts and heads to come about more common-sense solutions to the problem of homelessness. Importantly he notes that much homelessness is due to structural defects in our system and/or our laws.'

"The book is a good read and should be shared with people of good will wherever they may be found. He sees homeless people but not everyone does. It is a most thought provoking moment in the book, he raises the question that what if the homeless person you encounter is God who has taken that shape for that moment in time? He suggests that of course we all would want it known that if we had unknowingly had such an encounter that the record would reflect that we did the right thing."

—**Gary Bledsoe**, Head of the TX NAACP since 1991
   Attorney, Civil Rights and Health Care Law
   Acting Dean of the Thurgood Marshall School of Law since 2017
   Vicechair of the National NAACP

CPSIA information can be obtained
at www.ICGtesting.com
Printed in the USA
JSHW041925180222
22893JS00002B/2